Messages to Clare

Messages to Clare

FINDING PEACE, JOY, AND SPIRITUAL AWAKENING
EVEN IN LIFE'S DARKEST HOURS

**Received By My Wife During Her Inspiring Dance
With Cancer**

Clare & Jim Keating

Praise for "Messages to Clare" and for Clare Ruth Keating

The 'Messages' Clare Keating received from the other side will warm your heart, fill your soul, and occasionally inspire a smile. In this labor of love, Jim Keating shares with you the messages he recorded from Clare and adds a glimpse into her inspiring life. This book has the spirit of angels, the words of divine wisdom and a loving roadmap for life. Share far and wide.–J. Michael McFadden, author of Deidre's Dawn: Book 1 of The Enchantment

Few people on this earth have the courage to open themselves to spiritual messages, much less to admit to others that they hear "voices" or are "receiving information." At a time in one's life, when most of us are thinking of our legacy, Clare Keating boldly stepped onto a unique path. She abandoned all worldly judgment and criticism and let her soul take flight. She allowed her heart and soul to bring forth the divine for those of us who have "ears to hear." Listening is your choice. Clare choose wisely. –Catherine Lanigan, novelist, author of *Angel Watch, Divine Nudges, Angel Tales* and over 45 novels and non-fiction as well as the novelizations of *Romancing the Stone* and *The Jewel of the Nile.* www.catherinelanigan.com .

Experience comfort and help from the unseen world that is with you right now. Clare Keating opened herself to that realm, and she shares it with us with clarity and compassion. I recommend this book!–Mary Margaret Moore, spiritual teacher, channel of the Bartholomew teachings

Clare's messages present Truth in a way that resonates with every fiber of my being. What love is there for each of us, soft, yet with the knowing that cuts through. We're led to new ways of thinking about the ordinary and recognizing the extraordinary.–Kristen Hartnagel, speaker, singer, business consultant

Love it, love it, love it! I have read probably over 100 channeled and inspired books and I know this will be a comfort to many.–Jackie Balcom Lindrup, R.D.H., M.Ed.

Clare experienced the Divine all around her, in the people, Jim, her family, the flowers, the earth, all of creation. She knew that these messages were not hers to keep. She was called to share them as a prophet to each of us. She would not have used that word, too pretentious for her, but we know that is what she was. While never saying it, she knew she was answering God's call for her by sharing the gift. –Thomas J. Norris, STL (Sacred Theology), M.A.

When I first met Clare Keating, she had already been fighting breast cancer for eight years. She never let her treatments get in the way of her life, no matter how ill she became. She never let her illness consume her. Concern for her family and friends kept her going, even when she had no physical strength. We could all learn much from Clare. –Saundra Blanchard, M.D., Clare's family physician

Clare was one of the most courageous women I ever met and she will always be an inspiration to me.–Deacon Joe Schmitt, Catholic Diocese of Kalamazoo, Michigan

The spirit of loving that she lived and shared in her life was so powerful and truly moving for so many people. It seemed no matter what was going on in her life, she could bring forward an amazing joy in all things. I am very grateful to have known her and shared this inner walk with her.–Jim Gordon, spiritual teacher, President of Inner Light Ministries

She showed me with her choices and her attitude that beauty is about the way you see and approach the world, not in how you dress or the material possessions in your life. She was the most beautiful woman I have ever met and I am thankful every day for having been able to learn from her.–Paula Mierendorf, niece, information systems security analyst.

Clare really lived life to its fullest! As a strange gift, cancer seemed to be the vehicle that led Clare to a deeper spiritual understanding about life. She was a role model to anyone around her about how to live fully no matter what the circumstances might be. She had a connection to higher realms and was able to tap into deep wisdom. She lived with passion, love, excitement, and courage.– Gay Walker, friend, artist, former director of Holistic Health Program, Western Michigan University.

There are many people who come and go in our lives. Only a few touch us in ways that change us forever. Clare Ruth Keating profoundly affected my life and for this I will be eternally grateful.–Elizabeth McIntosh, friend, Oahu, Hawaii.

I have never known anyone who was so spiritual and such a "hoot" to be with.–Pat Denner, long-time friend of Clare

Library of Congress Cataloging Data
Title: Messages to Clare
Subtitle: Finding Peace, Joy and Spiritual Awakening Even in
Life's Darkest Hours
By Clare and Jim Keating

Original Publication Date 2018

ISBN:1635380251
Paperback 978-1-63538-025-5
E-book 978-1-63538-026-2

Includes bibliographical references:
1. Spirituality   2. Channeling   3. Peace   4. Joy   5. Cancer.   6.
Spiritual Awakening.

Cover design by Olga Shevchenko
Cover and inside photos by Jim Keating, unless otherwise noted

All quotes from *A Course in Miracles* are from the second edition,
published in 1996. They are used with permission from the copy-
right holder and publisher, the Foundation for Inner Peace, P.O.
Box 598, Mill Valley, CA 94942-0598, www.acim.org and info@acim.org

.

Publisher: Golden Sphere
Contact information: jbkeat37@gmail.com

Dedication

To my beautiful, strong wife Clare who joyfully allowed these messages to come through her during the most challenging period of her life. Her positive spirit touched all those she met in her 67 years on earth.

To her parents, Joe and Mary Mierendorf, who raised her so well.

To my parents, Jim and Dorothy Keating, who taught their nine children by loving example.

To our children and grandchildren, some of whom never met Clare. May they be inspired by these messages she received.

Acknowledgements

I wish to thank the many friends who contributed their advice, feedback, and energies to this book. These include spiritual teachers and authors Connie Shaw, Judith Skutch Whitson and Mary Margaret Moore who encouraged me to publish these messages for the world at large. Also encouraging and supportive were the Muskegon Thursday night "Miracles" group and my "Oxygen" Master Mind group who were the first friends to be shown this material.

I received much technical advice from authors John McFadden, Catherine Lanigan, Camille Albrecht, and my brothers, Jerome Keating and Dennis Keating. Graphic artist Olga Shevchenko came into my life at the perfect time to assist with cover design. Paul Littrell generously gave his time and suggestions in the early proofreading of the manuscript.

Most of all, I wish to thank author and editor MaryAnn Fitzharris for her positive spirit, as well as her invaluable editing and technical assistance, without which it would have taken much longer for this book to be published.

Introduction: How the Messages Came About

Sometimes gifts come in unusual wrappings. In summer 1991, my wife, Clare Ruth Keating, was diagnosed with an advanced stage of breast cancer. For the next fifteen years–with the help of traditional and non-traditional medicine, prayer, spiritual healers, and a very positive attitude–the disease went into remission and returned two more times. In January 2006, we received the most discouraging news. The cancer had now spread to her spine, liver, and three other areas of her body. It did not sound like she had much longer to live.

Just prior to this very depressing period, Clare confided to me that she felt someone was trying to talk to her—in a spiritual rather than physical way. Being a therapist by training and work experience, I was well aware of what psychologists typically think of people who hear voices, but in Clare's case, I believed and understood her immediately. During the 42 years of our marriage, this had happened at least half a dozen times and I had learned to take down the messages she was receiving as she related them.

Clare began to receive the messages after our morning meditation. For a few days I wrote down the messages, but then we decided to go immediately to the computer after meditation, and I would type as she dictated. When the messages came—and they did within about ten seconds—there was no change in her voice, posture or personality. Was someone channeling through her? It did not seem like channeling, as I had seen it. Instead, it was as if someone was talking to her on the phone and she was relaying to me the messages she was hearing. I would often ask a question to make sure I heard her correctly, especially since she would get the title first, and neither of us had any idea where the dictation was going, or how the title would fit in. Invariably, it would be clear about half way through the message.

During the next year, she received about one hundred messages and in the following three years, approximately one hundred more. As the cancer and chemo treatments wore her body down, and she was put on oxygen, her energy lessened, and it was harder for her to focus for long periods of time. She entered her nineteenth year after her initial diagnosis of advanced breast cancer. Her oncologist and family doctor considered her a "walking miracle." Clare passed to the other side December 19, 2009.

Despite undergoing eighteen different kinds of chemo plus radiation, Clare's life was one of joy, enthusiasm, and spirituality. Her positive attitude had a great effect on those around her. She had been a teacher, workshop leader, and therapist. She traveled to thirty-four countries and most of the United States, directed and taught Sunday school and sang in both an interracial gospel choir and a traditional Irish folk group. For excitement, she skied, parasailed, and sky dived. As one friend said of her, "I have never known anyone who was so spiritual and such a 'hoot' to be with." Together we raised five children, including a Japanese youth who lived with us for eight years. Family was very important to Clare and she lived to see all our children have children or be expecting a child.

The Source of the Messages

These messages were communicated to Clare from spiritual beings who once lived on earth. Similar to angels, they live and serve God from another dimension that some might call heaven. They have higher vibrations than we do, and desire to serve God in every way possible. As they stated, they are around us all to assist in our awakening to who we really are with God. They will aid us when we ask God or them for help. In fact, it is their joy to be asked and to assist. Simply put, they are God's helpers.

The first spiritual being to identify himself was named Jon. We were soon told that, in addition to Jon, there was an entire group or team of spiritual individuals who are here to assist us and others. They made it clear several times that their names were not important, and that several would often join to give a message using one name, like Ben or Serena.

It was actually harder for Clare to receive the names of the sources than the title or the content of the messages. For these reasons, unless the name appeared in the transmission, I have left the individual names off the messages so they would not be a distraction from the content.

The group identified itself as "The Arc of Infinity," an inclusive title we associated with a passage from "A Course in Miracles." The passage refers to "an arc of golden light that stretches as you look into a great and shining circle…Within it everything is joined in perfect continuity. Nor is it possible to imagine that anything could be outside, for there is nowhere that this light is not."*

Some of the messages were more personal and specific

*   *A Course in Miracles, Text- Chap.21, 1, 8*

to Clare and me. Still, I have decided to leave several of the personal messages in this collection. A college writing instructor once told me "the personal is the most universal," and I hope that some of those reading will also relate to the advice given specifically to Clare and me, especially those who are facing difficult life challenges.

Clare was often given a mental image to help her understand the words and I have included their descriptions here in italics within parentheses. Other italicized notations in the text are comments from either Clare or myself, or descriptions of what was going on in our lives at the time.

One thing that I appreciate most about these messages is the constant use of examples to illustrate points, making them easier to remember. Though the messages are recorded in the order we received them, there is no need for the reader to follow that order. The messages are mostly independent of each other.

I personally believe that we are at a time in history where spiritual help is more readily available to all and that the veil between the physical and the spiritual world is thinning, allowing individuals to connect more easily to the God energy. The challenges, pace, and distractions of modern life may be requiring this. These messages are offered as one more aid to all who are seeking.

I hope you will profit from them as much as Clare and I have.

Jim B. Keating, Muskegon, Michigan

#1   THE FIRST MESSAGE

Hello! Welcome today. This has been long put off and today is perfect. My name is Jon (*smiling*). I have known you for a long time. (*Feels like lifetimes to Clare.*) Together (*he and Clare*), awareness can be revealed. Time, as you know it, is short.

(Clare sees a vision of a thousand little birds with mouths open, hungry to be fed.)

Your chicks are waiting. First, dwell in peace. Let go of the garment of political figures and all of the "bad guys" from TV programs, as well as "Ain't it awful!" kind of thinking. Dwell in clearness; that is who you are. (*Clare sees clear water.*)

(Clare questions, "Why do I have cancer?" and Jon replies, "We will not address that now." It would be addressed in messages 152 and 189.)

Come home to me regularly. We will develop a cadence, a wonderful rhythm where truth will be unfolded, like a child's fan, one part at a time. Today, start holding your hand in mine. (*Clare asks "What areas should we cover?"*) You are being trained, guided. Lately peace is what you are to focus on. All is like clear water, clear open area—God energy, Godness. When there is not peace, it is because you have invited drama, intrigue, and adventure into the scene. That's cool! You are like a matchstick on the ocean, peaceful when it is peaceful. Even when the ocean is full of adventure like a storm, there is peace within, for you know where you are, with it, not part of it. You are still connected to the Oneness that is not the ocean.

The key is to remember, no matter what is happening, you are experiencing it, but not of it. Good, bad, or indifferent, it is only an adventure. Look around, you will see many match sticks on this ocean. Find your levity, gaiety, and happiness by commiserating with the other adventurers who hold peace like yourself.

Don't be sad. Sadness is an experience of value, as is joy, as is hate. The issue is to experience it while remembering who you are. (*Clare sees an image of a doll that, when flipped upside down, it becomes a different character.*)

We are both—one of God, one of the earth plane. It is so healthy to reveal the God-self frequently, to flip the doll, so you remember who you are.

It is done.

Jon

#2   COSTS

Hello! Today we talk about "costs." You have at hand that which you have paid for; in one way or another you have requested this. You, Clare, have requested to be apart from the world and so you chose infirmity. That has paid you well.

Jim, you have chosen to be in the world. The cost is your momentary fleeting depth of connection to who you are. The two choices are the same in value. One might look at the price you are paying. Each of you can get your desire without being overcharged. Seek ways to shortcut the cost to your goals.

Clare, you may want to commit those two hours a day to meditation instead of illness. It is quicker and easier and clearer.

Jim, you too seek clarity. Your goal is more immersion in the moment with laughter and friends. You express connection to the "now" through rejoicing with photography, music, interacting, and socializing.

(Clare sees a photo image of trees and rocks like Boom Beach, a rocky spot on Isle au Haut, Maine, that Jim enjoyed photographing.)

Each of you must clarify what you desire and how you can get it for a better price. Shop! Find ways. Each of you is embroiled in the path itself, and by the time you get to the goal, your energy is depleted. Chose simpler methods to your clear goals. Let go of past decisions. If it is not fun, let it go. It is a path of joy, wherever you are going.

(Clare sees many paths going off from one spot, all of them perfect.)

Clare, you are letting suffering go and it serves you well as you do so.

3

Jim, you have come up against a nemesis (*Clare sees huge white wall*) on your path. It is a wall of paper (*Clare sees Jim poking his hand through it*), not as challenging as you think. It is easy, like a big bm (bowel movement). There is grunting and pushing, then a big relief, a victory. It is joyful, successful. You will meet this nemesis regularly on your path, but it will be smaller each time.

(*Clare sees picture of it getting smaller, blocking less of the path. Although almost completely blocking the path now, later 50 percent, then only a boulder to the side. As far as she can see it keeps getting smaller, confronting Jim periodically.*)

Jim, remember you live in the path of Light. Each step is your destination. Don't look to the future. Now is where it's at. Picture yourself on your path conquering your little paper demons.

(*Clare's image: Little paper men warriors about three feet by two feet. She feels that demons don't experience pain, are artificial, easy to deal with. As Jim walks down the path, he pops the paper demons out of the way.*)

Freedom! You claim your inheritance—the whole path. Remember it's easy. To think it is not is only from past pain. Be in the now. You can do it.

Clare, be patient. That which you get from being ill is not finished. You have not picked all the grapes on the path. Your intent to find a different way to accomplish the same goal will shorten the path of illness. Get started.

Be happy. Be Love. Be sensitive. I am devoted to your heart.

(*Clare felt a huge expression of love, like an orgasm in power but 20 times longer.*)

#3   THE ADVENTURE

Hello, Clare! Welcome. Tonight I will be your guide. I am Serena.

Tonight we call "forever." Just trust for now. Tomorrow is free. (*She shows a view looking out a castle window into a valley, open and clear.*) Today challenges abound. (*She shows thick mud around Clare's feet.*) Think of them as video games. They mean less. Try not to take the situation so seriously. Laugh at it, laugh with it, get angry, get sad, and see that it is over.

Rejoice. Commiserate. It is all an adventure, nothing more. A choice glibly made to test your skills. (*Clare sees a confident, smirk-like smile.*) It is not important. It is only an experience. Don't lose sight of who you are.

If you are well grounded in this knowing, you can do this adventuring and yet be connected to the Peace. Take time, more time, out of the adventure and into peace. You won't be sorry.

(*Clare sees a picture of a majority of people who only know the adventure, but haven't had a glimpse outside of the adventure to know that they are not just the adventure, but much, much more.*)

As you go to the edge of the adventure, others will watch you and wonder where you are going. Their curiosity will bring them to the edge of the adventure and they, too, will look out, and some will venture forth and realize who they are.

The peace and joy of this reconnecting is boundless.
(*Clare: "I can feel it, it is so wonderful!"*)
The role assigned to you is important. You cannot fail.
(*Clare: "It's so peaceful, it's amazing."*)
There is nothing more!

#4   FORGIVENES

Welcome once more. Today we are happy to assist you in understanding. Forgiveness is what you can get your teeth into. Forgiveness sounds heavy but the result is very light, like a corn removed from a toe. Or it is also similar to lifting a large stone off of you—the light comes in, the weight is gone.

Forgiveness, as we know, is not acknowledging another person's mistakes and releasing them from the bondage of being caught, but rather looking at that very same person, seeing them as flawless, and knowing that they are God. It is being able to step out of your role that you have always played with the name that you were given, and instead step into the director's chair and know a production is in process. Even though one may not follow the thread of the director's reasoning, one trusts that it is perfect, steps back, and enjoys the moment without condemnation.

When we get good at this, our hearts will be light, joy will attend our path, and suspense and delight will be around every corner. A twinkle will be in one's eye and love will radiate, for fear will not attend.

This suspension of condemnation must apply to one-self as well as to others. Travel lightly. Avoid the snare of believing that everything is not self-determined. Do not believe you are powerless. It is your experience. You have all the power.

This understanding will not come overnight. Watch for related signs or areas of feeling powerless over your judgmental habits. Watch also for success displays that reveal themselves to you here and there. Acknowledge them and they will grow. It is a type of unfettering and one day you will be free.

Don't try to teach this so much as do it. It is very personal. If you are not happy, you are tied down to condemnation of some sort. Observe the source. Focus on the tethering; release condemnation and return to peace.

Peace awaits you. Peace is who you are. Come home. Amen.

#5   JOYFUL SUPPORT TEAM

This has been a period of relinquishment for you and for Jim. While dealing with death, trivia become inconsequential. You have come so far alone, within yourselves. Now is the time of joining. You travel alone no more. Around you is a team that supports and encourages and rejoices and even shares your sorrow (*tears from Clare*), and your joy (*wants Clare to focus on something more fun*) and your laughter. You are beginning to feel our joy, our love, our peace. Feel it around you now. Note the presences and recall the feeling frequently throughout your day and even when you awaken in the night.

(*Clare: Jim's right—one group helps us both. And what a team! Full of joy.*)

Be in the moment. Be in the moment. We are with you in the moment and we do influence plans for the future. This movement together is meant to be fun. But like any team going for a goal, there will be bruises and stressful times. But we are here even then and we do what we can to make things go well.

(*Clare sees image of a shout of joy.*)

We hold your hands, your shoulders, upper arms, back, as we go. Again, stop and feel how close that we are. Speak to us. You can call us "the gang" or any other title: "team"? "loves"?

Now for the moment we wish to express our pleasure in your connecting to other people and bringing our light with you.

(*Clare: They are complimenting me on accepting health this time around on the second series of radiation treatments, rather than illness. They are very pleased with Jim's disposition even in difficult times.*)

You, Jim, are good at avoiding fear.

(*Clare sees huge joy, like fireworks around that idea.*)

(*Clare asks about Jim's accumulation of paper and file boxes in his office. They won't touch the topic.*)

Jim, go for a clear look around your desk, three feet on each side. Nothing is loose. Clear. Neat. Feng Shui. You can do it. Stuff around the desk is like a pressure around your (*Jim's*) temple. By clearing, you will be more cognizant of them. Shut out those outside pressures to be more open. (*Clare sees areas of resistance in terms of piles of paperwork.*) Tough, but you can do it and will.

Hop into each morning with joy and expectation and devotion. Your day's activities will slide easily with intention. Join again in the evening for ten minutes with us; we would appreciate it. Go now and slide through this day.

Amen.

#6   UNTIE THE SHROUD

Light be unto you from your Father, Mother, and Self. Untie the shroud that is upon you. It is time to awaken to your pure God Self. Holy are you and through your knowing can you usher in the holiness of others for they are just as you.

(Clare sees a group of guides taking off their shrouds.)

What joy! Being in union with one another brings joy beyond understanding and peace. There are levels of joy and as we become connected to one another, our understanding of joy is heightened, and the experience is amazing.

It is a choice to stay as you are, but it would be ignoring the holy call of God. It is pretending to be happy in the, as you call it, video game. This is not happiness. The lotto you seek is the lotto of joy and it is available to you at much better odds than is the financial lottery. "Seek ye first the kingdom of God."

Change is required. Inner commitment must be brought to a higher degree. You think it is difficult, but you will be guided.

(Clare is shown a blind person with guides on two sides turning him toward a new direction.)

Daily intent is essential. Consistent commitment often will get you there. It is like going to a party of loved ones. You have been lost, circling the neighborhood for so long that you have accepted it as your life. But now, with strong intention and willingness to change patterns, though it may not be easy, you will be guided to the party. And what a party it is! You are being called; you have been missed. It will be so worth it!

We are here for your guidance every minute of every

day and night. Reach out for our hands; they will always be there. We are excited. We see you coming. Hurry.

Amen.

You, Jim, (*Clare is shown Jim walking head down*) must change your focus. Glimpse more and more frequently into the Light. These morning meditation sessions are good. Insert ten minutes in the evening as well.

(*Guide shows it to be a burden in the beginning, like a bird coming out of an egg.*)

Once you break out, you will have a whole new experience and it will be wonderful.

You will know the time because as the chick has an instinct, you too will have an internal nudging to begin. It will be soon.

(*Clare sees guide smile. Blanket of peace comes.*)

It will be revealed when you start giving the ten minutes at night. It is like you will see the Light behind the projects and the Light will be more important than the projects, though they are entwined as one, like spaghetti and sauce.

#7 LIGHT WORKERS UNITING

Beloveds, your place in my heart is ever warm. Today, crisis seems to abound—the world political situation, diseases being spoken of (AIDS, Bird Flu, and others), and many natural disasters. They are just the backdrops for your Light.

Light workers are uniting in a serious effort now to speak as one, of that which is not only of the earth plane, but that which exists everywhere—light, love, peace, and joy. The accumulated Light of the Light workers is quite bright. Its magnitude is triggering those who have been dormant to also open up their own Light and join, and then the Light gets brighter, and more people see it and are triggered to turn on their own Lights. They join the other Light sources and it becomes even more brilliant, which has a more far-reaching effect, triggering still others, etc.

It is a great time of awakening. The calamities that appear are a mere background contrast to the real happening, which is of great joy. Keep your focus in the Light. Ignore the other. Your focus can only be on one spot or the other. Know that it is always a choice. When you find yourself focusing on the background, let it be a reminder to refocus and merge into the Light.

(Clare sees it like a sideways trampoline that bounces you back into the Light.)

It is an amazing period to be alive. Your Light is needed, as is that of everyone who is called. Do not delay.

Do what you need to make your meditations more in the Light. Try music, incense, chime sounds, or repeating a phrase like "I live this day in peace," Some, like Jim, may benefit from a walking meditation.

This is for you both, Jim and Clare. At times, you settle for quiet time and not meditation. Ask yourself, "Am I in the Light at this moment?" If you are having difficulty, ask for help. Help is always available.

We speak to you in love, not to scold, but to guide. Your happiness will grow exponentially to the Light you open to.

Such joy! Such gratitude! Such happiness! Don't delay. Amen.

#8   JOYFUL SERVICE

Happy are those who serve, for that is the Kingdom of God. Loving and caring and giving, one for another is the joy found in the God Self. To have this revealed into one's life is such a gift, for without it, one will focus on grief and sorrows and pain and fears and shortcomings. But when one's bucket is strictly for giving, personal cares are minimized. As you become more aware of your God Self, you will delight in serving even more.

Show me your love in action and I will show you a happy person. Observe your community and see where true joy abounds. As your heart opens, your level of service will go beyond your home and family.

Such a simple lesson and such a seed of gladness!

The daily "to do" lists are the underpinnings of loving and giving. Mundane tasks done in love are also Divine service. Be happy as you serve one another.

Amen.

(Guide folds her hands at her chest and bows, as in a "Namaste" greeting.)

#9   DILUTE CARES WITH JOY

(This message came at a very challenging time in Clare's journey with cancer. Tumors had spread to her spine and she was forced to undergo radiation on her back, as well as chemo. Cancer had also spread to the outside of her liver and pelvic bones. The prognosis was not good.)

Look at us. (*Clare hears an incoming expression of surprise, humor and excitement*) Today, girlfriend, we are going to see the Light. Show me your cares and woes and I will dilute them by injecting joy. The more joy you bring in, the more insignificant your issues become. It brings us great joy to perform the little miracles that make your problems diminish. Review the lesson in "A Course in Miracles"* about being receptive to the Word that comes—you need it. We are by your side on other daily issues that you are facing as well.

Joining with Dian† is a good example of joining Light with Light workers as we have asked you to do. When Light workers join in one purpose, their Light is brighter than the sum of the individuals.

Read, but don't drive yourself crazy. The reading required for either of you is only for snacking, not for a full course meal. Appreciate the potential of the written word. You, too, will be sharing Light through the written word. Do it in joy. Do it with enthusiasm. And if it becomes blocked, ask for redirection from us. Guidance is always available.

Be careful not to be in the "someday" attitude about putting some writing on paper to publish. We are pleased

---

* *A Course in Miracles, Workbook, lesson 106*
  † *Dian is Clare's sister-in-law who does remote healing through Reiki*

to see that Jim is breaking that attitude. You will, too.

Be of good cheer on the healing on your back. There is progress being made. It will not be a dominant theme in your life. You are on the right track. Good things will come, and you both will sigh a large sigh of relief. Congratulations! (*Clare feels happy, light, joyful.*)

You are cheating by looking into our lives (*said teasingly*); we live this way. As you dedicate your life to giving and serving, you will be slipping into these qualities as well. Isn't it fun?!

Approach unknown experiences with a carefree attitude. It is not up to you to see that another person has a point of view that you want them to have. There is a great deal of growth necessary for Clare in this area. Trust that the fallout of any action need not be handled by her, but will be taken care of by us for the highest good of all concerned. It may not turn out the way she thinks it should, but releasing control will help it turn out the better way. This is a major lesson and one that needs to be worked on regularly.

Salutations of love, ever-present love, go to you now and forever.

Amen.

#10   VOLUNTEERS FOR THE HARVEST

Happy are those who are called into service for they are remembering the joy they have known on other planes. Rejoice for those who give. Ask and you too can serve at the banquet. Desire and a loving heart are the ticket for entry into such a service. Hollow are the energies spent on the mundane, such as TV, shopping, and impressing others. (*Shows Clare an image of people driving fancy cars.*)

Many volunteers are being sought now for the task at hand. It requires sacrifice of self-aggrandizement to be replaced by service, very rewarding service. The amount of effort will have amazing payback, similar to mining diamonds that are four inches under the surface of the soil, or picking the ripened fruit from the trees. The readiness is at hand for a great harvest, being the Awakening of your brothers and sisters in God. They are waiting in suspense and great anticipation for the moment.

(Feeling of great excitement and joy like a party is being prepared.)

The harvest will be bringing Light workers of equal value to yourself, doing equal effort as yourself, bringing equal results, causing a very rapid progression in the amount of Light that is present on the earth. It will be much more the norm to look at a stranger and smile at them, or have them smile at you. The levels of peace, happiness, joy, and laughter will all increase as the Light increases. It will still be spotty; percentage-wise a greater number will be awakening, but there will still be those who choose not to awaken at this time. (They are blessed as well, but it is not their time.)

Remember to take time to feel the peace as often as possible. Feel the presence of the love that is around you. In the beginning, it will have to be a conscious effort to remind yourself to do this. Perhaps artificial reminders, like a telephone ring, a stop light, someone sneezing, any time you pet your dog, or any other self-discovered stimulus can be a trigger to remind you to connect. One day it will be ever present and then you will know bliss.

Much love is here for you; much love is in your own being. Neither of which is fully accepted by you at this point. (*Image of a baby bird who can't stretch his mouth all the way open to be fed.*)

Now go through your day in great joy and blessings, triggering yourself frequently to connect to the great Love within and without. Blessed you are.

Gratefully yours.

#11   CHOOSE PEACE/ PERSONAL QUESTIONS

Hello from your friends. Today, peace is the topic, for without peace, you cannot be connected to who you are. Do you have any idea the percent of thoughts that you have that are not peaceful? This is a choice. Clean up your act.

Seek joy. When you find yourself lamenting over others' mistakes, pretend there is a bell in your hand ringing, saying it is time to get real. And reality is only in the now, in joy and in peace. This does not indicate being a Pollyanna. Spilled milk must be cleaned up, dishes must be washed, but the prevailing attitude is one of choice.

This is an old lesson, but it is one that has much more learning before it is complete. The goal is to maintain a loving attitude all of the time, but you could settle simply for improvement of ten, twenty percent. It is sloppiness that puts you in this state of ego versus Godliness.

Life is meant to be fun. Guard your attitude.

("Earth changes" question from Clare: "Can we relax and enjoy the dryness around our home and continue to spend money on improvements, or would our time be better spent elsewhere due to the likelihood that there will be major earth shifts, and energy for home projects will have been wasted?")

Times are changing. *(Clare sees swirling or fast movement all around the earth.)* Apply the peace principle to your daily life. Soon your energies will be more directed toward service. Your home projects will cease to be as interesting to you. The house will not be taking the energy it is now.

The earth changes will be moving at a faster pace than they are now, but not so fast that it will be alarming.

19

It will be noticed. You are secure in your home. There will be more dryness in this area. Lake levels will drop and there will be more sunshine. Records will be broken in sunshine and warmth almost every year for this area. You can relax.

(Question about Jim's writing) Intent will help your writing as well as clarity of purpose and clarity of space.

(They show a shovel pushing everything away from his desk, just Jim and his computer.)

Forty percent of your time, Jim, can be writing. The mess that's around you won't really be around you when you get focused on the writing. It won't tug at you. You are going to need clear surface areas to lay things flat and not lose them, related to the writing.

It is very good that you are moving forward. Keep the momentum going. Discipline is the key. The first attempts may not be your final destination. Be able to set aside and move into new direction when nudged.

(Clare says: "It feels like the book will be mainly yours right now.")

Your work will inspire Clare. You may want to write twice a day, once in the evening. You will know. Happy to be of service.

Your friend and brother.

#12 HAPPY ARE THOSE WHO ARE CALLED TO SERVICE (PART PERSONAL)

Welcome. Focus your attention gently on things that please. Struggle is not necessary. Come to each day in peace and joy, planning to uplift or be uplifted. Remember the feeling of this connection and go there frequently throughout the day.

You are admired for your efforts on the earth and supported with a team of fellow Light beings who love you without end and will assist in any way they can. It is important to listen to your nudges for them to be effective. As Mary Margaret Moore* would say, frequently go to the Oneness for a brief moment of "Ah!" It is like blowing water out of your snorkel tube. It clears communication.

Picture yourself everywhere you go with a group of about six people in robes, hustling along with you. They not only see what you do, they hear your thoughts and take on projects for you to shorten your struggles. Some issues they cannot take on, and you must experience them fully. Please ask often, though, for assistance because we get so much joy in serving you.

(Jim asks a question about using photography with future books.)

There seems to be a barrier in this country because of the cost of producing photos. Perhaps in India they could be produced in a cost-effective manner. Photography is a beautiful medium for reaching people.

As Catherine Lanigan† uses simplicity in her format of

* *Mary Margaret Moore is a spiritual teacher who channeled the Bartholomew teachings in books, tapes and talks.*

† *Catherine Lanigan is the author of several books about angels and angelic assistance.*

21

her books, it is wise to use simplicity also in your format, so people can read a little bit, then put it down. This material may be helpful in writing, perhaps more useful in writing published articles rather than published books. Articles will reach more people easily and touch a lot of lives. They can also refine your writing style and connection to *your* guidance in writing. After publishing articles successfully, a book will be forthcoming.

(Clare "I don't see the book being as widely distributed as the articles.")

The articles are hard work and very rewarding. Great joy can come through articles. Do go there soon.

Your diligence is appreciated.

#13 ROUTE WILL SEEK YOU/ QUESTION ON INDIGO CHILDREN

Joy unto you. Your devotion is noted and is rewarded for yourself and others as they will get the benefit too. Be peaceful on your path, not seeking for direction (*Clare sees a canoeist going down a river, asking if each tributary is the right one*).

When there is a correct turn, you will be guided effortlessly. Do not seek the correct route; the correct route will seek you. Your job is to keep joy in the vessel, like people singing in the canoe as it goes. The vessel is the body.

It is advantageous to seek spiritual strength in your meditation and prayer work. It helps you remember who you are.

There will be many parallel activities that you will engage in as you travel this path, like an outrigger with side canoes attached. You can be writer, parent, teacher, etc., but your main role is to be a vessel carrying the light.

Look up as you travel. Your guide, like an eagle above the canoe, is always with you.

(Clare asks a question regarding our grandchildren, and "indigo," "magenta" children, terms which are used to represent children born with special gifts for the current times.)

Each child that comes, comes with its own purpose, one no better than the other. Like in a soup, there is the meat, the pepper, etc. Each has their role and is equal to the other in importance. It would be unwise to hold one with greater value than another, although your ego would really like to do that. All crayons in the crayon box have the same value—indigo, magenta, brown, flesh— they are just used at different times for different purposes.

Each of your grandchildren comes into this world with a great deal of love in their hearts. Their service will be more easy and more enjoyable because of it, but not more important. These are blessed souls, even those yet to be born, because their service will be one of mainly joy. Again, remember that their work is not more important than that of the prisoner. We are all one. That is all.

Amen.

(Clare is told that their names seem hardly of interest to those communicating.)

#14   CHINESE DRAGONS OF LIGHT

Hello gentle folks. Happy are we who serve. You, I and those on the other side. Slow to anger, quick to laugh, patient, tolerant, and understanding are attributes of those on the path. Walking to the Light is not a solitary experience. Each step we individually take is like a carrier of a dragon in a Chinese parade. Each must carry their weight; each must go in the same direction, seeking the same goal. There are many Chinese dragons of Light, simultaneously heading in the goal of Oneness as we speak, all around the world.

Don't assume that you know who is on your team. There may be people you haven't met, different races, and different cultures, all lifting and going to the Light with you. They are grateful for that which you do and you are grateful for what they do to make this trip possible.

The trip itself is like the dragon carriers. The direction is uncertain to the carrying team, but the guidance is sure and trust must abound. As Light bearers then, one must be certain to carry their load, but at the same time be confident their direction is perfect because of the wonderful guidance. Enjoy the trip. Be sure to take pleasure in your connecting to the Light. If it is more of a task than it is a joy, your intention must be purified.

Again you are reminded to go frequently throughout the day to the pure Light, if but for a brief moment. This practice keeps away all gloom and reminds you of who you are.

(Clare feels Light; it is very bright and they remind her that going to the Light is a cheerful experience.)

It is on the same idea as light bulbs that help avoid Seasonal Affective Disorder, but it is more cheerful and convenient. You can do it in a car.

(Clare is reminded of the words of a Girl Scout and Brownie song familiar to her, "Take the smile out of your pocket and put it on your face.")
Yours in joy and love.

#15   HAPPINESS ABOUNDS

Everyone is the Love of God inside, like a treasure chest with blue/white light within. This is without exception in every person and is truly a great incredible treasure. On one level or another we know that it is there. We may have forgotten the combination to the lock, but we do have the Love of God within us.

When one desires to open the chest and be in the Love of God, they need but ask of their elder spiritual brothers and sisters from all dimensions for help. It will be given in great abundance. That is all you need to do, is ask. The rest will be taken care of and you too will live in the Light and Love of God. When you are in this Love and in this Light, you feel the joy of giving and of appreciation of others and their giving. It is a state of understanding, acceptance, appreciation, rejoicing and difficulties seem so small, almost like little ants or crickets that need to be dealt with but don't dominate.

Merging into the Beingness of God is the ultimate happiness. At this time there is no "I," there is no "we," there is simply a state of Being and all is well. Amazingly so, all **is** well. It is such a state of peace, no struggle, no goals, no failures.

(It reminds Clare of a cloud sitting on a lake on a moonlit night where the cloud is sitting on the water and glowing with moonlight, so serene, so beautiful, so peaceful, and so content.)

This state is our destiny and will come to us as we seek, as we ask for help, and as we meditate. It is a different dimension and it can't be reached if you don't still yourself to go there. On the order of brain waves—where beta is a very active state where you are thinking and moving and planning and implementing plans—in this state the dimension of being that we seek has a difficult time showing itself, at least at your (mankind's) level of development. But, as you slow your brain waves down in meditation, you come closer to the dimension of peace and love, and the Beingness of the Oneness. And with grace, God's assisting hand, we can go there.

There are few short cuts other than meditation and joyful service together. You don't serve alone, you don't meditate alone, and the joy you are tapping into is so bountiful, you could not comprehend the magnitude of it. Please try.

We love you. We rejoice in your seeking. Come home. Amen.

All of Us *(Loosely defined as The Arc of Infinity, when asked by Clare who they are.)*

#16   TOTAL FORGIVENESS

Forgiveness again is a theme. It has insidious levels of lack of forgiveness that one wears with him but without conscious awareness that he is doing it. They show up, emerge when we want to not forgive someone else, such as a disliked political figure. In truth, we are choosing to keep a piece of ourselves unforgiven and hidden. In some ways we feel unworthy that we have this ugliness and we try to hide it.

But as we bring out forgiveness for others, we are learning to see them and own them as our own and deal with them and let the Light of God erase them as reality, and then we return to a more purified state. As long as we can't forgive the other person, then we can't forgive ourselves. It is a litmus test to see how well we are purifying ourselves.

The day will come when we don't see guilt, only funny mistakes viewed with joy and delight. And then we will find ourselves in a more clarified vibration that can communicate with higher beings on a more ready basis. You are ready. You are there. So when Spirit speaks to you, you hear them and you can ask questions and hear answers.

So our purpose today is to observe our own behavior toward another and embrace our projections on them with understanding, acceptance, and love—total forgiveness. For that which we are doing for them, we are doing for ourselves. The efforts are worth it.

Amen.

Live your life this day in gratitude and you will be walking with the Spirits.

Lovingly yours.

#17   ALL THAT I GIVE IS GIVEN TO MYSELF

As we care for others, so do we receive caring for our-selves. Caring for us is in great abundance, but focusing and acknowledging that the caring is there for us is our weakness. But as we show our own love for others, we know it is but an echo of the abundant love sent to us. We need never feel alone.

Life is to be a dance and not a struggle—a perfected dance like you see in the Olympics where effort is made to make it beautiful. The process should be fun. You are always part of a team in the different roles. You play all the roles: the director, the choreographer, the dancer, the critic, all for members of your team and they for you. It is a joyful pursuit.

When progress is not being made for the members of the team, you become stagnant. Joy ebbs; conflicts may arise. Seek spiritual assistance to get back on the progressive track. Assistance is always available. You are very blessed.

Each person on your team should find spiritual food for thought in reading materials. These will be different for each person. There is a banquet of them out there. Just find one that is delicious. At the same time, don't be consumed by reading. Let it be a snack food. Pause before reading and when you conclude, to connect to the Oneness. The purpose of everything on earth is to birth oneself into the Oneness. Therein lies all peace, joy, and love. It is wonderful that you are coming home.

(Clare feels a powerful emotional connection.)

Welcome.

Amen.

#18   HELPFUL TEAM IS HERE

Welcome loved ones, family. We come together again to do what we can to break out cobwebs to clear thinking. The cobwebs from non-use have caused your channels to the Oneness to be marred, to be inefficient. The best way to cure this problem is to use this area of your connection, your communication with the Oneness. Use it often. Use it briefly and intently. Use it generally with a humming atmosphere over your existence.

As the song says, the very best place to start is the beginning. Start now. First have the intent to be open to God, and secondly request assistance, and then relax into it. Distractions must be under control. A grateful, appreciative heart is a requirement. Commitment to time, commitment to consistency is also required. These commitments can be started in small measures: five, ten minutes. Then they will grow on their own to fulfill your heart's desire. Uniting with another or others is a boost to the joy you will feel, for you share their joy and they will share yours. Again, intent is reemphasized. Should you desire to do this, you will be given much guidance and much success.

To work with you from the other side is such a joy. Those of us who have the privilege are so pleased. In a very loose way, it would be like taking a small child on their first Easter egg hunt and helping them find the eggs by giving them hints, bringing them close, offering suggestions, but yet the last motion for the child is to find the egg for themselves and have the glee, the excitement of doing so.

The heart of the assistant is as full of joy as the child, if not more so. So it is with us who serve you. You tell us you wish to find God; we show you where He might be. We bring you very close and wait for your discovery. We rejoice together. See how much fun we have. Now when your intentions are to serve others, we have the same desire to assist. We help you set up situations where there is need. We help you use approaches that will succeed. We supply time and space elements to make it work, and then when you succeed, we all have a party.

Clarify on paper the goals that you would have assistance with. Include a general time frame, the general audience, and the type of impact that you are looking for. Keep your intention pure in that you don't get the ego out there seeking for acclaim. Pure intent and willingness to strive for the sake of others will not fail. We will be helping you, no matter how small or how big the goal or task—dropping something off at someone's house to cheer them or developing a program for 40,000 people. Some programs are going to start looking good and then dry up or go into a dormant stage. Some will die, yet others will be revived at a more correct time, and will succeed beautifully.

Attachment to outcome is a motivator, but with guidance, must be laid down from time to time and perhaps picked up again. Just know that it is not up to the person that you are for all your goals to be met, but it depends on many things. First and foremost is your team.

(Clare hears "What a team!" cheering themselves on.)

In a way, you who are on earth are the pencil for the team's plans. We work through you and with you to awaken the Light within those on earth.

(Clare sees a picture of little toy figures that have a Tootsie Roll center inside them that are acting and moving and then, with this amazing team assisting, these centers are dispersed

32

throughout the figures. They are sweet everywhere.)

We would like to give guidance to you by saying first of all, congratulations on your meditation every day. Before you meditate, put on a paper three things that you would like this day to bring through your efforts. Hold those during meditation; then clean those up early in the day. Get right on those. This list will grow as you have success. Don't push it. Do it peacefully, easily, happily, with success. This will keep you as our team member happy, which will buoy the joy of the rest of the team.

Your brothers and sisters of your team in the Light

#19   VARRROOOOOMMMM!!!

Traffic comes and goes, you among the rest of the traffic doing your thing. The day's activities seem to have purpose and direction and urgency, but the core is peace. This peace can go through the traffic. It can be adorned with activity, with purpose, with sounds, with business. It still is peace and pure. It is the core of the vehicle that travels, which hurries here and there, to and fro. It is a good combination to have the peace within and the activity over it, but not diluting it. It is like the activities, business, goals, and interactions are all adornments for the core of the vehicle or being, which is peace. The purer the peace, the clearer the adornments of purpose, activity, time constraints, and relationships, like the old advertising jingle "Everything goes better with Blue Bonnet on it."

The busyness of life is not an enemy to peace. They are synergistic. Wonderful, wonderful peace can bring wonderful successful activities; much purpose of giving love can be accomplished.

However, the peace must come first and must be continually fed and nourished. If the busyness comes first, the space for peace is eliminated and the relationship between the two diminishes. Then the busyness itself becomes a major struggle, thus dominating the life force. Putting peace and the connection to God first allows the activity to be an overflow of the God love, assuring success and cooperation in the world to bring joy.

The old dictum of "start your day in prayer or meditation" is truth. It is partial truth. The day's activities must also be fueled by that love connection, so prayer and moments of God connection throughout the day are essential, and gratitude in the heart in the evening are all part of the package.

34

With this simple formula, joy attends you. Faith and trust guide you securely through your activities. You never travel alone. Your path may bring you into difficult and dark times, but you again will always have assistance. Lean on that assistance.

The adage, "the times are a-changing" will seem like the theme of life, but as long as you hang onto your guidance, it won't matter that the times are changing. Again remember to connect strongly in the morning, as frequently as possible throughout the day, and again before bedtime.

Feel the love of God through it all.

Amen

#20   WELCOME HOME, WANDERER

Welcome home you who have wandered a while. You are always welcome and home is always a perfect fit. When you are having trouble finding your way home, call for your brother or sister to guide you. It is their joy to assist one they love so much.

Remember today and always that you are living in two dimensions. One and foremost, of course, is your dimension of love, joy, and peace of God. The second being the medium through which you are experiencing your life, in this case, the earth plane, and all that entails with the ego and the feeling of separateness of one to another. In truth, there is no separateness, but a Divine Peace that settles over the Oneness of our divine natures as they rest in harmony one to another.

Challenges that come up to your awareness on the earth plane are artificial. There really is no cancer. There really is no mental illness or stress or fear. However, in this dimension you do see them and do engage in the dance as unpleasant as that may be. Be sure to ask for dance instructors. And ask for perspective, knowing that the Oneness, when experienced, is so profound, that the unpleasant dance is tolerated.

You are not alone. In difficult times look for, ask for, beg for connections that are more pure than your own. And trust that the help will come.

Each dance or challenge is different and requires different solutions. The one solution they all share is the intensity of God's Love as we feel close to it and dip from its reservoir. The profound experience of God's Love overshadows the difficulty being faced.

If one cannot experience the profound Love of God,

due to their own distress, then it is time to call in others to help. Most frequently we would call on Jesus, Mary, Mohammed, Buddha, but there are many favorites, each with a major desire to serve you. Hold their hand; do not walk alone. Ask for miracles and expect miracles. Then seek the lighter things of life that bring you joy. Go to what serves you. There will be assistance waiting and that which serves you, is probably you serving others. Find the joy in whatever way you can.

Have a blessed day.

P.S. Get enough liquid and sleep. Smile a lot.

#21 ALLNESS

Joy and peace be with you. *(Clare feels excitement.)* Today you touch upon the Allness that is adapted to your understanding. Passion calls and passion gives fuel for the intention of serving one another. Become aware of that which brings you passion in the spiritual realm.

Uniting with others gives stability and staying power. Be clear on your intention and find others who have the same intention. Unite in love and joy. If a project is being guided by God, by the Holy Spirit, it should flow fairly smoothly. Like sand burrs caught in wool, be willing to pluck out little entanglements of the ego, especially your own.

Look around for examples of people on Earth in service, like Ken Walker *(a minister friend of Clare and Jim's)*, Sunday school teachers, and other givers in local missions and charitable groups like Loaves and Fishes. Their zeal is what we are seeking.

Find small projects in your own life where giving is the idea, for example, Dian *(a sister-in-law)* doing healing sessions for Clare. The more you put yourself out in the name of God, the more use you will have for God. It can be just you and paper and working out like the publishing of a book, but if it is done in love and giving, it is a gift from your God Self.

Be conscious of what is going on with yourself. Record success moments. Plan ways to give. Build on your successes and unite with others who have zeal to share. Ultimately walking in the Light of God from moment to moment is the goal. Feel the joy. Attack problems with adventure. Ask for help and understanding.

When you ask in prayer, do know that your prayer

will be answered. There are such big problems around for which you cannot see a solution, but answered prayer will come. Ask for miracles. Pray more. Kindness and mercy will abide with you throughout your life.

Amen.

(Clare has the feeling of clear air and refined connection after these messages, like the air is a thin, refined vibration.)

#22 SERVING IN JOY

Joy-filled sister and brother, good morning. Service is subtle and best served are those who are served by joy. So in order to be a wonderful servant of God, fill your tray gift with joy and distribute it to everyone you see. No one has too much joy until they are totally merged with God and then it is not too much, it is perfect.

Serving God is like being the waiters at a party and you distribute the cook's good wares. God being the cook, having an abundance of joy, asking us to help Him/Her distribute the abundance of joy to those who are hungry for it. Better yet, is for the servants of God to call forth from the guests at the party their ability to distribute joy. In other words have them awaken to the joy they carry for God and distribute that joy among others.

No greater joy is there than to awaken to one's own capacity of joy distribution, the awareness of the God presence within and in reaching out with this joy, seeing it come back to you from others who are experiencing the same thing. This joy-giving is so more easily experienced in goal-oriented groups, for example, a play, Habitat for Humanity, cleaning up the east side neighborhood, Girl Scouts, a church service, or a family birthday party where the object is that many come together in love, sharing the love of each other for a common good. It is an opportunity for love to flow freely.

Take this day and insert love at every opportunity. Be happy. Interpret everyone's actions from the best light. Let your heart sing, your eyes twinkle, and walk with God. We walk with you. Let's have fun. That includes everything you do, including cleaning out a purse.

(Clare says "My heart feels dancing.")

How blessed we are to know the love of God and to be able to walk in the Love of God. So many long for that experience and even our demonstration of walking in the Love of God is a valuable demonstration for those who are seeking.

(Clare: They show a border of live white flowers, like gardenias at the bottom of the typing. They say to us, "Thank you for your time.")

#23 SACRED PRESENCE

The Sacred Presence of God is who you are. It is your fundamental foundation. It is that which you have always been and always will be. The experience of being away from that Sacred Presence is new and artificial. It is similar to enjoying the experience of a warm summer afternoon in nature with gentle sounds and pleasantness and then turning on an AM radio and listening to teenage music that is loud and active, or songs with drama and trauma, thinking and emoting, and knowing that it is just a momentary experience that one chooses to go into and that it is not real, but while one is into the music, one forgets the Sacred Presence that is the background for this input experience.

That is what living in this world is like. It is a choice to focus away from the ever-present sacred experience and briefly go into the soap opera of life, not that the sacred experience is not always there, because it is. The seemingly momentary experience of life—it is so short compared to the vastness of the sacred experience—is simply a focusing away from our true foundation, which is sacred presence.

It is only a simple momentary refocusing, it doesn't change who we are.

There is great delight in identifying both experiences at once, knowing we are the sacred and exploring the temporary. In doing so, there is much more peace to the drama of life because our true nature is ever present.

Because this is only an experience of choice, it is certainly wise to make it a joyful one. Make extra effort to find joy, laughter, the humorous and delightful. Again, this is an experience of choice. Make it a choice that you appreciate, not taking yourself too seriously. Remembering who you are can assist in this attempt and there is room for all kinds of experiences. It does not have to be a fun one, it can be any experience you wish to have, including sorrow, sadness, struggle, etc. Each one offers an experience. Each one has its own value.

Connecting with your sacred center, the true foundation of who you are, helps to take the drama of life more lightly. It is basically getting your priorities straight, recognizing what is important in this world. Meditation is so valuable to remind ourselves of our sacred center. Knowing our sacred center changes the perspective of life's meaning. We can travel the river of life more peacefully knowing who we truly are. It is like running a rapids with a raft that cannot in any way fail. No matter what the rapids brings, there is a confidence and sureness that all will be well.

The sureness of our raft is the sacred center within us. Being well aware of it through meditation and prayer can bring much peace to a very interesting life.

Amen.

Your friends of the Arc.

#24   PEACE

A peaceful center is similar to a white linen tablecloth. Keeping that which would spot it, such as regrets, negative thinking—be it our own or dramas from the newspaper or television or life—keeping these things swept clear of the tablecloth will keep the tablecloth clean or your countenance at peace. It is mainly the responsibility of diligence and the ability to forgive and to let go.

Observing the countenance when it is clear, observing yourself in a peaceful state will help you also observe when it is not peaceful and clear. Even noticing that there is a disturbance on your peace is the first step to clearing that disturbance, replacing negative thinking with joy is one process; another is working on forgiveness; another is working on understanding.

The ability to keep oneself in a state of peace usually takes conscious effort until the pattern has been developed. Then the awareness of peace and the joy and the love is forthcoming. Joyful assistance is always available if we but ask.

When the process is complete, we will be as Jesus Christ and live in a state of joy and peace forever. Don't make it a struggle; make it a journey.

Bon voyage!

All of Us

#25   FORWARD

"Forward is the Lord's Command." Holding the hand of Jesus one moves forward through life's destiny. Your life plan is scheduled for you. Relax into it. Go peacefully and happily on your path knowing I am with you and you are never alone. You need not stress about the bumps on the path or the turns it takes; just relax into the promise that you are not alone and it goes as planned. Fearing tomorrow or what may be down the path does not aid your joy of the moment. In fact, it takes away the enjoyments of the little joys that surround you at any given moment.

Focusing on the here and now and its delights is a training one must undertake to be truly happy. It is in the moment that joy is burst forth, like capsules opening. It is practice that helps you capture them. Noticing the magical joys that are around you and increasing the number you observe as the years go by, is a challenge or a talent. Observe laughter; tuning in to your own laughter and other's is a way of honing your own joy capacity.

Equally important in your happiness is the ability to not attend to unnecessary negative issues. These issues may be important for some to attend to, but if you are not called to make a decision on them, focus your attention rather on the light side. This is crucial for a joyful life. Try to be the observer and watch yourself in conversation. Note what you are focusing on and try to improve toward the joyful.

Releasing criticism is a moment-by-moment goal. Criticism is a national pastime and a large stream to pull oneself out of. All efforts are worthy and worthwhile. Take it on as a personal challenge in life to sidestep the engagement of criticizing as a pastime. That challenge in itself can be fun. Developing a grateful heart is a means to accomplish this.

Feel our love and our joy and our unending support of you as you seek for the good. We cheer for you, and your smallest efforts bring us great joy. Try to feel it.

Picture a nine-month old in a bathtub, splashing and having great joy. Look at the parents' faces as they see the joy in the child. It is similar to those of us who serve you. Your joy is magnified in our joy. Your struggles are vacant of our joy and yours. We love to see you happy. We assist as best we can. Remember us and the joy you bring to us. Be happy and look for our support.

You are deeply loved.

#26   TO SAND A SURFACE

Observation is a gift; to step back and watch life and observe what is going on is a must. In doing so, one can see the areas that are rough—places where love doesn't shine, similar to a wooden chair where the finished surface has been damaged and the shine has been marred. We can see this in areas of our life where there is no love present at the moment. For example, we might look at how we are viewing our political leaders or people at work or in an organization where we judge them to be in error.

How we can best serve the world and our souls is to bring love and forgiveness into the situation, one layer at a time, as best we can at that moment. We will, with effort, change condemning attitudes to understanding attitudes, change understanding attitudes to appreciating attitudes, merge appreciating attitudes with love. Each of these is a different layer bringing the change about.

The first stage of changing condemning to understanding is perhaps the most difficult. This will be more easily accomplished if we ask for guidance and help from God. All things are possible with God. That can't be overemphasized.

When love is complete, like the chair, our life will shine without flaw. Joy will be around every corner. Because we are all one, our joy is the joy of everyone on this planet and elsewhere. What a wonderful gift you give to God when you can replace a feeling of condemnation for love and appreciation.

That is our purpose. Much joy and peace and love attend you.

Give it your best effort.

Amen.

#27   THURSDAY NIGHT MIRACLES GROUP

Miracles Group*. Sweet! This is a group of like-minded seekers who joined together combining their efforts individually and as a group to better the world's vibrations. Each person is blessed each week of meeting, all in a unique way. Then that blessing is brought out into the world and others are blessed. The group's efforts are supported on a higher level. There are many groups similar, but this is an excellent example of this effort.

When there is a particular need, perhaps even unidentified, the leader will be guided to materials that will assist. Commendations are given to those who take leadership roles and their willingness to listen and adapt to spiritual guidance. Appreciation is also given to each individual that comes. They bring joy and a feeling of brother/sisterhood that is supportive to each other. In this world where oneness is hard to find, the strong feeling of connection is very important to assist in remembering who we are. Remember because there is only One, any additional joy brought to the world affects all. Be blessed in your giving and be blessed in your receiving. We who guide you are blessed by your efforts.

Thank you, your friends in the Oneness.

(Clare is shown an image of a cake with frosting, a gelatin with whip cream, and cheese with crackers to represent the idea that together we are one and neither is complete without the other. They play one role and we play the other.)

---

*   *Thursday Night Miracles Group is an open, informal group of spiritual seekers who meet regularly in Muskegon, Michigan. There are many similar groups around the world.*

#28   BROTHERHOOD

Brother/sisterhood is our goal because it is the understanding of the atonement or the oneness that we all have together. All activities that enrich are extending love and our connection to others, and are worthwhile. Barriers to that union must be noticed, found, and eliminated. These barriers can be such things as prejudice, condemnation, fault finding, ignorance of another's beauty, and lack of forgiveness.

Join me daily in surrendering to the Oneness within. Knowing this Oneness and rejoicing in its beauty can't help but extend into your daily living. Barriers will weaken and Oneness will be once again attained.

Merging with others on the same path strengthens the process for oneself, the community and the world. Celebrating others' successes in this realm strengthens their resolve and therefore the resolve of all. Joy is enriched. For all there is a celebration of the heart.

This process of atonement, or joining with each other, starts close at hand in the family, in the neighborhood, and extends out. The most crucial being, of course, that which is close to you daily. There you can feel the success and know that you are in completion in your efforts.

Without that lesson secured, the healing of the world can be more of an ideal than a reality. And yes, unfortunately, it is not always easy, but each lesson learned up close, through difficulty, will be a tool that will be yours to use in other realms. There are no mistakes; the lessons that you are asked to learn are the special skills that you are asked to learn to use later.

Gather your tools gladly and thank God for their acquisition. These tools will make life go with more ease as you go further down your path. Go boldly into your day, filled with the oneness you know. Extend love everywhere. You are blessed and we are blessed to be with you.

#29   JOINING

Join together with those you know and those you do not know, those you understand and those you do not understand, knowing they are you. You are they. Wholeness must be attempted, although its completion will not occur soon. Any barrier that can be loosened between two people, two ideologies, two religions, two races, genders, ages, etc, will aid in the eventual dissolving of separateness.

Like the metal mercury, when two parts become one, there is a greater completion in the new oneness. There is more understanding, more life experience in our case, when two parts join as one. Both parts benefit; more peace, more joy results.

There are two approaches to joining. One is internal and spiritual, emerging into the light of the Oneness for a brief moment, those moments to be extended as we develop our abilities to go into the Wholeness of being. The second approach is that of being alert and identifying areas where we see ourselves as separate, noticing and then consciously dissolving barriers between ourselves and another, be it real or imagined.

Often we see ourselves as separate from a fellow human being through some report of how they think or feel or act. These are taken out of context and we react to that part of the person and not to who they really are, for they are the same part of Being as we are. Our energies need be put into how we are similar, not how we are different. Their beauty is our beauty. It serves us well to make the effort to see the beauty. The opportunities abound.

Coming from a loving and understanding heart with patience will aid us on this journey. Know that every difference that we see is brought forth to our attention to aid in the development of understanding that is so important for the joining.

We hold your hands in this endeavor, for we too are one with you and the other. Take on this challenge, but don't make it burdensome. Work on it as you can in peace and you will be well rewarded.

Our love to you,

Your Support Crew

#30   CLEARING

Life is composed of details that would pull at you at every turn. Add to that the plethora of social options that are also calling for your time, and then the media, television, movies, books, games, email, so that the banquet table is filled.

For peace of mind, focus on purpose is essential. Clarifying of goals is important. When this is done, the banquet table can be more easily perused. And note when traversing the banquet table, there are issues there that are tempting, but are distracting to the goal at hand. The more passion for the goal, the easier it is to avoid these temptations.

Start with few, but clear goals. Write them down. Then prepare your room for those goals. Eliminating any piece of paper, any box of treasures, any unnecessary item of beauty, any item of distraction will all help keep the focus on the goal.

At your *(Jim and Clare's)* stage, you are not focusing on a clear goal for six hours a day. That will change. When the goal merges with you, the joy begins. Passion drives you; spiritual guidance leads you.

You are in the process of preparing for birth, and you have to get the room ready and the whole house. Look around the home and eliminate things that might get in the way when you are completely engrossed in the new goal. Do everything with joy. Wash the windows with joy, rearrange the cords around the TV with joy, paint the basement floor with joy, etc. The idea is that the house should be simplified, simplified, simplified, so that there are no hooks to draw you away when you become engrossed with the passion of your new project.

Create order and beauty around you, preparing the operating room for the new project to flourish. We are here with the white gloves, lovingly reminding you to simplify. Remove things as you can.

We love you.

#31   ASSUME

You see yourself as a package. You have an appearance that is given to those whom you feel are separate from yourself. Inside you have memories and fears that guide your separated self, but inside, beside all this packing paper, which everything is, is who you really are.

That is your core; that is your part of the Oneness. The more you focus on the Oneness, the more value it holds for you, and the less value everything else will hold.

Worries and concerns, plans, busyness, all can come to rest when the focus goes to Oneness.

#32 SOLUTION

Giving of one's joy is a path that brings the opening to one's own spirit. As you give, you peel off the outer layer of an onion and as you continue to give, joy increases and you get closer and closer to the core of who you are, which is the Oneness with God and with your brother/sister.

Giving of one's energy to another can be a solution to the quality of life. Some giving is done through prayer. Much giving is done to family and close friends. It always benefits to give even beyond the normal circle.

Maintaining a positive attitude is a gift in itself. Enjoying those whom you meet is another gift. Giving does not have to be difficult or burdensome. It is an attitude of joy and happiness that wants to be shared. Giving can and is often done with nature: caring for pets, caring for plants and yards, with love.

Happy hearts will find ways to radiate their joy. As happiness is shared, happiness is enriched.

Happiness comes from gratitude and appreciation. Disciplining oneself to take time to appreciate is beneficial for the growth of happiness, which helps the giving. It is a basic exercise in growing in joy, which helps the giving of the heart. Note other people's joy, no matter where it is found. Joy and love, in any guise, is always God. Like an Easter egg hunt, go through your day and observe joy and love in yourself and others and in nature.

Efforts on this behalf will be well rewarded,

#33   LIVING IN THE LIGHT

Blessings to you who seek the Light. Being in the Light is being in peace, in joy, being effortless, carefree, laughing a lot. Those of you on earth feel yourself in darkness. You have forgotten the existence of living in the Light. Happy assistance is ever at your bid and call. It is wise to call upon those who know the way to bring you back to where you need to be, back in joy.

You have become accustomed to living your life without Spirit as dominant. In such a life, the Light is dim, similar to the greys of winter. You become accustomed to the dimness and accept it and lose the urge for the Light, but remembering how magnificent life in the Light is draws you back to where you came from.

There is a pull from the darkness to keep you as you are, and there is the remembering that pulls you in the other direction. You need a lifeline to go forward. Ask for help. Jesus is a wonderful Source but there are many. Feel the Light of your Source.

Do happy things. Share joy and give.
Amen.

#34   GUIDANCE FOR THURSDAY NIGHT MIRACLES GROUP

Some strengths that are admirable in the group are their openness to other seekers, their strength in leadership, with John especially and others who take leadership from time to time, the reaching out for current and alive messages from workshops, materials such as this, good reading material, all truths that come together to help each of the members to grow and awaken.

(Clare is shown a tier of the group fanning out as if their energy is expanding, joining in the Oneness, which will never be taken away. It is a permanent accomplishment, a knowing of who they are. It is like a banyan tree; they have spread way out and have strong roots and deep understanding and provide peace not only for themselves but those who tarry there.)

The group* is an accelerator for awakening. The structure is good, thanks to John and others. The sharing of wisdoms coming from everyone, the heart-felt lovings, one person to another, and the joinings with that love become a unit with one purpose, to awaken to who we are in God. The format is an accelerator. Demonstration of the love they have for one another can be seen in the food that is brought.

This group has been assigned guides to assist not only when you are together, but when you are apart. They/we are honored and thrilled with joy to be in this experimental awakening group. Tapping into our energy, you will

* *The Thursday Night Miracles Group is the same group of spiritual seekers who were referred to in message #27. Clare and Jim were members of the group and shared these early messages with them.*

feel more buoyant. Reach out and touch Spirit whenever there is joy, whenever there is sorrow, and whenever there are concerns. Remember to lead your life with your heart and with your hand in the hand of guidance. Your joy can change the amount of joy of everyone you touch, and we can change your joy if you tap into us. Don't take life too seriously and try to look on the light side.

Change your thinking if negative thinking is irrelevant to your daily life, for example, if politics are something you can't do anything about, avoid "ain't it awful" games that do nothing but spin negativity. Try to catch yourself at least once a day where you change your thinking from negative to a positive by choice.

Go forth and be the joy that you can be.

#35   AWAKENING TO THE GOD WITHIN

God being Love is always the center of the candy tootsie roll pop, is always present within our being. Accessing the God within has a similarity to accessing the center of the Tootsie Roll Pop. First, you have to acknowledge the presence is there. Secondly, you have to desire to change the present situation to where you are connecting with that presence. The desire alone carries a great deal of importance to the accomplishment of such a goal. It is easy to become distracted and forget that goal in the rhythm of everyday existence. But holding the goal is a magnetic force in itself that will pull you to the connection to the Oneness.

Remembering that God is Love and God is Joy calls you home.

The journey need not be a difficult journey. Trying too hard can actually make the journey longer. One should have the strong intention to be with God and strong desire that you would unite with the Oneness once again. Then let go and let your higher self do the directing and enjoy the trip. The joy of the trip itself will hasten the final outcome.

An alert mind to the presence of joy and love in your life will expand that very love and that very joy. That then will hasten the journey to the Oneness.

Challenges will demonstrate learning for serving. As you go through the challenges, you will pick up understanding and skills in living that will assist you in assisting others to awaken to their own joy and love — to their Oneness.

Hold onto and treasure demonstrations of love in any form that present themselves throughout your day.

These will be revealed much more frequently when condemnation is diminished. This is a process that greatly reflects your own light. Be mindful and observant of yourself and others as you go through your day.

You are guided and helped in every way, and loved beyond measure. Be happy.

With much love.

#36   JOINING WITH SPIRIT

When expectation for Spirit Presence is here, you notice God's Presence. The awareness of Presence comes in many flavors—there are times it is very huge and fills the room and times when the awareness of Spirit isn't so grand. Of course, Spirit always fills the room. The amount of presence that we experience is proportional to that degree we can get ourselves out of the way.

There are times, with great effort, we cannot make a good connection. It is important to be accepting of this experience as well. Any condemnation would only put the ego in charge. Because it is all a process, we can't be one hundred percent all the time.

To appreciate the experience of God immersion, at whatever level, is our joy. The less we stress at this experience, the more successful we will feel. Having great appreciation for the God connection makes the connection stronger. Self judgment should be set aside, except for the wandering mind. Diligence to keep oneself present in the room right now is our responsibility.

Singing songs of joy, of connection, of brotherhood of man and love of God, and of appreciation for Jesus enhance the process of meditation. Singing, even during the day when you are not meditating, also enhances your love connection to God.

Intent and requests for assistance both strengthen your meditative success.

So today, keep your heart light, (still do the income tax or whatever you are called to do,) and feel the moment-by-moment connection to joy and love which is God.

#37 COMMITMENT TO JOY

As a Light worker, you are a member of a team. The team has a purpose, an intention to change the vibration of the world. Of course the vibration is to grow more and more in love and joy. Each of us is like a bubble in a fizzy drink. Each one has a job to do. If we do not hold our joy, our bubble, the drink will be flat and the vibration of the world will not improve. Left without distraction, we would feel our connection to joy and there would be no problem. Each of our Lights would grow and the world would be greatly blessed. However, we have a tendency to focus on that part of ourselves that we believe is separate. We worry, we have fear, we have condemnation of ourselves and others.

The issue then, is to find ways to keep ourselves in our Light. Daily meditation is a commitment to that effort. Without daily meditation, you concede that the separate part of yourself wins. Daily meditation is a reminder of our joy, of our oneness, of our commitment to the Light. One takes time to cleanse the body daily. One must also take time to clear the soul. The commitment must be made.

If necessary, the commitment can start off very small, say ten minutes in the morning and perhaps ten minutes at night. When considering your own personal value that you hold for the Light, your action should reflect that value. If you find yourself failing in this commitment, try again, and again. Keep trying until the habit sticks. It is very important. The part of us that believes we are separate would fight this commitment. In your heart, you know you are one with each other and with joy. One should be true to that knowledge.

Logically speaking, joy is the better goal than worry, fear, concern and busyness. Carrying the flag of joy everywhere you go makes for a more pleasant journey for yourself and others. Start each morning then in joy. Feel the love of God within yourself, and consciously bring it into the world. You are the vessels on this earth plane to carry out this responsibility.

Do it in joy.

#38   HOLDING THE LIGHT

Our love comes to you, and surrounds you. Never feel comfortless.

Within each person on earth, at all times, is the Light of God. This Light is often buried so that others don't see it, and there are times it is buried so far that the persons themselves are unaware of it. What a wonderful plan to have given everyone their greatest treasure within! Our purpose, since the separation, is to reconnect to our Light, grow it, and let it be dominant for our life.

Ways that help us rekindle our Light include primarily forgiving, which is the lack of condemnation. Another way to enhance our own Light is to seek it in others through the joy in their eyes, their smile, their gentleness, their giving, their loving. Appreciation also helps, not only of others, but also of circumstances, nature, guidance, and health. Celebrations are also very good. Anything that makes the heart feel light and full of joy. (Yes, cheering your team on in sports and sharing the excitement of victory counts.) Hobbies bring joy, volunteering brings joy, adventure brings joy, supporting when needed brings joy, singing brings joy. There are many individual things that each person finds to delight him or her. It is wise to take note of what these are and be sure to have time in your day for them.

The more we enhance our Light, the more we desire to do so. It is a life purpose. One can also benefit from observing which parts of our lives take us away from our joy. When they are observed, correction can be made. Sometimes it is a changing of our own attitudes and other times it is changing activities. Without taking stock of our "downers," we can live a life of mediocrity.

Yet another way to enhance our own Light is to find

spiritual companions and actively seek God together in joy. This is often found in a church family, but there are many other areas where this experience can be found, for example, meditation groups, healing groups, volunteer groups, and spiritual study groups.

Knowing that enhancing our Light is our purpose, we must take responsibility for ways to do just that. Daily observe your own demeanor. Are you happy? Are you shedding Light? Are you connected?

Your joy is so precious it blesses the world, as well as your family. The path of joy and Light is an important path. It is also one that is served with great appreciation from the Wholeness of God. Daily make effort to brighten your Light in even a small way.

Fondly.

#39   HELPING OTHERS

(This was started on April 9th, but Clare's tiredness made communication unclear and slow, one word at a time, so it was continued on April 10th in the late morning when communication flowed more clearly.)

From the instant you come to love, you desire to assist. Caring in and of itself does not show direction for assisting. Observation from yourself can clearly define the need of your loved one. No greater joy will your heart feel than to serve those you love, especially if it brings them joy.

Another way to serve others is to be clear in the joy of God within yourself. If you are clear and full of joy, you bring the sunshine where you are. Your sunshine will shine upon those you love and brighten their day.

A third way is to suspend any reaction to negative energy from those you love.

(Clare sees Jim's mother, Dorothy, as a good example.)

Holding them in the Light and in the view of who they really are, helps them to see themselves as a child of God. This may not happen quickly, but holding the Light for this person assists them into remembering who they really are. This is one of the more difficult paths of serving, but a very important one, a very valuable one.

Appreciation for your loved one at all times is a support that truly serves. The appreciation should be clear in words and actions. The loved one should not be able to miss the fact that they are well appreciated, even though they may be in a dark mood and very unobservant.

Joy expressed in any moment is bringing God to that moment, and the presence of God is always a gift for oneself and one's loved ones. A good sense of humor, laughter, smiles, twinkles in the eye, and a loving touch are ways of showing joy.

Helping in ways that are needed also serves. Perhaps a meal, cleaning, beautifying, childcare, yard work, any effort that lightens the burden for another shows love.

And lastly, sharing peaceful time together shows love. Sharing your presence with your loved one, merging your energy and their energy in a oneness lightens all burdens. Bringing your peace, your joy, your caring, your support and blending it with theirs, changes the density of concerns. It all becomes easier.

Because we are not separate, but we are one, our need is always to reach out and to care and serve. We are not complete alone.

Amen.

#40   GARDEN OF JOY

We do not awaken alone. Because of our oneness, we share the journey with each other. One can liken it to a garden of flowers. There are moments when it is our turn to bloom, to hold the joy of God, and in so doing, to encourage the rest of the garden to do the same. We will have periods where we are not in bloom, where the joy is not being manifest at a given time. At that same time, others in our garden will hold the Light in their blooming. Their joy will encourage us to bloom again.

It cannot be stated too firmly that we do not travel alone, so whenever you can encourage a brother or a sister on their path; it always benefits your path as well. When someone is not in bloom, it is easy to react to them from the ego state rather than from love and joy. Here is the challenge. To see this person as a vessel of God, in joy and love that will reveal itself in due time, may be difficult but valuable. There are times when both ourselves and our brother or sister are not in bloom. At these times, it is very difficult to bring the joy to each other.

Rejoicing and appreciation are ours when we take our opportunity seriously and change a moment without joy between two people to a moment of joy. As we grow and become more and more aware of our joy of God within, this experience will become more and more common to us. It will fertilize the garden of flowers and bring joy to ourselves, as well as to others.

How blessed we are to be on the path of joy and love. It is a fulfilling path and very pleasant. Understanding and patience will be our strong points and we hope our brothers' and sisters' strong points also as we grow in Light and love. As the song says, for each of us there is a "time for every purpose under heaven." There will be times when we are the strongest Light guiding others and times when we will be looking for a Light to guide us. It is a dance.

Feel the love of God in your heart and you bless others. Go there frequently and observe the joy of others equally. We are all in this garden together.

Love and joy.

#41   BE OF GOOD CHEER

Living on earth consists of a great variety of emotions. For most people, it is similar to the weather in Michigan. You will have your days of great joy and excitement and peace, and then the storms will come. This may be followed by days of gloom and cloudiness, and eventually the sun will shine again. The lessons that will bring us closer to remembering who we are, very frequently are not easy. Remember during that stormy period that the difficulties will not last and peace shall return.

Living on earth is like going to college. You sign up for different courses. Some are easier than others, but each lesson that you undertake is by choice. The ultimate goal of awakening can be reached through very, very many easy lessons or fewer, more difficult lessons. Often a person chooses the more challenging course with hopes to reach their goal more quickly.

Remember, just as in college, there are tutors available for the asking. So is it in life. Should times become difficult, there are many unseen tutors who would be very happy to assist if they were asked. And similar to a college situation, the tutor would not approach you to ask if they could assist. The tutors' purpose is to assist, but they can only experience this fulfillment if they are asked. Their joy is great when they can help you to achieve your goal.

Think of yourself helping a baby learn to walk. You hold their hands, you encourage, you smile, you share great joy at the effort that is being made, and when the baby actually walks, your heart rejoices. So is it similar to those who are asked to help you. Sharing their understanding is very rewarding to those who help.

Consider this as an advertisement from those who wish

to serve you. They have been down the path that you are going. They have great understanding and they are cheerful. They are honored to be asked to assist you and perhaps ease your burden and make your lessons come more easily.

Not all assistance will come from those who are unseen. Ask each other to assist as well. Any time we can help another, our joy increases.

Go into your world today willing to ask for assistance and willing to serve.

In love.

#42   LITTLE GLASS BOX

(Guides show Clare that they can come in more easily when she is in joy, rather than tired or having busy thoughts. It looks like a rainbow of curved light, like a slide that they can come down. There has to be a certain "wattage" of joy to receive these transmissions. It took three aborted attempts to finish this message because Clare was tired, lacking energy. It was resumed and completed the next morning.)

Each of us has within us special gifts that are ours alone. These treasures we have stored within us and are truly a delight to the soul. These are the gifts and talents that are ours to share with the world. Unless we take these out and share them, we won't know their true joy. As we discover what they are and begin to give them away, they multiply and they serve many, very much like the loaves and fishes in the Bible story.

Each of us is part of the whole, but our talents therefore vary, so that combined, they make up a complete set. It is similar to the pop pearl children's necklaces of old, where each individual pearl can be added or subtracted from the whole. But for the grandest, most magnificent necklace, they will all be used. It is so advantageous to bring your pearl of talents to the whole.

The responsibility for each of us is to discover what our talents are and to give them away. It is important that we seek to find ways to use our talents. They have been given to us alone so that we can use them in the environment in which we have been placed. To be "humble" and not acknowledge our talents is a disservice to God and to our fellow man. We are God's vessels on the earth and we have been given responsibilities to fulfill. In doing so, our joy is unearthed and our lives become very full of God.

Ask your friends and family to help you identify your strengths—your gifts. Look around and find ways to apply your talents. Every joy that you bring to a friend or a stranger helps God.

Never forget you are part of the whole. You are part of the strength, wisdom, joy, and peace that is of God. You will know you are doing your part when your life is full of joy.

As a coworker of God, you must assist others to discover their strengths as well, so your compliments must be very sincere and clear to those you are with so they may be directional. Never forget who you are and who your fellow man is. Live your life in joy and service.

#43   CIRCLE

Being in God is complete peace and love, like being in a circle that has a rosy glow in the middle. This area of peace is undisturbed by any thought, any action, any circumstance of life. It is always with us, but it can be shrunken down in awareness or can be enlarged. The goal, of course, is to continually enlarge the circle to where it dominates our thoughts, our actions, our choices, our giving, our Beingness. Those in life who strike you as incredible examples of God's Presence are those who have enlarged this Presence to be dominant over their whole existence.

As we continue to seek ways to improve our awareness of God, our circle grows. Each time we choose to change a thought from a negative thought to a positive thought or avoid negative headlines or negative news, or we chose to spend our free time in giving rather than being entertained, we will increase the size of our God awareness. Joy will follow.

Taking care of the physical body also serves, because to be of service to God, our instrument must be in good condition. This need not be taken to extremes. Comfortable healthy eating, moderate exercise, sufficient sleep, all are essential for the body to serve well. Getting carried away on any of these areas is a distraction to service.

Focus on taking care of one's own vessel and not on others. If others have a similar path, they will see your example, especially if your path is cheerful and non-condemning and self-contained. Again we mention meditation for God awareness. It cannot be left out. Spiritual reading is also an assistance to many. Being in nature enhances one's God connection as well. Remembering to serve in joy, no matter what service is asked at the moment, is also beneficial.

Watch your circle of God grow within you as your joy increases and you heart fills with love. How blessed we are to be on this quest.

#44   BURNING BUSH (EASTER)

Just as God gave the Israelites guidance out of Egypt with the burning bush, so God will also guide us to our remembering of who we are. This can be done in many different ways and some or all will apply to each of us. We can feel the guidance of God through prayer and meditation, through role models, through scripture and other spiritual writings, through dreams and miracles. Our responsibility is to look for the guidance and ask for it to be shown clearly.

Our journey home need not be long if we follow guidance similar to MapQuest on the computer. In days of old there were no signs on the roads and one had to guess which of two roads was the better choice. Today, our traveling by roads is so much improved over the past. So can our trip home to God be easier if we read the road signs, if we follow guidance.

The part of us that does not want to go home will distract repeatedly and try to make us forget that we are on our journey home to God. With "good" distractions, we can forget to look for signs, we can forget to ask for directions and guidance, and we can get lost. Being lost in ego pursuits can look like a busy life, a conflicted life, a worrisome life, a life with attention so involved that you forget your pursuit of God. Or simply put, the journey to God is secondary in importance.

A burning bush or any guidance is wasted if it is not attended to. Scan your daily existence for evidence of being on the right path. Are you taking time for guidance? Are you feeling close to God? Are you keeping this journey to God a priority in your life?

Help and guidance will always be there when you wish

to have it. It is up to you to wish to have it.

The priorities of your life are yours to make. Seek the way of God, of joy, of love, and you will be guided home.

#45 THE VISITOR

Picture yourself visiting your relatives. You have traveled from afar and are greeted with much love and joy. While you are at this home, things are arranged for you—where you will go, what you will do with your time, whom you will meet, and what you will eat. You can just be along for the ride. You may not always like the arrangement. Perhaps the food is awful, the bed's hard. Perhaps the toilet paper is put on the holder backwards. Whatever is done, however, you know is done in love, with your best interest in mind.

So, too, is it with the life that we are living. We are being cared for by a Loving Guidance that always has our best interest in mind. Learning to trust this guidance is a life lesson that most of us can improve upon. Can we truly know that where we are led is with our best interest in mind? Can we give up control and accept the "awful food and hard bed" knowing that they are lovingly given to us for our soul growth? The "awful food" in our lives may show up as an illness, the loss of a job, or the loss of a loved one. The overall experience is one that is planned for us very carefully. As we learn to trust, we can relax into the day, we can smile more, share joy more completely, and be at peace more frequently. We can know that where we are is where we are supposed to be. We can experience our life fully being grateful that everything is as it is because it is in our lives through love.

We may have a tendency to want to turn that toilet paper roll around, or in our life, change that which is given us. Of course, improving our life at any given time is ideal, but learning not to curse the challenges that we are being asked to confront, as they are lessons being set up for us, is the aim. As trust builds, each new challenge can be greeted, accepted, and dealt with, with a light heart.

Joy attends the trusting heart.

#46   BLOSSOM

It is said that there was a time in the evolution of plants when there were no blossoms at all. Over the centuries, a few species developed the ability to blossom, and then others. Then, when the time was right, almost all species blossomed.

The same is true for us. We call it awakening to who we truly are, but it is the human version of blossoming. Over the centuries there would always be a few enlightened ones that were known about and a few that were not known about. Their known numbers were in the single digits for the whole of civilization for centuries. In the last forty years, this has changed. People are awakening at an amazing pace. As many awaken in a year, now, than would awaken in half a century before. The time has come for each of us to "blossom."

We have been preparing for this period of time when the vibration of the earth is raised. Those who are uncomfortable here will leave and find another place to evolve that fits their pace of development. There are many places that will be wonderful for every spark of God that chooses this slower path.

For many, our destiny is to awaken to the God within during this period. The energy on the earth is enhanced and the time is ready. We are called and the call is urgent.

Let's do it!

#47   THE CRAYON BOX

In our life, we may find it difficult to understand others; for example, why is that mother not being kind to her child, why is that Christian not being more loving, why do people hate? The conclusion, of course, is that we are all so different one from another.

It can be likened to the crayon box of a thousand different colored crayons, no two alike, each one perfect for that moment and for their purpose. So there are colors we like very much and there are colors that have no appeal to us. Each one holds a place and a purpose. It is unfair for us who are not the creator of these crayons to judge these colors for their worth. We do not know their purpose. It serves no one for us to say, "Why is this grey crayon not yellow?" Knowing that yellow is more pleasant to be around.

When we are disappointed in another person, we are taking on an assumption that we know their purpose or we know the color they "should" be. But we don't. We ask the other crayons in the box to accept us and the color that we bear. We need to do the same for them.

Each of us, though, can purify and make our color more clear. We go through life with lessons. We learn to give our love more abundantly, and we learn to release condemnation. As we do, we purify our color to its most glorious presentation. And now we can serve each other more joyously and our service will be received more appreciatively.

Our differences can also be compared to the alphabet. Can we imagine ourselves saying the "n" should have another curve added to it or that the "p" is incomplete. It is not our place to condemn another for that which they are. We don't know the purpose that they will serve in the grand scheme of things being exactly as they are. If we want to increase the beauty in the world, we can work on purifying ourselves, bringing more love through us into the world, bringing joy. How freeing it is to accept others for who they are and love them just as they are.

Our task on earth is much more simple than we make it out to be. We do not have to evaluate every person we see. We simply have to find ways within ourselves to bring these people more and more love.

Go in joy to do just that.

#48   COME UP FOR AIR

The joy of God is just that—joy. People who live on the earth plane have a tendency to live in struggle and concerns, and if they do not have enough of their own, they turn on the television or read the newspaper, both of which are filled with problems and difficulties. Humans tend to engage in this kind of activity as though that were life. On the other hand, life could be so much more fun.

The joy and love of God should swirl in your veins, bringing you to a constant state of delight. It would be more reasonable to have the occasional non-delight moment that stands out in a life of joy. You have here instead the reverse: joy and delight that stand out as unusual in a life of struggle. This is a choice that is made mainly by your society. With mindfulness, one can rise above this milieu.

To do so, one must make conscious choices. Decide what brings joy to the person and do those things. Decide on being cheerful in one's work and in fulfilling one's responsibilities. Decide against situations that are not uplifting, for example, entertainment that is meant to scare or bring fear, news that causes undo concern, news about things that one is helpless to change. Chose to spend your time making joy. This can be in cooking and cleaning, yard work, volunteering, helping those who need you—perhaps the elderly, the widowed, the lonely.

Look over your day at the end and note where your joy came from. Keep a journal of the joy you found in your days. As you become more mindful of what is bringing you joy, you will find yourself automatically going there, and life will be more fun.

Your ability to serve God is enhanced by your degree

of joy. It is your desire to serve God and what a nice responsibility it is for you to improve your joy at the same time. It is a fringe benefit.

Because your environment is full of people who are in the lower levels of joy, you can be brought down from the joy that you have found. Be wary of making friends with people who do bring you down. Seek out the joyful.

Connect to your body. Use your body physically in service, or in exercise. Being in nature through walking or biking, swimming, or sports can help you connect to your joy.

Pets bring joy. They often show you how to love. Pets can also connect you to nature through walking, horse-back riding, or other experiences.

The song "Don't Worry, Be Happy"* is the concept in a nutshell.

---

* *"Don't Worry, Be Happy," by Bobby McFerrin, 1988*

#49 SPECIES

Each of us comes into the earth plane with a predeter-
mined plan. The plan is very unique to us and may contrast
to that of our neighbor. You can think of it as a similarity
to different bird species in the spring. Some will chose to
have their young early and perhaps build their nests on
the ground. Others can be very different. Some will have
their nests by water, others in trees, bushes, etc. Each bird
knows where his nest will be, even though it may be the
first nest ever made by this bird. The bird doesn't worry
about looking correct to the other species. They do what
is theirs to do, knowing that the way they build it will
be the correct way.

Our direction for our life may be very different from
the direction of others around us. The trick is to trust our
own path. Comparisons don't work because we are not
the same as anyone else. Our direction is unique.

How do we know we are on our own path? Are we
happy? Is there joy in our life? Are we distributing love
as we go? Is it fun? General measurements for success
may not fit. What is correct for you is not necessarily
what is correct for anyone else, except the joy.

This does not mean there will not be struggle and difficult times. We each have lessons to learn. But even
amidst the struggle, there should be joy and love if we
are following our own path.

If life is a continuous difficulty, and joy is hard to find,
one should reassess one's direction and perhaps try a
totally different approach. Perhaps you are trying to be
an eagle when you should be a woodpecker or vice versa.

It is important not to evaluate another person's path,
because we do not know their species. We can just love

and support them and enjoy them. They will find their own way.

Peace attends those who allow others to be who they are.

Peace be yours today.

#50   THE OLD LAMPLIGHTER

Just as in the days of old, when a person was given the responsibility of keeping light in a given area at night by lighting gas lamps, so are we given a responsibility to keep Light alive in a given area. The area, of course, is our life where we are, and we have been given a responsibility. The Light that we are to provide in our environment cannot be provided by any other. If we fail to fulfill our responsibility, the area is simply more dim.

The joy that we seek, the unending joy of God's love, is the presence of the Light of God, provided by all. When the level of Light gets bright enough, unending joy shall reign.

How can we improve on our responsibility? First we must feel the love of God and the joy of God. We must trust in guidance given us and remove personal concerns, worries, and fears. We must daily meditate and commit ourselves to love. Asking for and being open to tutoring will help us also.

As in a picture puzzle, we have a particular part to play. This part cannot be fulfilled by someone else. Without our part, the Light will be incomplete, but only momentarily. Eventually our Light will contribute to the whole. It is inevitable. It is our destiny.

We are so blessed to be an integral part of the whole, a part that will never diminish. We are needed and without us, God is incomplete.

Our destiny is a blessing, not one to cause concern or stress. It certainly gives us a focus, a joyful purpose, but what it is not is a condemnation of present activity. Guilt has no value in God's kingdom. It is simply a goal to attain, as best we can, as pleasantly as we can.

Any part of our life that does not appear to be a part of this goal can simply be observed and allowed to exist until its time of existence is done.

Sometimes our life appears to be like a ball in a pinball machine, from time to time going to places that appear to be undesirable. As time will have it, things will change. With prayer and constant desire, the Light you wish to bring will shine forth.

Find joy in the moment and your Light will shine.

#51   HOLD PEACE

Early in the morning, looking out upon a small lake, you see reflected in the water the trees from the bank across the way, a small mist rising on the water, a seagull circling. The Light is beautiful; the scene is peaceful. You see and feel peace.

As you look upon this very same scene, however, there are situations going on that are certainly not peaceful. For example, the seagull pursuing a fish in the lake is not peaceful for the fish. It is not peaceful for the insects that are being pursued by the turtles or for the chipmunks that are being pursued by the hawks.

In the world that we live in, we can choose to see peace or the day-to-day struggle. We can choose to know that the whole scene is a picture of what is, and allow in our hearts the experiences that are going on to be neither good nor bad. We can know that what is at any given moment is what is meant to be. We can distance our judgment from the individual situations. We can know that the peace that we look at comes from the focus of our heart. Trusting that all is working for the good, we can relax and see the whole picture as one of peace and joy.

Just as the fish was engaged in a struggle with the seagull, so are there struggles in our world. The trick is not to focus on the struggles, but to focus on the peace of God that prevails in our hearts. Learning to allow without judgments that which will be can bring great peace.

When our peace is disturbed, we must take a moment and check our focus. Are we observing the individual struggles or the beautiful scene of God in action? Whenever we find ourselves in consternation, we need to observe where we are focused, refocus, and choose peace.

Where we focus is a matter of training. We can train ourselves to see peace. Today try to refocus at least once and choose peace instead of concern.

#52   THE CURRENT

The energy of God can be felt like a beautiful, gentle electric current that is there at all times. The energy is somewhat like a musical chord that is ever playing. Its presence can be noted more particularly when your mind is at peace or when your mind is not active with competing ideas or concerns.

The effect of this awareness is simply a reminder that we are part of God. We are never separated from God and belonging to the Oneness is the dominant theme of our existence. Holding this knowledge keeps at bay ego thoughts of competition and comparison. It reminds us of the love that we carry, like the vein of chocolate fudge in chocolate ripple ice cream. This knowledge draws us into the purity of love that God is. It also draws us into great appreciation of who our brothers and sisters are. This knowledge brings us peace.

Because life is busy and demanding, we often fail to sense the current. We can do things that can enhance the awareness of it, including taking time apart from our daily world to notice how we are always merged with the Oneness. Listening to beautiful music may enhance our awareness of our own God-current, as well as laughter, light heartedness, and joy-filled experiences with those around us. Spending time with those we love in giving and receiving also refines our awareness. The process of allowing life to unfold, without fighting the direction it is taking, is beneficial as well.

The current is a gentle delicate experience that can easily be overrun and unnoticed. As one learns to center oneself, the awareness of this gentle energy emerges. Watch for it in quiet times, like in the moments at night before sleep sets in, in church when you are having moments for personal reflection, in the early morning awake times, or any time you can avoid mental activity long enough to just feel.

The current is a blessed reminder that we are not separate from each other, or from God. Find that reminder today in your sacred space.

Your sacred connection is my sacred connection. We are one.

53   HOME

So many phrases that you hear spoken of referring to your childhood home also apply to the home of your soul. For example, "homesick" is a longing to be in the place where you are used to being. For, in truth, you have been in this spiritual home forever, but your awareness has left and you carry within you a longing to have that awareness of your spiritual home again.

"Childhood memories" also refers to our spiritual home. It speaks of a sense of well-being that one feels when everything is in place. In this world it would be when everything was arranged for us, all responsibilities were taken care of, and those who loved us deeply were with us. In the spiritual sense, we subliminally remember being in the space where love dominated, where joy was the order of the day, where there was no struggle, no responsibilities, no failure. We were completely surrounded in love.

"Extended family" is another term that can also refer to our spiritual selves. Humanly, extended family refers to additional love that comes toward us and from us to others. Spiritually, it is the extension of ourselves in all those that we see or have ever known. When we become aware that we are part of a Oneness that has no end, we can appreciate the connection that we now feel between those who were previously considered as "other."

Forgiveness, patience, and understanding are dominant in our soul family, as they often are in a human family. When we truly realize that everyone is a part of our family, we will see them through loving eyes, and feel at home in their presence. The warmest family on earth is cold compared to the love that exists in our spiritual Oneness.

Go forward today and observe each other through loving eyes, knowing they are a part of you, and you of them.

#54   CLOUDS

In a typical weather pattern, there will arise clouds that block the sun. This can be likened to distractions that hide the Joy of God. Because the clouds come so frequently and in such a varied presentation, we think that they are normal and have no problem with their presence in our lives.

In fact, these clouds are distractions that have been accepted in our lives to keep our minds busy and to keep us from being with God. These take on the disguise of jobs, family, health, political issues, friends.

We have all had seasons in our lives where the clouds were few and our closeness to God was memorable. As we let the clouds in, a few at a time, we become used to them. We distract ourselves and forget to seek the warmth of God. Upon awareness of the presence of the clouds, we can make effort to remove them or to lessen their importance.

As we start to seek the Light of God more consistently, we feel the brightness and strength of God's Love and desire to hold it near. We start to seek ways to diminish the power of the clouds. We start to focus on laughter, on peace, on joy. We start to assure our day of moments that are private for just ourselves and our God. We develop habits that bring the closeness of God more in focus. Now we see the clouds, but know they are just that. They are not how we must live, but are distractions in a much more pure form of existence, an existence that we know and choose to focus on. We can live with the distraction of clouds, knowing they are only that.

A key to staying aware of God is to acknowledge that there are clouds that interfere from time to time.

Keeping a clear desire for the Presence of God will help us remove them.

Clouds can be enjoyed and observed for their individual beauty, knowing that each cloud is temporary and brings a gift of its own.

The trick is to continually hold the desire for connection to God and allow the distraction of the clouds, knowing they are only momentary. When our main focus is the clouds, we need to shift our focus back to the Joy and Love of God. Our lives must be dominated by the Light of God.

Go forth today observing the clouds of your life and appreciating the God Light that is in your heart.

#55   STRETCH

Joy that we know comes to us more frequently when we give. Joy is God. The experience of giving then is an avenue to connecting to our own God self. The giving has to be done in love, of course. Giving can be done to fulfill the other person's needs, for example, help fix their car, run errands to the grocery store, bring people to the doctor. Or, it can be an expression of your own talent that is given in joy. This can be through art, music, acting, or humor.

The result of our giving is then two-fold. It enlightens or lifts the other person's life as well as our own. To be able to serve another is a privilege that one earns through life experiences. To take advantage of this privilege brings great joy.

Television is an enticing distraction from service. Millions of hours a week are spent in idle entertainment that could be spent assisting someone or sharing your love. The middle road is the best, where you have some TV and some service.

Anonymous giving is always good, as in the theme "random acts of kindness." When one can give without expecting or without receiving appreciation, then the giving is pure. Other kinds of giving that are ego-less are those that serve the earth to make it more beautiful. Examples of this are demonstrated on Earth Day. This can be carried out daily, weekly, or at any given opportunity. The giving doesn't have to be large, but consistent. This also applies to animals. When we humans can ease the life of a wild or tame animal we are being privileged to serve. Sometimes serving the wild or tame animals that are human is our privilege.

When mining for a happy life, remember the wonderful vein of service that brings great happiness. So check your life. Are you happy? Are you serving others? This service need not be a burden or large and onerous.

It should be included in your life with joy and pleasure. Start small and let it take its course, like perennial flowers that continue to multiply and bring more and more beauty. Service will be like that.

So have a day of love and joy and do some delightful service.

Amen.

#56   BIRD HOUSE

There is a place within your heart that is full of peace. It is your home. When you go there, you are surrounded in a gentle, safe, encompassing embrace. It is where you belong.

You are drawn to this place. From within you have the urge to go there. Similar to the bird that goes to the bird house, you go to your inner home.

Joining others can strengthen the connection for which each of you longs. Communal meditation brings harmony in your social world as well as your spiritual world. The joy you each feel is multiplied and everyone benefits.

This is a period in history where small groups are forming. The groups not only benefit yourself and others, but the society as a whole, and even the world. The vibration that is set up in the group counteracts and balances lesser vibrations in other areas of the world. For the world to advance in its awareness of the God within, the higher vibration has to be in greater proportion than the lower vibration on the earth plane. So not only is it a wonderful experience to merge in meditation with others, it is a contribution to the united goal of awakening for the world.

As the saying in the Bible goes, "The last shall be first." It is our desire to help those who are in the dark that their inner lights may turn on and they too awaken to the God within. Therefore, the urgency is felt to experience the magnificence of God for ourselves and even more so for others.

We are each led by what feels like instinct to go to God. Our major responsibility is to find time that we are willing to commit consistently to this pursuit. Simply holding the desire and taking the time will bring us home.

This day, reward yourself with a piece of quality time that is reserved for you to go to God. When you do, you bless us all. Thank you.

#57   RENAISSANCE

We are all connected as part of God. We are like a blood
family. Individually we may think that we can be apart
from our family. We may change locations, declare ourselves independent, and let fear and ego control our lives.
This does not take away the fact that we are part of the
family of God. We can run, we can fight it, we can play
the game of confusion, fear, struggle, but we can never
stop ourselves from being part of the family of God. We
are part of beauty, of peace, joy, and laughter. Distracting
ourselves from this does not negate the fact of who we are.

Accepting our part in the family and taking our rightful
place is like a renaissance. Each of us who quits fighting
the fact of who we really are awakens to a new life, a life
of joy and service.

Part of the joy is in knowing that we are not separate
from each other, and knowing that each person we see is
a beautiful blessed part of the whole family. We are all
loved very deeply. The family is incomplete without any
one of us. Rejoice; you are home. Rejoice; your brothers
and sisters are home. Let the love flow.

Acknowledging there is no one outside the family reminds
us to remain in a state of allowing. We don't know the
part our brother plays, but we do know our part, and that
is to allow and to love.

There will be days when we temporarily forget our
connections to the family. In these times, we focus on
our separateness and our egos. Competition and comparisons come into play. Demands on us do seem difficult.
Laughter subsides. Then we once again remember who
we are. We step into the wholeness of the family again
and are received with great love and joy. We give back in

the same manner. This stepping apart from the family will occur less and less as the true knowledge of who we are becomes apparent. You will know if you are connected to the family by observing if you are happy.

This day observe your joy. Extend your connection to your fellow travelers on this earth. Join the family of God, for in this connection you are home. As your love shines forth, you bring God's joy to the earth.

Amen.

#58   WORKING FROM HOME

When we come home to the presence of our God Self, we find great comfort and a sense of well-being. A peacefulness settles over our countenance and fear leaves us. We find that we are not alone, and as we look, we find great numbers in the same situation we are in.

From this place of home, we take our guidance to go forth into the world and to remind those who are unaware of their home, that it is within. The actions we will take may be very small ones, almost inconsequential, or very large ones, but the direction that we take will come from within in an almost surprising manner. It is not a plan that we make with our minds, but with clearer and clearer nudges from our Spirit Self. The work will be easy and fun. We will step lively and effortlessly along the path that is being laid out for us as we go.

It will feel like the winding of the ribbons of May Day, where each will go a direction assigned and joyfully pass another, and in so doing, weave a tapestry that is God-sent. Our responsibility is to trust and to move. One will know they are on their correct path by synchronicities that will show up more and more frequently along the way. Miracles will show up more and more frequently also. You will be continually reminded that you are not alone in carrying out God's plan, and that Jesus, or whomever you perceive your guidance to be, goes with you on this journey.

When the burden of the journey seems too heavy, we must make some alterations, spend more time with God, ask for more help, look for the beauty in others, and increase gratitude. The journey will be as wonderful as you desire.

This day, start and end by connecting with God. Listen for the guidance throughout the day, rejoice in the simple things of life, spread that joy, feel your blessings and they will flow into the world.

#59   WINGS

Connecting to the God within and without is in the moment. It is desirous to fly away from yesterday. We need be similar to the birds in the field that fly with their wings, but they are in the moment. They are accomplishing a great deal. They are expressing great appreciation and joy. They are continuously in the here and now.

Humans in this period of time have the practice of being many places other than in the present. Much time is spent on memory and television and electronic games. Each of these can bring a blessing if they are tuned into in the present time frame, or they can be a numbing to the world of reality.

It is as though each of us is being sent on a mission to work in the garden. The garden has many weeds, is wilting from not enough water, and needs tender loving care. As we head toward the garden, it is like going through a corridor at a school. Some of us slip off into the rooms on the side as we go along. We may step into these rooms momentarily to be entertained and then find that we are there much longer than we expected to be. The garden's needs await us, but we are not anywhere in sight. We still hold a commitment to the garden in our hearts, but have become so taken up by the distraction that we feel the urgency to serve less and less.

Not only is it important for us to be on our guard for the lure of these distractions, but we are obligated to also assist our fellow travelers and remind them of their purpose. As we disengage from the entanglement of time-wasting, we demonstrate to others the joy of serving. They can see the results in the garden of our dedicated service. They are then influenced to feel the joy of service in their hearts.

As the pace in this world picks up, so do the temptations to be distracted from our goal of service. Be on guard and ask yourself "Is this activity I am engaged in helping me to reach my goal of service for God?"

Many times it will be a joyful "yes," and other times a signal to change. In the morning, set your day where your goals reflect service. Check from time to time to see if you are on track. Your personal joy will reflect your success in reaching these goals.

Have a happy day.

#60   THE RETURN JOURNEY

Certain things will catch our attention as we go through our day. Identical twins raised in the same family, going through the same day in the same locations, will have their attention brought to different things because their spiritual self is presenting each of them with that which is of importance for their soul growth, or awakening to the God Self within. We can expect perfection in this training, for we will receive as we have requested at a higher level.

The final outcome of our awakening will be to find ourselves in a God-aware state equal to Jesus Christ. Notice we will not be inferior to Jesus Christ, but equal to Him. Our God power, the power of love, will be also at the same level as the Christ consciousness of Jesus. It is a very happy state, full of laughter, joy, friendship, and deep devotional love one to another with no one excluded from this depth of love. Life in that state is so easy. The term "will be" is not necessary, because on one level we are already there. In this experience we are having on earth, we are wearing a blindfold to the joy that is ours, like "temporary amnesia."

This aspect of ourselves that we are now experiencing has come about by free will and a desire to know other than the purest form of joy and love. However, we have been in this state for a long time and the amnesia feels permanent. Our higher selves are now helping us to reawaken to the pure state. Because of the ego involvement, we are fearful of this change. It becomes a challenge to turn our sights and habits from ego control to our own personal Spirit control. This change need not be long and arduous, but it typically is. Every step that we draw closer to the love in our own heart notches us up closer to the Joy that is Universal God.

There are abundant helping, loving hands willing to assist in this return journey. They are honored to be asked, and wait patiently for such an invitation. So, as you take your time to be quiet and go within each day in meditation and prayer, remember these loving assistants.

We are on a wonderful journey back home. Each lesson learned is worth the struggle to learn it, because it draws us closer and closer to pure joy.

Congratulations on attempting this journey. You will be successful and we will join again.

#61   PURIFYING

The God State is a state of purity. As our intentions lead us back to the state of Oneness with God, we must purify. "What does this entail?" you may ask. Purity is of the mind. It speaks of love instead of fear. Just in this day alone, there will be many opportunities to look with loving eyes rather than judging eyes. There will be opportunities to offer complete forgiveness for even very small things and feel a heart pure with love.

The purity that one experiences is never about the other person, but only about how one approaches that which is offered to them in a given day. Can we be at peace and full of joy and laughter, or do we feel a little offended, perhaps a little rejected, or even condemning of the other? Setting an intent for purity and asking for assistance will help a great deal on this exacting journey. The beauty of this effort is the instantaneous reward of joy.

It is as though we have a hot air balloon full of love and appreciation, but wanting to attach to it are lead balloons of the ego, such as jealousy, comparisons, resentment, feeling hurt, and condemnations. As we snip the lead balloons free by catching ourselves and choosing another path, we allow ourselves to feel from a higher nature: love. We are not always talented enough to disengage all the lead balloons, but every time we do disengage one, we rise in our own nature to a higher loving. Once we have begun the process of purification and continue to ask for help, progress will be made.

Noticing and appreciating persons around us who have a forgiving nature and a loving heart are good ways to remind ourselves to continue our own personal quest. People who have successfully disengaged the lead balloons of the ego are a treat to be around. They have a magnetism and a comfortable presence, and frequently these people who have purified their own nature are able to communicate with entities beyond this plane.

Purification is a lovely goal, but there should not be struggles in attaining it. Set your intention, ask for help, and eventually it will come in its due time. Fighting for it is the antithesis of what you are seeking, so don't try too hard. Trust in God and you will be well rewarded. Replace each frown with a smile and life will get easier.

Have a beautiful day.

#62   CANOPY

As a canopy shields you from the harshness of the sun, so does the presence of God soften the challenges of life. The act of going through this world is not a sole activity. You may have suspected as much when you have seen the coincidences and synchronicities of life, such as the person you run into in the gas station while on a trip or at a particular store you rarely frequent, or the inner feeling that you should go a certain place or buy a particular book, or many other unusual happenings that bring you just what you need at a particular moment. You have Godly assistants. Some might call them guardian angels, some might call them guides, some might think of them as relatives who have passed on before them.

Being grateful for that which comes into your life gives wonderful joy to those who serve you. It is not important, by any means, to know who serves you, because they serve you selflessly. They are instruments of God. You may simply thank God for their assistance, for it is the God within them that serves you. It is not crucial to be specific in your requests of how you need to be helped, but be clear in your ultimate goal. You can trust that they may find even better ways than you can imagine to assist you in reaching your goals. Sometimes it is only necessary to be clear about the goal, incorporate trust, and get out of the way. The details will fill in as you travel forward in joy.

Keeping your vibrations high, avoiding worry and fear can keep the channels open for service to be given you. As a blood vessel is constricted during fright, preventing the flow of blood, so is your ability to receive gifts from those who serve you constricted by fear and worry. Trust not only feels good, but opens the channel of guidance given to you. Those who serve you maintain a delightful attitude. Their hearts are full of joy. They exude love and happiness. The closer you can get to that vibration, the easier it is for them to transmit blessings.

As you speak to God, you speak to those who serve you. As you center in your peace and trust, and you relax and spread joy, you receive at an even greater rate. When you are frightened and ask God for help, you still receive. It simply is more difficult for those serving to help you. There are times it must be so, but when you can, seek the peace and joy of God to enjoy and to share, and your blessings will multiply.

Have a blessed day.

#63 PRESENT

Being in the now is being in joy. God lives in the present moment and whenever the mind takes you to the past or the future, you go alone.

Because God is in the present, there is your power, your creativity, your ability to give and receive. It is also the place where you will learn and draw closer to God.

Pictures from the past in our mind are delightful to visit, but the experience should be limited. It is like leaving your path and briefly taking a side trip. The same can be said for the future. Concerning ourselves greatly with what will happen in the future can take us away from the present, and the present is where we desire to be.

Each person should look at one's own thought system. Some will have more of a tendency to look at the past, others to look at the future. And, of course, others will be tending to stay in the moment. Once one analyzes their own habits, and if they find them to be wanting, they can make conscious efforts to return to the present. For example, if one finds oneself planning incessantly, he or she might return to the present. Or if many moments of the day are spent in memory of past experiences, again one may try to discipline oneself and return to the present.

Being sensitive to your senses—the sights, sounds and smells—keeps you in the moment. Even your aches and pains can keep you in the moment. When you check to see where you are, and you realize that you *are* in the moment, be grateful.

Think of yourself in a play on stage. Each moment things are to be done by this person and that person, inter-actions flow, all as the script requires. An actor on stage would be ill-advised to take a moment and remember his high school graduation or to plan the grocery list. The moment is where the attention must be, for a successful depiction of an artificial life. So too, do we benefit by keeping our presence ever mindful in the major play we call life. There are so many lessons to learn, why take time out? We are on this earth but a short time to gain many experiences. When we allow our mind to not be present, we diminish the number and quality of the experiences at hand. We will never be without thoughts of the past and plans of the future, but to discipline the quantity is advised.

Be present and be in your joy this day.

#64　THE SEED

There is much work to be done before we all go home again. First we have to realize that we are not home and that there is a loving, joyful place where we belong. The whole of mankind is starting to be sprinkled with aware-ness of the Light that they carry within. It is likened to the night satellite photography of the different continents showing the electricity on each continent where the little white lights appear in the darkness. Unfortunately, there is not quite the concentration of awareness that this would show in big cities. Each spark of awareness has much work to do, albeit work of love and joy.

Each person who awakens to the wonderful Light that they contain must then send out awareness to many, many others, similar to a dandelion that comes to seed, and then sends out hundreds of little starters that go forth into the environment. Everyone knows how dandelions can seed far and wide. So can God's teachers.

Those who have awakened to the Love of God, which is their essence, will be brought into many circumstances that allow the Light to be seeded and to spread again. Cross-fertilization is very desirable. This indicates help-ing people awaken in situations that are different from yours. This can be different religions, cultures, national-ities, locations, socio-economic classes, and age groups. The Light within you will direct you into your path. It may surprise you where you are being led and may confuse you as to why you are in such a setting. But as you let your Light shine in all settings, you enhance the ability of those around you to connect to the Light within them. This is not a purposeful conversion of another person's life. It is like a rolled up newspaper on fire that touches another rolled up newspaper and lights it. Then the two go forth and do more of the same, etc. I want to stress again that the Light itself, the Love, the Joy do the work. It is not a mental conversion to one way of thought. This transcends all religions. It belongs everywhere.

Life is meant to be happy much of the time. It is meant to have lessons, to help us awaken to the Love and Joy that is within ourselves and others. Some lessons are difficult and may be repeated many times until they are grasped. This is the Holy Spirit serving you with boundless Love.

It may seem different when you struggle, but the lesson you learn will be a beautiful gift and worth the effort. Gratitude will replace resentment.

As the Spirit of God burns within you brighter and brighter, you will find yourself trusting more and more. Life will get easier. You will be more open to guidance and gifts from the Holy Spirit. You will find yourself a giver of gifts for the Holy Spirit. Your service will increase proportionately to your joy.

Daily take time to connect to God. At least twice a day is recommended. Whenever you are in Peace, Joy, or Love, you are serving God.

Amen.

#65   TEAM MOVEMENT

Each of us is a Holy Part of God. We are all connected. No matter what role we play in this world, we are still equally Sparks of God. Think of a school of fish. They turn and move together. With grace and intent, they all move as one. So, too, is it with our souls of mankind. We are all connected as a school of fish. We move forward to our awakening "en masse."

Even as we move forward, there will be some that are at the front, others partway behind, and others at the back. All movement forward affects all. "A Course in Miracles" states that "Every act of kindness affects everyone." Because we are one, no one can be left behind. Through choosing to serve our senses, perhaps through drugs, alcohol, or other choices, we can only change positions within the group, but we can never disconnect, and as the group moves forward, we will be pulled along as well.

We are all being called to awaken. Some hear the call clearly and feel urgent about answering the call, and many others are experiencing lifetimes that are not intended for immediate awakening to God. Each person's lifetime is a perfect experience. They are on the path to God, even without understanding. Each of us should be peaceful in our journey, certainly peaceful about one another's journeys. As they said on the moon, "One small step for man, one giant step for mankind." As we learn to love more clearly, more purely, as we learn to forego condemnation, as we learn to appreciate the moment and appreciate our fellow man, we draw ourselves closer to God and we help all mankind.

Like tobogganing down a steep hill, we may start our path cautiously, slowly and hesitantly, we may have fear and uncertainty, but as we go down the path, it goes more quickly and more easily. Instead of feeling fear, we feel joy and trust. We know our destination is out of our hands and out of our control. We know that it will end well.

Even this day, be at peace and trust your path. You don't travel alone. You are part of a large massive movement to God.

Live in joy and appreciation.

#66 THANKS

You who toil in the darkness are never alone and are fully appreciated. You volunteered to reveal the Light from within not only yourself but from within others. You knew the task would be difficult when you came. You have come upon many unforeseen obstacles that you have relentlessly reduced to stay on the path. Because you have come from such Light and Joy, your continual struggle is even more appreciated.

We walk with you on your journey, pulling you up when you stumble, sending miracles to encourage you along your path. Don't get discouraged. All steps toward the Light are progress and there is only the One involved. It may not be the ego that you have identified as "self" that carries the journey forward at another time, in another place. Simply appreciate each step that you take that brings Light. The whole picture is not yours to understand.

The most appreciated service you give is your unconditional love that you give to others. This "others" includes other Light workers, family and friends, and those who are lost. Love in any form is a step along the path in the journey of service to God.

Be gentle with yourself and with others. Try to let your life unfold in front of you; avoid working at unfolding it. Relax into the blessings of the now. Don't take yourself seriously. Keep and respect your commitments in joy.

Your movement in this commitment is watched and supported. You give us great joy, simply by being who you are. Your very presence and involvement on the earth plane fills us with delight. You are doing a wonderful job. Give yourself unconditional love.

Be in peace today.

#67　WHAT MAKES YOU HAPPY?

As you go through life, you will find yourself in many different situations. Some will be employment where you are helping other people.

Some may be employment that is dealing with things or numbers. Some experiences are strictly adventure, others socializing, others being entertained. Each experience will have a gift for you or you would not call it into your life.

Look over the different experiences that you do incur and find the ones that please you the most. This type of activity is for you to spend more time in. When you connect to that area that pleases you, life should become easier. When you are in your joy, you are in the Joy of God. This joy radiates to others and calls them to go to their joy. Life is not meant to be difficult, not that there won't be difficult times. In general, our lives should be joy-filled and giving and sharing.

As Kierkegaard* expressed, our lives are like a spiral going up a mountain, and we draw closer and closer to God as we progress through our lives. There will be new challenges as we move forth on our path, but there will be joy as well. Life should always have some challenge or we are not experiencing the fullness that is ours to know.

Look around you and see people you admire. What is it that they are doing that brings your admiration? Can you incorporate that experience into your life? Our lives can vary from one to another in the pace that we set. Some may move very quickly and have a very full life. They may touch many people's lives, they may bring great joy, great service. Others may take a much slower pace, perhaps the garden and family are the extent of their

* *Soren Kierkegaard, Danish philosopher and theologian*

giving. They may choose to be very peace-centered and non-hurried. One is not better than the other. As I may have mentioned before, one color of crayon is not better than another color of crayon. Each one has a purpose that only it can fill.

The life experience is not very long. One should make every effort to get into the activity that makes them happy. Happiness is service, even if no one else sees it. A single person canning pickles and having a good time benefits the whole of mankind on earth. The happiness radiates into the atmosphere and it all blends together.

So the best way we can help is to be happy. Don't settle for an "okay" life or a surviving attitude. Seek out what tickles you, what pleases you, and go in that direction.

The world needs your joy. Be happy.

#68   GATHER ROSEBUDS WHILE YOU MAY

Imagine a mother with a set of quintuplets about eight years old, on a Saturday morning. She gives them each a rather large identical basket and says to them, "Go into the neighborhood and fill your basket." She doesn't say what to fill it with. The children merrily go forth. One is particularly fond of flowers and seeks out flowers. Another is more interested in bugs and small living or dead creatures he pursues at great length to find enough to fill his basket. Another is fascinated with smell. She seeks out objects with interesting odors—good ones, bad ones, unusual ones. Another child becomes fascinated with textures. He finds hunks of cement, moss, leaves, gum wrappers, etc. The last one also finds a niche of interest that is an expression of herself as well. When the children come home, later in the day, some have filled their baskets to overflowing while others have only a few or a medium amount of different things.

Their Mama calls them all to the kitchen table and says that each should dump what they have onto the table for the whole family to see and experience. Each child then tells of each item why they chose it and how they found delight in it. The items will be left there to be permanently shared with the family. Mama has a way to permanently preserve these items so that they will always be fresh. Anyone at anytime can go to the table and see the items, and think of why they were brought there to be shared. Each of the family can experience items they didn't collect. Their wealth is of the whole family, and not the individual.

Similarly do the lives that we experience bring blessings to the whole of God. Each personal experience becomes a part of the experience of the family of God, adding richness and understanding. Positive experiences as well as negative experiences add breadth to the composition. All experience is welcome and has value.

Being born on the earth, we have each committed to bringing memories, sensations and understandings to the whole of God. Nothing is wasted. Each experience, although equal, can have different value for you, the receiver, so choose your activities carefully so that it may be a pleasant trip. It is like choosing the path that goes next to the ocean instead of the one that goes through the swamp. Neither is wrong.

Chose well.

If we consider ourselves a team, all working together for the glory of God, we can see how different tasks will be taken by different members of this group. Let's look at the servants of God as a construction crew, putting up a home in the country. Each of those who serve on this team has responsibilities. Some are shared and some are individual.

If it is my responsibility to build a basement, I might share this with ten others. We understand each other. Our goals are the same. We support each other when we can. We encourage each other. We take pride in the work of any one of us, for it is clear to us that we are a team.

On the other hand, we see part of our overall crew spending time in what appears to be questionable activity. Is it really necessary? Two or three of them walk around in the back yard area or others get in a truck and go to town. Yet others might be looking in books.

Just because my area of expertise does not include everyone's area of expertise, I do not have the ability to determine if these other workers are on task or not on task. Because they are part of my overall crew, I can but trust that they too are loving and serving God in the best way that they can, even though at times it appears to be quite the contrary. I learn to allow. I learn to trust. I learn to let the love in my heart be the dominant force at any given time. Appreciation for the commitment of the workers to God helps me turn from judgment and relax in trust.

So as I go through life, I know that we are all part of the same "construction company." Many are given similar tasks to myself and I can understand their work and appreciate them for all that they do. However, there are others who are taking on responsibilities I don't know. These persons may be going in directions that seem wrong to me, but knowing that we are on the same team, I can only trust that they are doing the best that they can and remind myself to appreciate even that which I do not understand. My job here is not only to do that which is assigned to me, but also to appreciate and encourage all the other laborers on the task we share. Love and appreciation should be the energy I dispense to all fellow workers. Trust that they know what they are doing will bring me peace.

When I am not in trust, I am in ego, and I am shirking my job and my boss will not be pleased. My job is to love and not condemn. As I and my fellow workers get better at this, our environment will be one of joy.

Thank you.

#70   COME HOME BELOVEDS

Congratulations to each of you who read this, for you already feel God's Love coming through you into the world. You are a willing servant of the God energy. However, your talents may not be as well honed as you would like. With the intention and request for help, this can be changed and you can improve your ability to serve. As you do improve your ability to serve, the amount of love, joy, and laughter in your life will increase. You will be happier.

It is interesting how advertising shows you how to find happiness. It seems that a beautiful expensive car, a beautiful, trim, youthful body and volumes of gorgeous hair, will certainly bring happiness. The happiness that comes through these things, and happiness does come through these things, is shallow. Seeking this happiness takes much energy and the happiness itself, being shallow, does not stay long.

The parallel to this happiness is the happiness of giving God Love. Contrary to the short-lived happiness, the deep satisfying happiness of giving even a small gift of love is felt deeply and remains with you. For example, compare taking a turtle off the road so he doesn't get hit by a car, versus buying a new pair of sandals. The sandals will wear out or go out of style and be out of your life; whereas the memory of the love you gave the turtle stays in your heart.

This can be notched up to higher and higher levels of giving. Helping someone fix their car, making a casserole for someone who is ill, lending an ear at an inconvenient time, etc. are common, simple ways that stretch your capacity for giving God's Love. As you continue your attempt to assist others, you become addicted to the love

127

that flows through you. You find such joy in giving God's Love that you seek ways to give more and more of it. As you do, you become closer to God and closer to coming home to the experience of Being—the Oneness.

Those who are reading this are already on the path to going home to God. You can hasten the journey by asking for assistance in doing so. Joyful, brilliant, loving beings will assist you at any time you wish. Not only will they help you, but they will thank you. They will hold your hand and guide you as you hold the hands of others and guide them.

We are all going home.

#71   OVERSOUL

Welcome beloveds. *(To Jim and Clare after a thirteen-day absence.)* You may have heard that a breed of dogs shares one soul. This is true, more or less. It is also true that you share a soul with others. In truth, you share your soul with all, but for today we will speak of the smaller group with whom you share your soul. This soul family urges each other along in their awakening. The family may not all live in the same time period or same location. Some may connect from other planes. Each one pulls the others along when they go closer to God and they slow the process for each other when they get distracted from their true purpose, which is merging into the Oneness.

It is very much like a family here would be, in that the joy in one heart can be felt in the hearts of their family members. Inexplicably, we may have a day that feels out of synch, a day that does not move along as usual. This sometimes can be attributed to a period when another family member is having a difficult time. Perhaps something traumatic has occurred. The difficult emotions can bleed into other family members as well. This also applies to joyful, sad, or other experiences.

What a privilege it is to know that as we take time to connect to our spiritual selves, we not only benefit our individual entity ourself, but also our whole family. Part of our family will be disincarnate at all times. We each take turns playing the roles of assistants from the plane that is not embodied. The love that is given to you from those who serve you is very deep, because they are family and they know and love you very much. You, too, will play the role of assistant to those on earth, doing your best to ease the journey on this often difficult path.

It is like a hidden partner to a magician performing on stage. Things must be handed to the magician at the exact correct time, things removed, other things brought in, and seeming magic happens. The hidden partners are very, very busy, but they are having a lot of fun.

Being in joy, or in love, is being in your God Self. When you are in these two emotions, you are making wonderful connections for yourself and for the rest of your family. This day, overcome all odds and be in joy. Spread love.

Lovingly yours.

#72   HORSES

We are all teachers of God for each other. It is our strength that allows us to carry another to truth —strength of conviction, strength of character, and strength of God. Seeking God on a regular basis is all that is required to be a teacher of God. Filling your heart with joy, with song, with appreciation and love as you go through your day makes you a teacher as well.

A solitary meditative experience is required to know God. This knowing will change your own vibration, which will change the vibrations of the world. As we feel the Love of God in our hearts, we desire to share it with others. We go out to others with great joy and excitement and love. We love those whom we see and in loving them, they feel the Love of God.

Another avenue that will help a person awaken is to read the many wonderful books that are out there today, dealing with the subject of awakening. Joining discussion groups of these books is helpful. The Holy Spirit often works with these authors to speak directly to your soul. And the beauty of books is their convenience, being with you, allowing you to spend as much or as little time daily as you desire. A warning regarding books, though, they can keep you in your head and become addictive. If the book does not touch your life, it may be a substitute for spiritual connection.

Again, service is a wonderful way to strengthen your connection to God. It can be paid service, but if done with a willingness to give love and God, it can assist in your own spiritual awakening and that of others.

Appreciation is a sign of a teacher of God. It will start to happen more and more frequently that you appreciate the people around you and the people that you hear about and may not even know. You appreciate their efforts, their smiles, their laughter, their presence, their thoughts, their kindnesses, and other qualities. You will take delight in them as members of the family of God.

Just as horses are strong and can naturally carry a rider, so are the teachers of God in their Power given from God able to assist each other on the trail back to God.

Give and take and hurry home.

#73   JUMP ROPE

Living in the realm of spirit-self versus ego-self is our goal. In the spirit-self, we desire to live in peace. We live in the realm of ego and having spent most of our life in the same area, it is very easy to slip and conflict with others or judge, condemn, criticize, gossip. As we are living in our spirit-self, we will be similar to a child with a jump rope. When we see conflicting situations coming at us, we will jump. We will rise above the trigger of the ego and go into peace and let the situation pass. Very shortly thereafter, another temptation will come and again we will rise in patience, tolerance, and understanding, and the situation will pass. Our life will go on like this, and thus we will be able to avoid the ego's temptation to be separate from one another.

Living on the earth plane in our spiritual self at this time will be different from our past. We will find ourselves so much more in peace. We will see the spark of God in those we talk with, work with, and live with.

Life will be easier. We will feel connected on a constant basis with those who guide us and assist us on another plane. We will see our connection to everyone else on this plane also—yes, even the political leaders.

In our state of grace, we will be called to serve in big ways and very small ways. As "A Course in Miracles" says, we will be teaching that which we need to learn. We can only teach ourselves.

New levels of joy will come, and at times it will feel like you have just fallen in love. You have. You have fallen into the Love of God and it fills your heart. The world looks rosy and all is well. This love and joy you carry with you. It is like a secret signal to others to tap into their own love and joy, because each of us are the same and every one of us has the Love of God within us.

Knowing we are a piece of the whole and that all others are equally a piece of the whole, helps us to appreciate those we are with. Just as Source uses us to help our fellow travelers, so does Source use our fellow travelers to help us. In truth, they will lead us home. And we will be eternally grateful.

Amen.

#74   SEEKER'S SOUP/ A COURSE IN MIRACLES

(Personal note: Jim and Clare were preparing to make a presentation on "A Course in Miracles" at a conference the next day at Dumont Lake, Allegan, Michigan.)

Congratulations on securing a speaking position at this upcoming conference. Through this teaching you will learn, and as you draw closer into your awareness of who you are, you live that awareness and through your living does the real teaching occur.

It is also a wonderful thing to have people speak lovingly of "A Course in Miracles." The attitude you hold, the love you give, is what will spark interest in the Course itself. You two are loving and joyful and we are delighted to have you represent "A Course in Miracles" to those who are seeking to go home.

There are many paths to God. Many will be represented at this conference, and each person there would benefit by knowing and loving the Course.

The Course may seem to some as difficult or cumbersome, but the difficulty it may present for a very short time until one is comfortable in this material, is a very short amount of time for the thousands of years it will save in going home. It may be compared to a six-week's intensive language course, where one only speaks this foreign language. It may be frightening and difficult at first, but very effective.

The Course is not as demanding as that, but it too calls for concentration and commitment, and its rewards are vast.

Don't worry about the results of your teaching. Much of its benefit is mainly for you. There will be those who will change their lives due to your efforts. There may not be many, and it may not happen immediately, but it will be rewarded.

Your peace, your joy and love for those who are there are the greatest teachers.

This conference will be attended by many on the other side, many more than are coming from the earth plane. Those who instigate fear are on the wrong path. Condemnation is not an aspect of loving. Seeing oneself as separate from another delays the return home.

Don't worry if many go into that experience. It is only an experience. Their allotted time will come when they, too, will return to love and joy and the Oneness of all. Be totally in peace knowing there are no mistakes. We all travel by our own road map, and fortunately we all end up at the same place. Because we are all One, how could it be otherwise.

Work on your acceptance and joy and confidence in your path as Truth. The rest will be taken care of by Spirit. We go to this party together.

Let's have fun.

(The Guys and Gals) Your Team

#75   PEACEGIVING

The first step to internal peace is acceptance of what is. That is opening yourself to understanding, asking for help for understanding and accepting that sometimes you may not understand. But you do accept.

You accept because of the trust you have of God. You know the Love that comes to you continuously with no break. With this Love that is so abundant with you, you have no need of significance, and therefore can rest in peace.

When peace becomes who you are, people long to be near you. It may not seem logical. "What do I have?" I may not be wise, I may not be funny, I may have little charm. "Why do people want to be near me?" you may ask. It is because of your peace. Your peace is like a big shade tree on a very hot sunny day. It is a welcome relief for those who have not attained their own peace yet. Being in peace welcomes everyone or no one. Being in peace is a very blessed state of being, whether others come to you or not.

People in peace rarely feel anger. They don't condemn, and they are bemused by the antics of others, but not discouraged or depressed in any way. Trust for what is dominates and patience abounds.

Peace is a by-product of your major connection to the Spark of God within. This beautiful connection is there for the asking. For many it is a journey and a degree of achievement. Like candy, the more peace you have, the more you want. *("Oh, my teeth" they joke!)*

Heartfelt thanks for all aspects of life carry you swiftly into the center of peace, and with the peace and gratitude is joy. It may not be a giddy joy; it may simply be a peaceful joy, but joy is present. Interaction with a person of peace will reveal the joy.

Peace may seem like a natural experience when nothing deviates from the norm, but the true test of peace is when challenges abound and difficulties come at you at a rapid pace. In these times, the peace deep within buffers the impact of the adverse experiences.

Blessed are you who know peace. You are the peace givers for God.

Thank you.

#76   SWING

As you go into the joy of knowing God, it will be like a swing, in that you will go higher, higher, and higher. It is a joyful ride. As you submerge yourself in the experience of your God Being, you will change.

The higher you go, the more beautiful the view. Everything has more beauty. People bring joy instead of frustration. Nature takes your breath away. You find yourself loving all animals. Your joy just grows.

Then, in the typical human experience, you swing back to where you were, or further behind that, it seems, only to return again to the ascent of knowing God. And as you reach your peak in knowing God, there seems to be a stop in time. This period will last longer and longer as our ascent goes up. The descent will become less and less as well.

As sure as a swing set is well grounded, so is the Truth that you will ascend. It is your destiny. No one will fail to do so, although some may choose to do so in another play date *(lifetime)*. We can be at ease knowing this. We can trust the sureness of the plan. We can observe others to show us how to swing high and we can be examples for those who would follow us. We teach by example, not by desiring to change someone.

This activity of swinging is meant to be pleasant and effortless, like growing in a physical body. We need not encourage another person to grow for them to be taller. It will happen in due time and correct time. This concept of allowing and not imposing on others is very important, not only for your happiness, but for theirs. If we spend our time in joy, seeking greater and greater heights of joy, not pushing or pulling others, our lives can be effortless and happy.

That doesn't mean that if someone would ask for a push, you wouldn't give him one, but you don't impose your evaluation that they might need a push upon them. They will get the hang of it in due time, just as you have.

Keeping your mind focused on your intent will make the ascent quicker, and the degree of ecstasy surprising, but you can't go wrong.

Enjoy your pursuit of God, as you will.

All is well.

#77 STABLE

You belong to God. He loves you dearly and cares for you daily, momentarily and always. Just as in a riding stable, He provides for you and watches over you like the owner of the stable would for her horses. The horses, in return, serve their master any way that they can. Of course we, too, serve our Maker, our God, who cares for us. We willingly serve any way that we are trained to do so. Our desire to serve and our strength make us valuable to the Master because there is much to be done in the present time. The Master is looking for many willing servers for the task at hand.

The time is at hand to remind those who have previously committed to wake up. There is a large wave of people who have planned to awaken to their God selves. In many cases they need a reminder and guidance back to the Master. Those who are called to serve know who they are and eagerly and anxiously answer the Master's call to begin the search for the others to come home.

The responsibility for those who would serve is great, but at the same time, they cannot fail. The plan is clear, though as with a horse and master, it seems to be of a different language at times, but each will be guided carefully for their success. There is great joy in being part of this magnificent vibration that comes from so many lovely people awakening to the Light within themselves. It is a beautiful experience for those who call and those who are called. Interestingly, the roles often reverse, so that you are on both ends of the call. The call asks us to go higher, to become even more aware of the potential that is within, as well as the vast amount of love.

The difficulty for both caller and called is that both

are heavily engaged in a drama they call life. To part from the routine and change vibrationally is new and difficult for most. It has the similar change of focus as when a person who is on the ground goes up in a hot air balloon, especially if you can imagine the hot air balloon going up in small increments, first twenty feet, then fifty, then seventy five.

Each level helps to release the focus on unimportant things and to get a larger picture of what is. It happens gradually so that the change can be assimilated before the next ascent. There are many of these ascents that are required for each of us before we get the perspective of the Oneness of God.

#78   HALF SANDWICH

Today as you look around yourself, enjoying the good life, you feel near completion. There is a satisfaction in feeling that your plate is full. Your life has friends, fun, family, financial well-being, and future dreams. You know love.

Soon, however, you will realize that what you have is like the first half of a sandwich. There is equally as much yet coming as you have already. With the new additions to your life, you will feel more abundant, abundant to overflowing. With this sense of overflowing, you will have this strong need to share. You will share your gratitude, your joy, your love and understanding. The understanding will be a clarity around the connection of yourself to others. This clarity becomes a driving force for the direction of your life.

The connection you feel to others is a reflection of the deepening connection you have to God. The extent to which you are connected to God is in an equal extent to which you are letting go of your focus on yourself. Your joy now comes through understanding love, and the practice of extending that love.

A major part of this new understanding is not in sending love to another, but observing that spark of God, that Love force that is within another. Suddenly you are able to see good, joy, and beauty in people that before you had judged as perhaps failures, or unworthy. Patiently, you now look around and instead of condemning, you find yourself appreciating. Not that the people have changed, but with this new gift of God Love within yourself, you are able to discern it in all others.

It is as though you have been given a magic lens that, when you choose to look through it, you see beauty.

When you forget to look through it, you are back into the self-serving attitude of comparison and condemnation. This self-serving attitude now feels more and more abrasive to the heart. You much prefer the harmony of understanding, acceptance and "allowing." The soul celebrates the new awareness.

Congratulations on your awareness of how your God Light/Love merges into God. This strong awareness acts as a guideline for your future; it will direct you and hold you as you go forth in your life.

#79   THE RAILS

Guidance for you is strong. It is similar to the rails for a train. They will give you direction and assurance that all is well.

To not trust guidance and know its strength gives a very uncomfortable feeling. Imagine if a train could go off the rails and chose to find its own way from city A to city B. Perhaps part of the trip would go very well, and confidence would be built upon relying on one's own directions. However, at other times, personal guidance can lead a person astray, while thinking things are going well. Then, when it becomes clear that the personal path without guidance isn't going well, help is urgently sought. The guidance that was rejected is now desired.

Typically, guidance will come in a very gentle manner. There will be times when it will be very, very strong. The more you ask for guidance and then relax and trust that it will come, the more you can be at peace with where your life is taking you. When you have asked from your heart for guidance to come, you can relax and know that you are being guided now, and all is well. Granted, it may not always appear to be so. When there are bumps in the road, know that they are not a mistake and in some way they will bring you a blessing. Stay in joy, stay in peace, stay in trust.

Many of us have set our trip plans, rails, to go over large valleys or rivers. On our own, this would be impossible, and even with guidance it can be frightening. But these experiences are the route we have chosen to reach our destination. When faced with these frightening chasms, be they cancer, loss of a loved one, loss of a job, or other seeming tragedies, it is wise to speak to those who have gone over similar chasms before you. Knowing it can be done brings reassurance. Trust your path with God; it is your destiny and you will not fail. Try to insert joy as often as you can on your journey. It need not be miserable.

The more you trust the rails, guidance, the more at peace you can be with where you are and where you appear to be going. If you can be at peace, you can relax and enjoy the moment, like those on a roller coaster who raise their hands and cheer. The power of your life is in the moment when you can relax, trust, and give your attention to what is at hand. Joy will follow.

Today, try to be in the moment in trust and cheer.

#80   TAKE A BREAK

Take this moment for God. Look about you. Find peace, find joy, find gratitude.

Life seems to be full of "hurry-ups," "must-dos," deadlines and projects unending. In the middle of these pressures, take a moment and breathe in the Peace of God. Make this a habit and do this throughout your day. In the beginning, as with any habit, it will be infrequent, but as you develop the habit more completely, you can insert these little breaks more than once an hour.

This habit of escaping the pressures of life and relaxing in the Presence of God, will grow stronger and stronger as the years go by. They will extend in duration and will color the vibration of the person doing it. Eventually, of course, it would be wonderful to stay in the awareness of the Presence of God at all times. Projects can be accomplished while in that Presence; deadlines can be met. The Peace of God can thread through your life, bringing peace and happiness to the person who carries this peace as well as to those around him or her.

It is amazing how the vibration of a group can be altered by one person. This could go either to the positive or to the negative. If, however, a person is able to raise their vibration to that of God-consciousness or a state of loving, the vibration of the room can change ten to fifteen percent. This movement can often be just the amount necessary for joy to be expressed for everyone. If the reverse were true, it can be enough to change the conversation to condemnation and "ain't it awful" games.

The experience of taking a break and merging into the Oneness of God Love is an enhancement of one's own life, but is an assistance to others as well. When we catch ourselves criticizing others, perhaps it is a tap on the shoulder to remind us to take a break and be in God Love.

Be observant of others who are your teachers. See them guide you into positive direction. Let them be an example for you to follow. Appreciation is often the clue to their loving nature. Watch them closely for they are there for you. Be grateful as well.

With love

#81   THANK YOU

We who also love God are grateful to those of you who intend to serve Him. We, like you, serve God with all of our hearts. We have so much love to give, but have our hands tied on earth. We can only give love in a manner that is recognized and received. We, on this other plane, work with those of you who are willing to receive the love of God in the higher vibration, and convert it into the vibration of the earth plane. You then distribute it for us and for God.

Singing, meditation, reading, praying, listening to CDs and speakers are ways you heighten your normal vibration so you can receive the higher vibration of love and then distribute it to others. When you get that feeling of really being connected to God, you are. You are pulling in the Love of God in a higher level than you feel from moment to moment in your daily life. Yes, it does feel so good. It is a beautiful sensation. Certainly this higher vibration of love can bring tears to the eyes. It comes into your normal vibration and raises it. As you go about your day, you distribute it.

As you receive it, you stretch your own ability to contain it. Those of you who connect on a regular basis, and we do mean *connect,* become noticed because of the Love that you carry, and spread.

Those who have learned to bring in large amounts of this higher vibration will become the teachers of others. With the Love comes understanding of Peace and Joy. This *understanding* of the higher levels will want to be distributed as well. Books will be written, seminars and workshops given, etc. All of the giving aids the willing receiver. Their ability to hold and express that which is

149

ever present, will grow. Their joy is great. It is heaven on earth.

The quantity distributed isn't large, usually. It is sort of a glowing that can't quite be seen with the eye. Those who are glowing are very receptive to others that are as well. Everyone benefits. More understanding of what Love is results.

Everyone has so very much to learn. Fortunately, as you understand Love more clearly, you suffer less in your lessons. Often you chose easier ways to learn, and when a suffering is on the path, you accept, and move through it more easily, knowing that love gave you this as a gift. Love your path.

Be at peace.

Your loving Family

#82   SNAKE EYES

"Snake eyes" thrown on dice usually indicates disappointment. The double ones have often been used in that manner—indicating the loss of all gain or other unhappy outcomes. On the same dice you also have the sixes. They are often very welcome because they represent gain (the "good" life). Then there are the numbers in between, each offering something a bit different.

We hear that we are all one. Look at the die and imagine it represents God and that each of us is represented by one of the sides. All coexist. Each is an equal part of God. Each will have a different experience. Each is constructed somewhat differently. From our point of view, one may have more value than another, but in truth, they are equal parts of the one.

Our egos would have us believe that societal constructs determine value, but no one is more valuable to God than another. The holy man has no more value than the prisoner. They are like apples on a tree, each ripening at its own pace. The apple that ripens first is not necessarily the sweetest apple on the tree.

Our souls can be at peace when we look at our fellow travelers on this earth in a non-condemning way. We can trust that they are part of the Oneness and in their own time, will awaken to who they are. This earth is a school for training and for helping us to remember. We have our tutors here and we are tutors to others. Ultimately we will merge as one.

When our hearts are not full of joy, we are not living in the Oneness of God. We must be patient with our learning process and that of others on the same journey. Be aware of those on the other side who assist as frequently as their service is requested. Take time to be holy. Ask of God for the help that you need. It will be forthcoming.

Suspend condemnation and replace it with words of praise for others. It is a gift to your heart. When choices are to be made, live in the giving of joy.

Suspend evaluation for those who are playing parts of God that are different than your own. Trust that it is all as it should be, and the snake eyes are as much a part of the dice as the double sixes.

#83   RAINBOWS

The joy that comes from rainbows delights your day. It brings the unusual beauty into your life. So is it with the awareness of God's Love. Opening one's heart to the Love that is within and being in that instant of purity is a thrill and is more exciting than rainbows.

A major difference of the two experiences is that the rainbow is outside of one's person and the experience of God Love is within. It is actually an awareness of God's presence that resides in the heart. It is like suddenly becoming aware that one is part of a family of royalty. There is a knowingness that you are part of this magnificence, but only a part. The family of royalty is in no way exclusive. Everyone is welcome to belong. Actually, everyone does belong, but until they awaken to who they are, it will not appear to be the truth. The day will come when all will joyfully awaken and rejoice in the connectedness to each other and to the awareness of the great glory of being part of the royal family of God.

Because a rainbow has many colors, the relationship of the colors brings the beauty. So also in the wholeness of God, each of us represents a part of the whole that will not be complete until we are all awakened and the full beauty of God will then dance in relative magnificence, one with each other. It is so important that we all remember who we are, because just as a rainbow would be incomplete without the color green, so is God incomplete without each of us and each of our brothers and sisters.

God is the sum total of all of us. Just as a rainbow is a singular item, so is God. There is only One. God is all there is. There is nothing that is outside of God. The only thing missing for us is our awareness and our joy.

God is Love, we are Love, and the vibration of Love is such a magnificent experience when resonating together with all its parts. We will be astounded by the joy of our hearts when our awareness merges once again into God.

Whenever you see a rainbow, let it remind you of who you truly are within and that everyone you see is part of that same royal family. Let the beauty of the rainbow be a dim reminder of the magnificence of who you are and who your brothers and sisters are.

#84   DISHWATER

Each of us as pieces of God is whole and complete. How-ever, having lived on the earth plane, we have forgotten who we are and have covered ourselves with pieces of unrelated items from the ego. Actually, we have so many upon ourselves that the purity of who we are is barely visible, if at all. It is like the surprise find of an antique silver spoon where the tarnish has made it black and uncomely. Its appearance is the opposite of what it really is. This, too, is ourselves. We have covered ourselves so completely that our brilliance, our light, has very little chance to shine.

Into the dishwater we go. We take on lessons in our daily life that help us to remove blocks. We know we have succeeded in removing these blocks when we feel joy radiate from our being, when we look at others with joy and appreciation, when we feel like smiling. In the dishwater with us are many other parts of God; they, like us, seek to be pure once again.

Our degree of cleanliness or awakening does not, how-ever, depend in any way on those around us. They cannot keep us back, although they can, and often do, lead the way.

It is through our own desire to be pure again that we go into the dishwater or the lessons of life. Every lesson is by choice. There are no accidents. We are never the innocent victims. Every situation has been set up by our own spiritual self for removing the blocks to our own brightness, our own clarity, our awareness of who we truly are.

Some choose to spend their lives with very little change, very little cleaning. Others will scrub and clean diligently and through struggle. Yet others will choose to learn their lessons, to brighten their soul through painless ways. This is the rarer path, however. Unfortunately.

As the debris and tarnish comes off of ourselves, we will radiate light and joy, but most miraculously, we will see others past their tarnish and see the bright, beautiful souls that they are. This will be a continuous joy and a connected feeling. We will start to feel the Oneness of God.

As we willingly go into the experience of clearing and cleaning the debris from who we truly are, let us count the blessings of the joy we experience and know that it will continue to increase as we awaken.

#85   HOPSCOTCH

Choose to make your life one of joy. Lessons can be learned while having fun. The game hopscotch is a fine illustration of how we can view our earth experience. We go from moment to moment intentionally with challenge and delight, then come upon a lesson, or in the case of hopscotch, the stone.

In hopscotch, the challenge is to deal with the stone while keeping your balance. In life also, we come upon our lessons and the challenge is to learn the lessons without losing our balance. It is all a game. Take care to enjoy the game.

As the saying goes, "Attitude makes the difference." And so it is. One can choose to approach life's lessons with delight and challenge or can choose to feel victimized and fearful. It is a choice.

If we find ourselves miserable and unhappy with our daily lessons, those challenges that come upon us, we can learn to adjust our attitude. This will not be done overnight. One can work on small issues first. Instead of dread of cleaning the car, choose to find joy in the result. Become the observer and identify areas where an attitude adjustment is necessary. Then make attempts to change your attitude to one of success and victory. It may be necessary to break down large tasks into small ones to have this feeling. Structure it as necessary, so that pride of accomplishment is assured.

Take time for yourself. Take time with nature and be a responsible steward to your body. Take time for music and friends. Watch the sunsets; smell the flowers. Life is not meant to be a dirge. Most of all, take time to connect with the Love that is given you by God. Feel the Presence of God's Love. Pour it abundantly upon the earth and receive it appreciatively from others. That is our nature.

Draw yourself willingly into a space that brings you in where you touch the Spirit part of yourself. Just as you take time daily to brush your teeth, to brush your hair, to bathe, so should you set time aside for the holy purpose of connecting to God. Keep it small until you are ready for more space. Don't make it a burden. Let this time be anticipated in joy. Let the amount of time grow as you feel the connection deepen. Most of all, be consistent. However, do not have guilt. Work toward these goals in your own rhythm in a peaceful state. You are blessed, you are loved, you are Joy itself.

Friends of the Arc.

#86   CAVE CRAWLING

Envision yourself on a spelunking adventure. You have walked inside the caves, you have climbed up walls, and now you are embarking on a period where you will make yourself as small as possible and crawl through a low tunnel. You do this with the idea that there is something to be discovered, something you haven't seen yet, something that will be wonderful. So it is in the path of seeking self-awareness. The path is not straight. At times it is easy; at times it is challenging. At times you find yourself doing things that you don't know where they will bring you, but you trust that they will bring you to a better understanding. It is this trust that leads you through life.

So you find yourself in a difficult situation, yet you have no desire to quit. You will move forth, you will conquer this situation in hand, and you will have a new understanding that you develop because of your experience. Much of our seeking for God feels like spelunking. We go through such varied experiences, all with trust and anticipation, all feeling close to our Guide. Some parts of the path may be difficult and may have to be done more than once to understand the lesson in that experience

Our path that is outside of ourselves is one of doing, and it appeals to our body-mind. The other path, which is simply going in, in silence, with no doing, is more challenging because we are not trained to be still. Of the two paths, the immobile path is the better. Connecting to the Light within brings great joy and peace.

The silent path of meditation is a commitment accepted by those who are seeking God. Habit must be formed from this day forward and without guilt. Similar to a diet, if you get off your rhythm of daily silence, you simply go back and start over again. Know that you are not so busy that you cannot take fifteen minutes to half an hour out of your active day. The peace it would bring would reward you tenfold.

When your intent is to understand God more, to be conscious of the Presence of God, and you ask God for help, you will be guided and helped in all that you do. Both methods will work to find God.

One is a path of activity where learning is incorporated into the journey and the other is being still with the Presence of God. They are meant to go hand in hand. Try to find joy in both. The journey can be interesting and fun or it can be difficult. Either way, seek God. God is seeking you.

Amen.

#87   BULL'S EYE

Life on planet earth offers a great variety of experiences. We meet people every day who are similar to ourselves or quite dissimilar. Each person living here, though, desires to be happy, desires to be at peace and to experience love.

Imagine that there is an invisible multi-dimensional target that is in place on earth, and at the center of this target is complete and whole connection to God, a place of utter joy, of peace and love. Think of the rings of this target using fifty rings, not five. These rings represent ever-improving places to be as they draw closer to the bull's eye. These can also be thought of as vibrations. So each of us is on the journey to change vibrational levels and become closer and closer to our target goal of being with God one hundred percent.

We change rings by accomplishing learning tasks that are given for that particular level. It could be a degree of patience, understanding, anger control, generosity, consideration and on and on. As we master the lessons given us, and we awaken at that given moment to a better way and can maintain that level of awareness, we progress. There is much work to be done and our journey is guaranteed.

Some may choose to linger in one of the outer rims and just experience that area, that vibration. There is no right or wrong, for we will all be together as one at the end of our journey. There is no time with God, so it doesn't matter if one goes quickly to be with God or slowly. The choices that we make for this journey and the speed with which we awaken to a higher vibration is all planned by our soul before we come. With free will, a journey can be delayed.

One of the characteristics that we must overcome is judging another. Because we are all at so many different places on our journey, it does appear that some are so very right and others so very wrong. But in truth, everyone is where each needs to be and their being where they are is planned to help us. The response to another's actions that would best serve us is gratitude. The only journey we need be concerned with is our own.

Taking time apart from our daily activities for connection to God is a short cut to reaching the bull's eye. Make it a habit.

#88   REGARDING LAND (Personal)

(This message was received as Jim and Clare were preparing to go to court over a dispute with a neighbor over a drainage ditch on both properties.)

The land is smiling. It feels loved. It can give love. It doesn't need anything changed. It is happy the way it is. It likes the moisture and the ability to grow grass easily. It appreciates the deer and the wildlife that come there. It wishes for no change.

(Guide smiles and says...)

When you go through your experiences here on earth, we are always with you. Know that we love you and support you in every way. Rest easily in our love. Give us your worries, your concerns. If we live in the love that is given to us in this present moment, and approach the whole thing while we are in this state of love, the results will always be acceptable.

(Clare sees a group of guides with a twinkle and happiness about them, as if they are getting ready to go to court with us, putting on their suits.)

This is a bridge that we set on our path and one that we are now crossing. Do it in style. Be honest, forthright and use a sense of humor.

You are blessed.

(The dispute was resolved by mutual agreement after the courtroom hearing.)

#89   DISCOVERING A PEARL

See yourself snorkeling in shallow water, enjoying the beauty of nature therein. Your mind is on the beauty of the day, the warmth of the water, the beautiful fish, the sun, the way your body moves in water. You are having a very pleasant time.

Then you see something. What is it? It looks like an oyster. "Hmmm. I wonder if there are more around here? No, just this one. I will take this back to my family."

Later, when opened, this oyster is kind enough to have a beautiful pearl within. What grace to have this brought to me!

So it is in life. Our life goes on, day by day. We are into the moment and then a gift is given from God. This may be quite unexpected, but thoroughly appreciated. It can come in the shape of many possibilities—an opportunity to love a child or to assist someone who needs it, or to have expressed to you full appreciation, or to come upon a job that is perfect. And on and on. This pearl that is in our path is no accident. Those who serve us await the opportunity to bestow upon us such treasures. Our clear appreciation of their efforts causes them to repeat more frequently.

You, too, have the opportunity to bestow pearls of joy on the paths of your fellow travelers. It is almost like a "secret Santa." You look for ways to make people happy and do kind things unnoticed. "Random acts of kindness" is a term used for this. It brings as much joy to the giver as to the receiver.

Holding your pearl, or memory of a wonderful experience that happened to you, will remind you to spread the joy. One of the most delightful ways to be kind to another is to be listening to those who guide us and work with us. They will put us in the right place at the right time, and will use us to do miraculous things. Reaching out to another to bring joy is very rewarding. Once you make this effort consciously, you will be inclined to do it more and more frequently.

Share your love abundantly to all that you see. Seek those who need help and are not in your awareness.

"What you do unto the least of them you do unto me."

#90 LEADERSHIP

Put one foot in front of the other and move, if you want to get something done. The challenge of bringing in new ideas is not an easy task. It takes many hours and much love.

Those who have committed themselves to serving God, alongside Jesus or anyone else, are assisted by the Holy Spirit. As you go through the world sharing your new ideas with joy and with enthusiasm, the Holy Spirit adds light, happiness, and understanding to the ideas you are trying to spread to the world. The Holy Spirit will lead you on your path to those who are going to be receptive. Your path should be fun.

Our responsibility as spreaders of the new ideas of forgiveness, unity and living in the present moment will not be difficult. It may be very quiet, subtle, and almost unrealized by the self. Humility serves well to keep the ego at bay. Confidence in the Presence of God assures the clarity of your truth. The truth will always be distributed with joy, for God *is* Love.

Music is a beautiful way to spread the understanding of God, because music itself is joy, and in that medium, God truths can be laid pleasantly on the melodies and given in small doses with repeated emphasis on one concept. It is also a means of joining one person to another in sharing a truth joyfully.

Children have truth within them. They are coming into a society that is often blocked to the love of God that is within each person. Open hearts of children can be teachers to us. Reinforcing their truths of goodness, connectedness, and trust will help them hold the ideas as they grow older. Missions to children are twice the value of those to adults because the children are so open and so clear. In children, many truths need only be strengthened, not introduced.

The delight in service for Truth is that there are so many fellow travelers who share the same responsibility. Each may be given specialties to teach. One may teach tolerance, another generosity, another trust and faithfulness, etc. As you teach, so do you learn. One is not above another. Like streamers connected to the same May pole, we all are connected to God and are on parallel paths, weaving together.

Enjoy the dance.

#91   SPIRITUAL CO-PILOT

We may travel this world alone for a period, but when the time comes, we may accept the Holy Spirit to go with us. Putting our life into the hands of the Holy Spirit will make our whole journey a much more pleasant one. Now our desires are triggered by the Holy Spirit's guidance and our desires are then much easier to fulfill. The Holy Spirit has a master plan to bring us to the ultimate goal of awakening to who we truly are.

When we accept ourselves completely as a part of God, then the Holy Spirit will only be a gentle guide, and we will know where we are going because the love within us will direct us. Joy will be the order of the day. We will be magnetized to others who are on a similar path. Our connection will reverberate in love and joy and it will bring momentum to assist others to awaken.

After many, many eons on the earth, mankind has reached a level where it can bloom into the awareness of the Spark of God that lies within each person. In centuries past, one enlightened one would come along very rarely, perhaps every hundred years. But gratefully, times are changing. The maturation of the soul and the refining of the energies of the earth are unfolding so that many, many souls can now open their eyes to understand what Jesus and Mohammed understood—that God is Love, that there is only One, and that we are not separate.

The change in our belief system needs to be vast. We must let go of past beliefs and turn inward to our God Self for guidance. This is not an easy transition and the ego part of us exists only if we deny the unity. Ego has been in charge for a long time and does not want to give up control. There will be many lessons to help us make the transition.

The best teachers are those on earth who already walk with God. Their joy has been acknowledged and people flock to them for understanding. Just being in their presence triggers your higher vibration to awaken. There are more and more of these people available to assist us in this metamorphosis.

As we awaken, we typically do it in stages, although it is not necessary. But as we go through the stages, we can be assisted by those who have gone further than ourselves and we can assist those who are following.

Intent to awaken and the Holy Spirit are the two main tools for happy living. Be sure to daily commit to both. May you drive swiftly into the full Light of God.

Amen.

#92   ONION

Within each of us is the vibrancy of God. We have covered this over with ego for eons. Just as one might anticipate Christmas because of its incredible connection to God and to each other, so is it for the time we are entering. It is like Christmas. For those who chose to, there is a window of opportunity to change levels of awareness and shorten our journey back to God. This experience is not for everybody, and because there is no time, there is no value set for those who come closer to God now or those who chose to do it later.

We can liken ourselves to the onion that has layer and layer and layer placed over its heart. This could be compared to our forgetting of who we are. Over much time, we have placed numerous layers of forgetfulness over the purity of our being. The opportunity is now to reduce those layers rapidly with the assistance of the Holy Spirit, if there is such a desire.

Once the desire for God realization is clear, there will be great amounts of help for this intention to become a reality. You will find yourself walking with your teachers. Teachers often come in many disguises, many of whom you might judge only worthy to be receiving teaching from yourself. This could be a neighbor of seeming un-enlightenment, or a non law-abiding citizen, or someone who is very outspoken in ways that contradict your own beliefs. The teacher could be anyone and, in fact, is everyone. There are no accidents, and those who come to you bring a gift to help you remove another layer of density to your remembering of who you really are.

Being aware that everyone is coming into your life in one way or another to assist you will help you have a warmer attitude and appreciation for their willingness to serve. Being willing to release your own judgments and take things lightly with joy is a sign that you are getting closer to knowing the truth about yourself. When you reach the point of living in amusement, happiness, and delight, you will be home.

As long as we have judgments of wrongdoing of ourselves and others, we keep ourselves from total awakening. Even having moments in a day without any judgments can signal massive awakening. It is as though we have peeled off many layers of the onion and the radiance of the heart of the onion is now able to shine through. Watch for the joy and laughter.

Walk in love.

#93   CONTRIBUTING YOUR TALENTS

We are the family of God. Each has been gifted with certain talents that have been selected carefully so that all needs can be met in the family. One will have the gift of humor, another of financial understanding, others will be wonderful with children, some will be quick to contact Spirit, some will be builders, others teachers, others will shine as cooks. Some are outstanding in repair; some have a tenderness for the elderly. The whole family is meant to benefit by your gift, and you are, in turn, to benefit from the gifts of others.

When one fulfills their giving role, they will feel full of joy. It is their purpose, and until they give this gift to others, they will not feel complete.

Because this is a truth, talents should be discovered early in children and developed fully. When a soul is developing their true talent, there is joy, as in pursuing a hobby. There is true zest and eagerness to learn. The student will have an ease in learning these skills. It will be like going with the wind, not against it. Individuals will find themselves at peace around time. If a related endeavor becomes time-consuming, most days it won't feel burdensome, but interesting.

True respect for each talent is desired. One talent is not a greater talent than another, although the financial rewards may be much greater. There is a balance in the family where each of our talents is required. If we choose to develop a talent that is not our own, we may find it very difficult, perhaps unpleasant and burdensome. Life won't be easy. Not only does one do a disservice to oneself, but also to the family as a whole, when one does not develop his or her given talents.

Be aware of pitfalls to self-discovery. For children or adults, they can be anything that consumes their time too much. This can include sports, electronic games, television, reading or any other excessive form of self-entertainment.

Your time on earth will be filled with joy if you allow yourself to give to others of your talent. As a successful person, you will be a pleasure to be around. Develop your talents and *glow*.

#94 MERGING

We can think of ourselves as a lone instrument playing the music of God. But when we combine our music with the music of another, even more beautiful music is made. In life, this can be demonstrated in working happily in the kitchen with a friend or raising a family with a partner. Then this same theme can be carried further and we can merge in harmony with many—those at work, those in church and other groups that we work well with. The blending of love is a warm feeling to the heart, and in fact, that is what God is—a blending of Love.

When we completely merge ourselves in God, we lose our personal identity and become the symphony, the music of the spheres that is vast and melodic, full of love. Love merges. It is like air. It seeks to go outward and continue like the scent of warm bread that fills the house. It continues to flow outward if it is not encumbered.

Being children of God, we carry in our vessel the pure Love that is God. As we learn to remove our blocks, we will find our love flowing more and more, first to family and friends, then to neighbors, coworkers, strangers, and whomever comes before us. Our hearts will overflow with love in nature, to animals, trees, flowers, clouds, sky, birds, light and everything.

When our hearts open completely, it is an overwhelming feeling of infatuation. You feel "in love!" with everything, indiscriminately. Unfortunately, it doesn't usually last in the beginning. Just having the feeling, just becoming the symphony, is such a treat that you long for it again. Your strong intent brings much help from those who serve God, and the recurrence will come closer and closer until you can hold it continuously. Then you will

be a Master teacher of God. All who see you will feel
God. You will feel God in all whom you see. It's a happy
place to be. Gaiety follows. Silliness abounds. Barriers
that were once monumental are simply issues to deal with
that will have perfect outcomes, whatever that looks like.
Peace is ever near.

As you go about your life today, watch for barriers that
are keeping your distribution of love from being complete.
Suspend judgment, accept, love.

The symphony awaits.

#95 CIRCUS

Living our everyday lives can often be like a three-ring circus, giving attention to those who are not with you by phone, email, or snail mail; dealing with plans for the future; dealing with the current environment and other details of the present. It is a very busy time, easy to make busier by adding television or other stimulating parts of our society that are there for us to tune into. So where is the "Department of Peace?"

The Department of Peace is found not in a physical location, or in an adjoining tent, but within. How can this sense of peace be dominant, when so many things are demanding attention? First and foremost, it has to be your intention to have it dominate. When the intention is strong, focus will be sought for peace. Putting aside daily a time to connect to this space of peace within is essential to set the pattern and recognize the focus, and also to familiarize yourself with the vibration of peace to the point that it is home. It becomes a familiar place to be and can be easily returned to when it is gone.

It is jolly to be active in the many interests that your life offers. To be holy does not mean one should desire to sit on a mountain top in pure meditation. The time will come for that later. You have chosen to be in the environment that you are in. You came for what it offers. So feel free to pick from the banquet table, but do not gorge. The trick or discipline here is to only take from the banquet table that which can be enjoyed, but not throw you into forgetfulness. If the sense of peace does not come readily, while you go through your life, then you must cut back from the choices that life offers until the balance comes.

When peace can be attained, as well as interests being

indulged in, all is well. Balance is at hand. It is not unlike the dieter and the scale. One must keep vigilant so as not to overdo. At the same time, one can add activities as long as that peace is dominant in the heart. Again, it is not necessary to keep apart to maintain peace. It is a self training that one must undertake with full intention to keep the peace and the wonderful connection to God.

When the peace of God is dominant in one's heart, that peace is then found easily in the hearts of others and the separation between one another diminishes. The stronger the sense of peace, the more one flows in the Love of God.

Joy prevails. Let us flow together.

#96   HOLDING HANDS

In this life, we see many examples of togetherness. We see teamwork in an office; we see harmony in a choir; we see sports teams with one goal to share; we see large families connected by love; we see the government chosen by us to improve our lives. These are all examples of how we join with one another and share our identity.

The practice of merging is valuable because it helps us to get away from our egos and our personal identities. The more completely and purely that we can forget ourselves and become one with another or a group, the sooner it will be for us to realize who we are and that we are not actually separate from one another.

Even though we are connected, we still maintain leadership abilities and responsibilities for the group, as does each group member. We have been each given different talents that, when applied, will meet the needs of the whole. Knowing which talent is ours is not always easy, but upon much searching, one would know they are in the right spot by their joy in giving. It will feel less stressful and very warm and satisfying to be giving of the talent that we were given at birth. Receiving from those who are equals on our team is also comforting and heart warming.

God is the Oneness of all. There is nothing but God and therefore, everything we see is God, everyone we meet is God, and we, in return, are God as well. Learning how to merge with one another on the earth plane in teams, in families, and in units aids us in awakening to the true identity of who we are. How amazing it will be as we draw closer and closer to this realization. Judgments will cease. Appreciation will be dominant; humor and love will be everywhere. The rewards for seeking awakening will be great. Just as today, as adults, we have learned a more pleasant way to get along than to bite each other as we did as children, every level of harmony that we find brings us a step closer to the realization of the Oneness.

The rewards are great for releasing the ego and the feeling of separateness between our fellow travelers and our selves. Like a magnetic force, the closer we get to truth, the faster we desire to get there.

Daily meditation, at least once, is essential for this journey. The destiny is bliss itself. Join with me this day in setting the intention to harmonize with others to the glory of the Oneness.

#97 LOOPS

Are you enjoying your travel through your life's journey? Has this trip's plan been one of joy or one of struggle? Your life's journey was established before you came to the earth. It was picked from endless possibilities as the one that would serve you best. That does not mean that your journey is easier than another's, but rather it helps you in ways that your soul desires to be helped, for the optimum goal of awakening to who you are in the heart of God.

When you are on your path, things go fairly easily. When you are off your path, it is similar to a train that is off the track. It can move forward, but it is very difficult.

Typically, we come to the earth to learn how to drop barriers that prevent our God Light that is within from shining forth. There are many lessons that we learn to accomplish this, and the lessons will be learned by degrees. If the lesson is not learned one hundred percent at the first presentation, it will come again. Like a loop, it will repeat in a different form. This can go on for loop after loop after loop. Or if we are fast learners, we can go to a different lesson for the next loops.

The lessons are not necessarily difficult, but as the loops are presented over and over, they become more and more difficult, so that the lesson itself cannot be missed. With daily connection to God in the form of designated time for prayer and meditation, the sensitivity to the lesson at hand is enhanced and it can be learned more easily. It's like traveling through the densities of the earth plane to connect to the sacredness of God and then, when the lessons come from God, they can be recognized and embraced in understanding and gratitude.

Without our connecting to God, the lessons are presented and disregarded, then presented again and again and again, until they become challenging and impossible to ignore.

Taking time to pray and meditate is like oiling the wheels of your vehicle. It makes the travel smoother. This does not mean that there will not be hills and valleys and bumps on your journey. Let's face it, some have chosen a very adventurous journey while others are content to travel more peacefully. There is no path, no journey that is not perfect. Each has been formulated before we were born by that part of our self that is God-conscious.

There is no room for judgment of another, for we do not know the perfection of his life's plan. Releasing all judgments of others can clear the smog away from your thinking and help you enjoy the clarity of a beautiful life. Travel with a song in your heart and a kind word on your tongue. Travel with joy as your friend.

Amen.

#98   WARM LOVE

Beloveds. Our love for you is so encompassing. Think of it as a soft fleece blanket that is four inches thick. It wraps you; it snuggles you; it protects you; it gives you peace; it takes care of your needs. Our love for you is unending.

Like a favored aunt that serves you with great love, we are delighted when you ask for assistance. What honor to us that you remember us in your time of need and that you trust all our love to be there for you. And, of course, we respond to your requests and aid you in a way that best suits your soul.

Just as you trust our love, you know that your prayers are answered, even though it may not appear in the present to be so. We will never fail you.

The love that you see in us is God's love. This is the same love that you carry to the capacity that you are able. By working with us and feeling the depth of love that we carry, you will learn to also be a distributor of God's love in an incredible way. And as you know this great love, you recognize it in the hearts of your fellow travelers, and it reminds you how we are all united in the love of God.

What a joyous responsibility to give and receive the love of God as is demonstrated by the Holy Spirit. Be of great cheer as you distribute your heart full of love to your brothers and sisters on the path. You are never alone.

(Clare feels a huge column of white light being released from far above and flowing down through her head into her body.)

It never ends. We are one with you and God.

Arc of Infinity Friends

#99   JUMPSTART

(As Clare feels the presence of spirit messengers, there is an atmosphere of joy—"party time!" They are thrilled to have an opportunity to express and be heard clearly.)

Spiritual growth is often an "on again, off again" experience. During difficult times, people turn to God for they remember that God's Love is always there. Life takes over in the business of the daily responsibilities, draws you away from those moments you have set aside to connect with God. Of course, the Holy Spirit never stops being with you. It is impossible that the Holy Spirit would ever leave you because we are all linked together as one through the Love of God, which is in our hearts.

When those around us are radiating the Love of God, it will jumpstart our sincere connection to God. If we have ever developed a relationship with God, it will immediately come to the fore with this reawakening. Our focus changes and once again, we swim in the flow of God Consciousness.

Born-again Christians, devout Muslims, Hasidic Jews, or any visible serious religious commitment reminds us of our connection to the One.

(Clare feels a wave of wonderful light coming in.)

Loving God and letting that love show enhances the connections to God of those around you. This service is appreciated by our fellow man and by God.

God wants us to be happy and our happiness is exponentially increased when we are connected to the Love of God that is within our hearts. The greater the connection, the greater the joy. Heaven on earth is present in those who carry God's love in their hearts, in their actions and in their smiles.

Let's each of us serve God and our family on earth by bringing to each other's awareness the great Love of God that flows through our hearts. In doing so, the world is greatly served. We can think of this as a subway that travels underground totally unnoticed by those in its vicinity. Then think of this same subway coming to the surface, becoming visible to many. Then, better yet, this subway becomes elevated and is seen by an even greater number of people.

So it is with the Love of God that is within us. It is our service to bring that Love into the awareness of as many people as possible. God will be served and so will they.

Go forth and elevate the Love of God in your life.

#100   GAILY WALK

The closer you walk with God, the more readily you let would-be offenses roll off your back. You live in a world of understanding and compassion and have no desire for condemnation. If you can successfully sidestep resentment, hurts, condemnations, anxiety, and fear, you can walk lightly. The song* that says "forget your troubles, come on get happy," is exactly true. If you can release from your basket of woes each of the burdens that you have carried with you for a long, long time, you will find yourself walking with a lighter step.

The process of release is two-fold. One way is to deal with each individual burden in the basket, develop an understanding of that burden and release it. Another way is to fill your basket so full of love, joy, excitement, enthusiasm, giving, and gratitude that there is no room to hold resentments and pain. Your heart is simply over flowing with God Love, and there is no room for heavy burdens.

It is like the words of another song† that says "stay on the sunny side, always on the sunny side, stay on the sunny side of life."

Walk with a joyful step, knowing there is much joy to be shared.

---

* *"Get Happy," Harold Arlen/Ted Koehler*
† *"Sunny Side Of Life," Ada Blenkhorn/J. Howard Entwisle*

#101 SPINNING COLORS

As you *(Jim and Clare)* read in "A Course in Miracles" this morning, we are each connected to the glory of God.* We may think we travel alone, but in truth we have a bridge that joins us to the great Beauty that is God. It is so beautiful that it is pure joy. As we awaken and clear the barriers from our awareness, we will feel that joy. It will feel like riding musical streams through the air.

Each of us is an integral part of the whole. It is like we are colored disks that swirl about in cooperation with each other to make beautiful scenes. The gift we give is cooperation and awareness of who we are. The pictures would never be as glorious without us. The glory of who we truly are is so magnificent that the color that we spin adds greatly to every painting we are in or every life experience we are a part of. And just like us, others are equally magnificent when they connect to the glory of who they truly are in God. What beauty we give to one another!

Our gifts that we give to the world are enhanced greatly by blending them with the loving Presence of God in our fellow travelers. It is like harmonizing magnificent voices in a duet or choir, and again it is similar to using beautiful colors together in a piece of art, one setting off the other where the beauty plays between the colors.

We are given such an opportunity to bring great joy to the earth plane if we but merge into our God Self and bring back that magnificent beauty that is ours to steward. In recognizing others who are doing the same, great harmony and beauty can be obtained. This beauty may show up in many ways. Sometimes it is simply working together on a project at work. Other times it could be a project

* *A Course in Miracles, Text, 9, VI, 3:9*

where cooperation is requested in service—perhaps a used coat drive or a clean up day for the neighborhood. God is glorified whenever you are serving in love and there is greater and greater harmony when you work with others easily and with joy.

Merge into the Oneness of God as frequently as you can. Set a time apart daily for twenty minutes to a half an hour. Use music, incense, a holy space, whatever it takes for you to get into a deep connection with God. Don't settle for simply having quiet time. The glorious harmony of many begins by the glorious connection of each of us to our God Self. Plugging in to our God connection is a must.

Go forth into your day with a strong God Charge.

(This particular message was beautiful for Clare because she saw the colors of individuals blending together in a huge painting. The colors were radiant and beautiful and complemented each other, harmonizing in their own ways. The last piece was interesting because she was shown that connecting to God through meditation was like plugging into a wall socket and receiving a beautiful energetic charge. Like rechargeable batteries, if we are not plugged in very long to a source, we don't maintain a good charge.)

#102   FIRST SNOW

Looking out of your window on a winter's day, you watch as the first snow falls. At first a few flakes, then a few more, and before long, by evening, the earth is covered in a blanket of white snow. This is very similar to the awakening of man on earth. First a few come full of love and peace, then others join and more and more, and one day the earth will be covered by the peace of God that is being expressed from the hearts of awakened individuals. It, too, will be beautiful and bring joy to the heart.

Again, it can be likened to popping corn. First a few, then many more, then all have come to bloom.

Our part in the experience of the awakening of the earth is guaranteed. We have entered into a path with a certain destiny. We needn't stress about it or concern ourselves. As the saying goes, "life is about the journey itself, not the destination." As we live our day to day, connecting to our God Source and reaching out to merge with our brothers and sisters, our path will find its rewards in our experiences of the moment.

Our job is to "make happy." As we reach out to make others happy, we will find the result to be our own happiness. Our teachers on the earth plane have demonstrated the next step in our growth. When we are ready, we take it on as an area to be developed within ourselves. As we open an area of our life, we start to see that area being developed in other people, similar to a pregnant woman suddenly noticing other pregnant women or someone buying a blue car and noticing how many blue cars are around.

As we pursue this area of development, of course, we are demonstrating it to those who would follow our example. As in leapfrog, one teaches, one learns, then the teacher learns from the student, and so on. We move on to a new game, or area of development, and again one teaches and then learns from the student, and on and on and on. Ultimately, one awakens, as does their teacher. The destiny is reached while the mind is on the game.

If we can learn to take life lightly, though at times it seems we can't, we can reach our destination of total Oneness with God. As a by-product of the games, the closer you get to the goal, you will find yourself more and more aware of the learning situations that are being offered you. Your heart becomes more full of joy and gratitude.

The end is a slippery slope into the magnificent experience of being all Love and part of the Oneness.

#103 FLOATING

Picture yourself a feather, a very small downy feather that has been dislodged in flight. You are blissfully drifting to the right gently, to the left gently, carefree and in perfect peace. So it is when we merge into the Oneness. Trust then is complete. Life is viewed as an interesting journey designed for the enhancement of your soul. You go from one experience to the next, catching the beautiful blessings that are imbedded in each experience.

As we have our moments of connection to the Oneness, we know total trust. At that point, we have no worries. We are imbued with peace. Unfortunately, few of us are able to maintain total connection to the Oneness for great lengths of time. However, each experience, each connection makes the next one more easily accessible and more long lasting. Even with experiences of connection to the Oneness, though, we are not guaranteed to easily access it at will. There may be long periods when the connection seems to elude you. Patience and trust and continuous commitment will assist its return.

Setting the atmosphere for a good meditation can't be overemphasized. The time of day should be consistent, in the same location, and free of distractions. If music, chants, or incense help, then they should be used. Reading a spiritual piece before meditation is a value to some people, as well as meditating with another person. Each individual must experiment to find what draws them into their deepest self.

Know that any attempt on your behalf to draw closer to God will be greeted with a thousand times your efforts by those who are assigned to assist you in your awakening to who you are. The assistance that comes to you is loving and compassionate. It will draw you in the direction you desire to go. It is a situation where they are blessed to be able to serve you and you are blessed by their presence. All is for the glory of God. Upon your commitment to connect to God, comes a connection assuring you will be embraced in the Light of God, in the Wholeness of God. This connection is one of complete trust, as the floating feather.

The challenging discipline of meditation will lead to a time of peaceful merging with God. It does take practice, but the results are sure.

#104 CHRISTMAS

(Clare is shown an image of Jesus walking as a ten-foot-wide tunnel of glowing, wispy light forms around Him.)

Christmas is a time of great celebration. At this time, we remember the man Jesus who came before us. Jesus is our brother and shows us the way. He had the opportunity to demonstrate the Love and Joy of God. He truly was aware of His connection to the Whole of God. He saw that He took a part in being God, while at the same time being man.

He was aware of the great joy, great peace, and great love that existed continuously in the higher levels of awareness. And, because He loved His brothers and sisters on earth, He wanted them also to know this great peace, this great love. He wanted them to focus on the sacred feelings, rather than the struggles and sorrows of this world. He saw the vast richness that life could offer if people would tap into the Source that is available. Jesus realized that the others did not know how, and so He desired deeply to teach them. He wanted to share the Love in His heart so that all could feel this experience and be part of the family of God.

It was a very difficult goal He was trying to accomplish, like the "jaws of life" that take a person out of a crushed car, so was Jesus attempting a very difficult task of releasing people from generations and generations of struggle with very little Light. The task was monumental, but because of the Peace of God, Jesus had the strength to give it His all.

It is right to celebrate the discovery of God within. It is like finding the very beginning of the vein of gold in a mine.

(Note: Clare sees the image of people in a dark mine scratching at the walls for treasure with no success.)

Jesus revealed the beginning of a vast endless vein of Gold for the whole of man that had been mining for Gold—God—forever. Much love and joy has been brought to earth thanks to His efforts then and now. He continues to live and assist us when asked. Others who have also discovered the Gold, or the Love of God within their souls, have passed on and also continue to serve us as Jesus does.

We are all connected like a huge amoeba. Motion forward from part of us instigates motion forward for all of us. We will not be content until the last part of the whole awakens to the glory of the God within. What joy and celebration there will be! Christmas is nothing compared to that celebration.

Sharing love, forgiveness, understanding, and delight for each other helps the whole amoeba move forward. Giving love in any circumstance is fulfilling our part of the whole. The giving of joy at Christmas is a wonderful symbol to remember Jesus and the significant role He plays in our lives.

Amen.

#105 BOX OF TREASURES

Just as a child may have a box where she keeps wonderful treasures—perhaps a feather from a blue bird, a huge acorn, a dried flower, and other little gems that bring joy to the soul—we each in our hearts have a box of treasures as well. These are memories that are highly valued. *(For Clare, it was singing "Up From the Grave He Arose" with her Dad in church at Easter, and the awe that Christmas lights always bring.)*

There are many, many more that each of us have in our treasure chest. Let's be sure not to bury our treasure chest too far down where it is only enjoyed once a year, if that. The joys that can be awakened are gifts for the world, not in the gift itself, but in the joy that is released into the world.

How valuable to the world is the individual joy; the genuine smile of another can notch up the vibrational level of those who receive it. As our ascent into the Light proceeds, our level of joy on a moment-by-moment basis increases. Those who are very close to God are so much fun to be around! They are kindly, forgiving, and genuinely loving. And those of us who are further behind down the path may have only momentary releases of great joy and love, but when we do release our love and our joy we assist everyone around us. And their release, on the other hand, benefits us greatly, as well.

Laughter for laughter's sake is fun, but is not necessarily a spiritual vibrational shift. For example, those who tell jokes that degrade another person do not enhance the vibrational level of others.

Some joy is quiet. Assisting an elderly aunt who needs help may be done with such love and gratitude for being able to assist that the vibrations of both parties can be benefited. Any gift of service enhances vibrations of both the giver and the receiver. How blessed we are to be able to serve. Canadian teacher Ken Killick once said, "You earn the privilege to serve."

Feel your joy in meditation and bring it into your day and spread it around. God leans on you to save the world, a privilege that should not be ignored. Continue to climb the ladder of joy and spread it further and further into the world, blessed one.

You don't go alone.

#106 THE WHEELBARROW

Your present love propels you along a Divine plan. The course that you are taking is less difficult than you imagine. Filling your heart with love, being happy, seeing joy and love everywhere is your path. It is meant to be easy and filled with joy.

When you find yourself troubled, you are on the wrong page. Our troubles will be cared for. We need not concern ourselves heavily, but rather trust the solution will joyfully and miraculously come. You can depend on it. Picture yourself going down a path and behind you is a servant with a wheelbarrow. When you come upon a problem on your path, you pick it up, turn around and put it in the wheelbarrow. The Holy Spirit is your servant. He will hold all the problems for you and will dissolve them as you go. All of this is to free you up so that you can fulfill your life's purpose, which is to distribute joy and love and peace to those that you see, that you come upon.

Your purpose is to be happy. Seek happiness within each task that is given. Attitude is chosen from within, so seek to choose a positive attitude, one of appreciation.

If you find yourself struggling, turn the struggle over to the Holy Spirit. He "has your back." Trust that you can release your problems to the Holy Spirit. Realize you alone cannot solve your problems well, but the Holy Spirit, in His endless joy, has strength unending.

Releasing control for the resolution of your problems to the Holy Spirit, also releases the outcome. How often we don't want to let the outcome be out of our control, and we hang on to the problem. This does not assure an outcome to our liking. The outcome given by the Holy Spirit will be the best outcome possible, although it may not appear to be so. Truly releasing your problem to the Holy Spirit assures comfort with the results.

If you picture humanity living in winter in Michigan, you picture many clouds and some storms and some break-through sun and even some sunny days. So it is with most of us dealing with burdens and worries, but our job on the path of awakening is to be the sunshine for all. Our path is to be joyful and to develop trust for ourselves and others.

Have a happy hour, day, week, month, year and life.

Be the sunshine.

Your Arc of Infinity Friends

#107   WE ARE NOT ALONE

Wishing to walk with God assures us that we are walking with God. And as we walk with the Master, we know that all of life is a blessing. The incredible Love of God surrounds us, guides us, directs us, and brings us into experiences of great joy. Some of these experiences may not appear to be gifts of joy when they are given, perhaps as a father might give his son a lizard for a gift. The gift may appear to be unpleasant and not understood, but as the child gets to know the lizard and understand the joys this lizard can bring, appreciation can be forthcoming.

So too with us, gifts are given us daily that seem questionable on the surface—perhaps a disease or a car jacking or a dismissal from a job. But as we, too, trust in the Father's gift and his intention to bring love and joy into our lives, we can learn to suspend doubt and seek the blessings of that which is given us.

This lesson of trust in the Love of God is one of the harder lessons. Our ego wants to make the decision of what is right or wrong, but look to the holy people, like the Dali Lama, and see trust and total joy—the knowing of the presence of God even in adverse situations. Being totally aware of Who walks with us, holds our hand, and surrounds us incredibly with Love, we can relax and look forward to a life that is interesting, full of joy and service.

Some of our greatest joys that will come to us in this lifetime will be from giving. Perhaps the most satisfactory giving is service, filling a need another has. Others also get great joy in serving us. If we are willing to give fully, we need but ask for guidance. Our Joy Maker who walks with us will bring us to areas of need. These may be difficult areas, but the rewards will be great.

With our great desire to serve and bring joy to ourselves and others, we can be disappointed because life does not turn out the way we expected it to. Remembering the Love that carries us through life helps us realize that whatever comes our way is the best for us at the time. Our job is to totally trust God and laugh and enjoy the moment. As the saying goes, "Bloom where you are planted."

So we must put our ship in the hands of the Master, and go along for the ride, trusting that the Master knows where all the treasures lie and will lead us into a life of joy if we let him.

Amen

(Clare sees guide playfully dressed like a pirate.)

#108   FIRE

Greetings of love.

As a child we are loved and adored and the world revolves around us. Then we go to school and it runs differently. We have to learn to adjust to the unpleasant awareness that the world does not revolve around us. It isn't always easy to understand, and tears and bad feelings may come along the way of total understanding. It is similar for us as we awaken to the Oneness.

Often there are parts of us that have not awakened to the concept of Oneness. It is desirable to remove these blind spots from our being, so that we can understand the Oneness completely. Because these spots have been resistant to removal by the lessons learned so far, one might call them "stubborn." They need more stringent methods of removal. The more challenging lessons will have been selected by our soul for such removal. Although unpleasant, the means for removal will be appreciated as they help the individual person reach the wonderful goal of total awakening.

As we go through life and run across the parts that are difficult, we can remember the kindergartener in tears as she learns her lessons of being part of the group. We, too, are attempting a new level of merging and have adjustments to make. There are trials by fire that are magical in removing spots of darkness that prevent total awakening.

Although the trials themselves may be difficult, appreciating that they burn off the hindrances to our growth makes them more tolerable. Accept that there are no mistakes on our path and that, although the fire may burn, it is serving us wonderfully and we will be grateful for it when the trial is over.

This remembrance is hard to hold when engulfed in the fire of removal. It is a kindness we can offer each other to help each other remember that there are no mistakes and that this difficult period does have a purpose. We can trust that the Love that is tenderly guiding us will hasten this experience and find ways to lessen its difficulty.

Be strong and know that your best outcome is foremost in every experience you undertake.

#109   FAMILY

It is not hard for us to acknowledge that a spark of God is within each of us. We see our relationship to God, and of course we realize that each of our brothers and sisters also have a spark of Divinity within them. The time is coming now when we shall see the relationship between the siblings as clearly as our individual relationships to God. We will acknowledge more and more frequently the similarity of our familial characteristics and goals.

We will see how God uses the older siblings, in soul age, to teach the younger siblings His values and His Love. As we become aware of that which is asked of us, we feel the honor and commit ourselves to doing the best job we can, as do our older siblings. Whereas once we felt loose and unattached one from another, we now form very fine bindings within the group. These bindings strengthen until the family unit of love has formed. Now this large gelatinous family unit moves toward God together. Some will be faster and others will be slower, but the family will still travel as a unit.

At first, there will be many, many family units. They will reach out and incorporate those siblings that have not yet found a family, and the family moves forward, closer to God. As families travel, they will join other families until all families have joined and we realize that we are all part of the family of God. No one is left out. No one travels alone. And although there are members of our family that we might deem "lost sheep," they are still part of our family and our love is still required to support them and to help them in their struggle. Our love will not fail, and even the "lost sheep" will one day awaken to the family love and to the embrace of the heavenly Love of God.

As we move into putting the value of love for another in front of our own wishes and desires, we hasten our journey back into the Oneness of the heavenly kingdom. As we travel, we will look around, and notice many, many others on the same journey. The time is hastening when all of us "wandering souls" will be united in the Oneness.

Reach out today in love to put another person before yourself. Know that your expression of love is the expression of God, because God is Love. The privilege is yours to help another.

Your reward will be great.

#110   BOUQUET

"A beautiful bouquet of spring flowers!" This bouquet has been selected for harmony and beauty in sight and smell. Each individual flower may or may not have been beautiful as a single flower. Its beauty is likely to be enhanced by being put into the company of other flowers. So it is with us. Each of us has our own individual beauty, our own talent for serving. The talent and the beauty we carry become enhanced when we combine with others of similar purpose. Together we assist and beautify each other, and as a group bring great service to the world. We unite as families, not necessarily blood families, but families of souls who care about one another and share in the desire to go back to God.

This bouquet of flowers will be assembled from the garden year after year. Some years, particular plants will be chosen to be together in the one bouquet of beauty and service. The flowers that have not been picked will bring beauty where they stand. On another occasion, they will be joined with an assortment of those in the family who are in the garden for another bouquet.

You too, may be living your life with people you have lived with many lifetimes. You have been together for many seasons—many lifetimes. Some of the people from your garden family will not be joined with you in the bouquet of this lifetime, or the group that you work with in this lifetime. However, from time to time, you will see a face and feel as though you know this person very well. They may be part of your family that is not in your bouquet this time around. You probably have spent many other times when you two were working together. Your garden is big enough that there can be multiple bouquets, or multiple groups that have assembled at any given time, and then yet in another lifetime may reassemble in yet a different way.

Because of our strong interrelatedness to each other, we want to be careful to learn lessons that are presented to us, often from each other, and be grateful for the lesson. It also serves us well not to retaliate or hold a grudge, because each family member that we interact with is doing it for us, more than to us. Just as we wish to be understood and forgiven, so must we understand and forgive all our family members who serve us so that we can become more beautiful and more capable of service. We may not love the lesson that is being presented to us, but it will serve us well to remember that love is behind the lesson, even though it may not be recognized.

Daily trust the unfolding of your life and its lessons. Through the lessons will you develop your full beauty, your full capacity for service. The day will come when you will be grateful and only grateful for all events that come to you, good and bad, because you truly know they are sent in love. Until it comes automatically, we must make an effort to go in that direction as best we can. Love yourself on the journey.

#111   TWINS

As we go through this world, it can be very lonely. However, when we do reach out and ask the Holy Spirit to guide us and be with us, it will be so. Our intention is all that is required for the blessed relationship of God and us to be strong. The Holy Spirit will be a part of you. A thought will come and you know not whether its origin is your own or from the Holy Spirit. You have ideas of where you are going with your life. Perhaps these ideas do not fit your ultimate desire of service. If that is the case, you will find yourself being nudged into a different direction by your twin, the Holy Spirit.

In our Oneness with God and our brothers and sisters, we merge into one unit with the intention of Love, which is God. There are times in our lives when we can't see the difference between the Holy Spirit's guidance and our own. A sign that will aid us in telling if we are being guided by the Holy Spirit is the feeling that the Love of God is present in the moment. Because we do have matter on our glasses and our vision is not always pure, the Holy Spirit may bring us down paths that are not strictly joy-filled, but serve to better our vision and ultimately bring us into greater joy.

How blessed we are to have the Holy Spirit as our twin and companion! The Holy Spirit never leaves us and is there for anything we need. We simply must ask. The joy the Holy Spirit experiences is very great when we call upon Him. How fortunate we are to have a twin with such amazing capabilities and filled with love for us. How can we be alone? The Holy Spirit has a magical connection to everyone. Knowing this, we will want to treat everyone as family because we are all linked in the

One. Being unkind to another person is being unkind to the Holy Spirit, the One who loves you so. Being generous and helpful to another is being generous and helpful to the Holy Spirit.

As we walk this journey with the Love of the Holy Spirit in our hearts, we are guided to be as holy as He. We desire to help everyone, to share joy and love this day. Ask the Holy Spirit to help you find your own love that you can share and make others happy.

We are privileged by the Holy Spirit's companionship and Holy service. Have a day full of joy, laughter, and song!

Amen.

#112   JELL-O

Imagine the spiritual unfolding of each of us taking place in a huge parfait of Jell-O*. We start out in the color purple, and in this atmosphere of understanding we put ourselves first and foremost. It matters to us what others think of us. We seek praise. We fight to be acknowledged as better than our fellow travelers. We often fear rejection. Our main energy is to shine the light on ourselves in a favorable way, or if not favorable, at least on ourselves. Life is difficult. People are hard to get along with.

Through lessons that have been brought our way, we learn that loving others has value. We switch from purple to blue. In this layer of the parfait, we are still very strongly self-oriented, but we are merging more into the Light. Life is still very difficult and still most of our energy is focused on ourselves. Again, lessons are brought our way and sometimes over and over again. Lessons are learned, new awareness forms, and we are able to graduate into yet another color of the parfait.

The same process goes on and on through the various colored layers of the parfait, until we come to the bottom where there is no color because all the lessons have been learned. This is the point where we have actually developed love in our hearts for others that completely outshines our love for ourselves. We are ready to merge into the Oneness.

Going into the Oneness is like going home into an environment where we disassemble our molecules at the door and merge into this space of Love. Here there is no identification, but totally a sense of unity. The Love is extremely beautiful and resonates throughout. When it is

* Jell-O is a registered trademark of Kraft Foods

208

time for us to serve others in the Jell-O, we will reassemble and go back to assist them in their awakening to the total Oneness, as others have done and still do for us. Not one soul will be left behind, because God in the Oneness would be incomplete without any one of us.

We are grateful that the path is sure and that the Love of God is strong in calling us home. Today, stretch your willingness to put another person ahead of yourself. Stretch your willingness to forego giving criticism, even if it is a national pastime. It is through making effort that we move through the different levels of the parfait and go home.

Speedy journey.

#113   THE MAZE

Our soul, which is part of God, has chosen to experience life on earth. The life that we live on earth does not define our soul in any way. The soul's value is maximal, no matter what experience it chooses while on earth.

The soul is complete and the lessons here are for experience and understanding and then for remembering who we are. The soul comes on to the earth plane and gets immersed into the experiences that are here and can easily forget the purity that exists within itself. Once the forgetting occurs, efforts are then made to help the soul reawaken to who it truly is. That is where most of us are today. We desire to be merged in the Oneness of God, but see ourselves as something else. So our objective here is to reawaken. This calls for many a varied path that will surely lead us through the maze and out the other end, back into the awareness of who we are one more time.

The life experiences can very well be likened to the maze. We see ourselves going forward with great enthusiasm and then run into a dead end where we feel lost and without hope. Then through guidance we are put back on our path and, sooner or later, the experience repeats itself. However, all of it is progress and we are being led through the maze to the other side where we will be in total clarity, total awareness, and total love.

As you get near the edge of the maze, you can start to feel the Love that you are being drawn toward. You will notice joy in your heart and satisfaction with all those who travel similar paths. Living with the end in sight can be very pleasant much of the time. However, there are still lessons to learn, turns to make in the maze, but the progress is sure.

When we enter the maze we don't go alone. There are those on the other side who delightedly, and with great honor, volunteer to assist us in this wonderful adventure. The path we take through the maze has been planned ahead of the journey. We will be guided to go forward or turn as we venture forth. Poor communication at times makes the signals foggy. At times we don't listen to our guidance and we make wrong turns and feel totally lost. We need but ask for clear guidance and it will come. The end is sure.

After the adventure, we merge once again into the family of Oneness. This family will not be complete without us.

Remember who you are and all the love that goes with you. Your travel plans are complete and you are guaranteed to arrive at your final destination of joy.

#114 SNOW BLOWER

(Clare was thinking that this transmission might be diffi-
cult because she felt weak and tired. Then the spirit guides
told her "This is easier than your life. Don't make it hard.
Lighten up and let it flow.")

Today is a winter storm outside the home. Much snow
is falling to the ground, covering everything. So is it in
life. Everywhere you look are concerns layering upon
concerns, upon concerns. They tend to pile up.

Then it is time for the snow blower, that which is going
to push aside the concerns of the world. In this case, it is
meditation. There are many qualities of snow removal.
One of the poorest is sweeping with a broom. In this
case, the problems don't go very far and it takes a lot of
effort. This might be compared to panic praying. The next
method is the snow shovel. Here one prays connected,
but not with much length of time, only enough to get
the job done, and it is a lot of work. Then there is the
snow blower, or meditation. Here, just connecting to the
method of snow removal brings one easily to the bottom
of the many layers that are covering the path. This is done
easily and pleasantly.

Then there are levels of snow blowers. As the power
of the snow blower goes up, so does the snow that is in
your path, or your concerns, get blown further away. This
does encourage one to go for the "super duper" snow
blower. This, in meditation terms, is a commitment to a
time slot where the connection to the Holy Spirit is clear
and strong. Using this high-powered snow blower on a
daily basis, during a snowstorm, will ensure your path
is easy to find and you are less likely to get stuck. If we
can see the path so simply with the layers of snow being

sent away by the snow blower, we should be able to also see how the layers of concerns that pile up can be cleared to keep our path sure with meditation.

As man has found a way to make the burden of snow removal light, so has God made the burden of life concerns light through meditation. In our time away from our concerns, we merge with God and get power and clarity that is beyond our own strength. For getting through our challenges, it is wonderful to have assistance. Just as with snow removal, it is not necessary to take advantage of that which is offered us. It is simply a short cut to meeting our needs.

Use the snow blower in the winter snowfall and have time to enjoy the snow for what it is. Take time to play. And in life, take the short cut to lessen your burden so you have time to enjoy life to the fullest.

Go have fun.

#115 LIGHTEN YOUR JOURNEY

Blessed are those who are called to serve. Welcome.

Daily life can be taken gently and peacefully. Struggling within daily life constricts your ability to receive. That is why it is so valuable to give your burdens to God and trust that the best will come to you in blessings. Daily life will be sprinkled with joy, similar to the manna given in the desert. The gift of joy will be sent to you on a frequent basis and it is your responsibility to be able to lay your burdens down to catch the joy. Your responsibilities that you are sharing with God can then be picked up again. There is always the time to lay your responsibilities down, a moment to gather joy, and then to resume your work with the added joy.

The greater your clarity, the greater your joy. The greater your clarity, the greater your love. The greater your clarity, the greater your peace. These will all be brought to you as you intend to draw closer to God. God's help is ever near to assist when blocks appear and your joy, peace, or love is not abundant.

There is so much fun to be had when one becomes clear. To become clear, you must trust God and unite with everyone, blending their beauty with your own. You must learn to not care that they are not one hundred percent beautiful in their qualities, but simply seek for the beauty that is there to unite with yours. It becomes like a party where love is given and received freely. Judgments are released. Trust is everything.

To light your way down your path so that you can move fast into your understanding of who you are, watch for your personal guides. You will know who they are, because they will appeal to you. You will like the way they live their lives. These are your spiritual way showers. They can tutor you through your observing them. You will notice that they take life less seriously than you do, or at least they have more fun. As we get a clearer view of what our goal actually is, we will want to run down our path to the Light. As we get closer to the end, the joy gets more and more real, love abounds. There is less to worry about and a greater confidence that everything is where it should be.

Today, peacefully handle that which is given you, stopping from time to time to gather joy. Know that your way is sure. Be mindful of the spiritual presence that goes with you on your beautiful walk back to God.

Amen.

#116 LIVING JOYFULLY IN THE ZOO

The easiest way to bring joy to your self is to bring joy to others. This can be brought with humor, or assistance in time of need or attention to another. The task is very simple and also easily overlooked.

World problems, if brought to you through wonderful media, easily distract your energy and instead of dwelling on the joy, you dwell on fear or frustrations, which you yourself cannot solve. The "simple-minded" people, perhaps having Down's syndrome, don't get mired down in problems that cannot be solved by one individual. They go through life smiling and hugging, distributing joy and appreciation, and we call them "simple minded!" Let them be our teachers and let us be single minded, focusing on the beautiful, not the ugly, in the world and in each other. Life isn't meant to be difficult and challenging most of the time. Our attitude can color each event, and as our heart fills with love, all experiences will be acceptable and appreciated for the gift they bring.

Being on the earth plane is like being in a zoo. People here are at all levels of understanding and awakening. There are large groups of people who are like-minded in all vibrations, and yet there is a large discrepancy between those who have chosen to awaken to the Light and those who have chosen not to, and the variations in between. When there are such diverse attitudes, due to the amount of love that is within, there are also diverse opinions. The best harmony we can hope for would be that each group would be tolerant of the opinions of others; however, this is not likely to happen.

We will get along best if we appreciate the differences of each group that is here in the zoo with us. There is no value in condemning another's point of view unless it directly affects your own life. A wonderful exercise for our own spiritual growth is to be aware of the many groups which are present, and the great diversity of opinions and thought processes. Knowing that others are patient with our ideas and way of looking at things will encourage us to do the same for other groups, even if still others are not patient with us. We still must respond to our own knowing and show understanding and love for those of a different mind set. Each group has the same base intention, that of increasing the Light within. Some groups choose to do this very slowly, and others are taking different speeds to arrive at awakening to the God within.

How interesting it is in the zoo! Such a diverse combination of characters! Without bars we mingle, but we must be careful not to hurt one another.

#117 SNOW

There is a similarity between snow and the human experience. Each flake of snow joins together with its brothers and sisters and creates an effect so that snow can be seen and experienced. So it is also, with each part of God that comes to earth. We come one after another, after another, bringing a part of God with us, and when those parts of God are expressed, the picture of God can be seen. And like the snowflake, the picture is incomplete until each person presents his or her part of God. You can see how important it is for each person to remember who they are and to express that beingness to the whole. Of course, others are expressing their beingness at the same time, reminding us of who we are and making it more likely that we will remember.

This presence of God can also be expressed by the departed souls that serve God from a different dimension. Walking into a place of worship can often bring the sensation of the presence of God, as we sense God from the many who represent God from different dimensions. Their presence only holds the awareness of God for us to behold. We can behold God more easily when those who are on a similar dimension to us hold the presence—not that God isn't heavily present in every place at all times. There is no doubt about it.

But, we can feel God when others like us hold God within and are close by. This is why we can usually feel God in church. The others present are revealing the God within, and the combination of many makes the room alive with God-awareness. It is the difference of a snowflake and a snow bank. This can also be felt in spiritual music. The person or persons singing are expressing their

God within and you can connect that to your own God within and express the Love and Joy of God that is yours.

Setting up a sacred place in the home can be beneficial to developing the connection to God. This place can be anywhere. Some use aids to assist them in their time of devotion, like candles, incense, spiritual music, bells or chimes. The most important piece to making this a holy spot is the disciplined daily practice of coming there and connecting to God.

Connecting to the God within and bringing that connection into the world is more important than you realize. You are being counted upon. Your smile is God's smile.

Go forward in peace and bring God's blessing to the world.

#118 MELON (MEDITATION)

Meditation is a skill that has to be developed, like ice-skating. In ice-skating, your first attempt may not be so pleasant, but if you try and try again, eventually you can skate, and then with more trying and more practice you can skate well. Then with more hours and more practice you can skate beautifully, and so on.

Meditation can also be likened to growing a melon plant. The intent is anchored; the seed is planted. Daily the seed gets sun and water, and daily your meditation is given time by you. This goes on and on for quite a long time, and then, one day, an amazing thing happens. You have a connection to God like you have never had before, a miraculous experience. Just like the plant, it will develop a magnificent fruit that will bring great joy.

Meditation is more than just the original intent. That intent must be nourished. If there is a long period of time without it being nourished, the intent dies, similar to the melon plant. You plant the seed, and you water it, it has sunshine and it grows. Then if there is a long period of time without water, the plant will die and the melon will not form. One can get a melon by planting over. Start anew and keep the intent going by nourishing it with water as needed, and never let it die. The same goes with meditation. If you had intention before but wandered away, simply start again. Maybe this time you will be the good steward and be able to nurture the meditation skills so they may ripen and become amazing as they open up to the God within.

There need never be regret if the first intention has failed; there is always time to start again. This can also be likened to people who wish to quit smoking. They may have that intention and after a short while give it up. Later they may have the intention again. Again they may fail. And then, eventually, they keep the intention long enough that their self-discipline is rewarded with the results they seek. If the intention is strong enough, for example, when a heart attack occurs, the motivation rises and success is at hand. With meditation or spiritual devotion, people are often drawn to God during times of calamity, but they are drawn to God.

How much more satisfying it is to give up smoking before the heart attack or serious health problem arises. Also, how much more peaceful it is to build a closeness to God when there is no worry involved.

If you don't have a daily devotional time, set your intention and begin again today.

#119   DAY OF LOVE

Welcome, emissaries of joy. Let hearts of those who seek God rejoice. Today is a day filled with love. Let love be in your every step. Let love shine through your eyes. Read the love in the eyes of everyone that you see, even if they are not intending to send love at that time. You may need to imagine the true Love of God that <u>is</u> in that person shining through. Imagine a haze that has descended upon earth and the haze is love. As you go through this day, do your very best to incorporate your personal God Love everywhere you can. And, equally important, receive God's Love through everyone and everything that you are able.

To live a life aware of love calls for an open heart and a strong desire. To live a day of love is equally challenging. To experience a day of love would be a preview of life in a dimension higher than earth. *(Clare feels a huge swelling of joy that comes from the next level.)*

There are many levels of awareness of God Love. There are different locations for developing these levels of awareness. We could liken it to elementary school, high school, college, graduate school, post-doctorate school, etc., for there are many, many levels in our awakening. Many of these levels can be accomplished on earth; then we go to a different school in a different location and work on the next higher vibrations. As our vibrations become clearer, we are able to connect to more beautiful pure joy.

The speed with which we matriculate through the different levels varies vastly. There is no right or wrong in the speed that we have chosen as our own. There is more struggle on the lower levels and less joy. However, there are also many, many interesting experiences.

No matter which speed we choose to travel back to God, we never travel alone. Even in post-graduate school, there is a team of higher light beings who are there to guide us, assist us, and comfort us. No matter where we are in our evolution of awareness, our task is to bring God's Love in through our hearts to share with others and to receive that Love from others.

Lack of forgiveness is often a stumbling block to our achievement of this particular goal. As you go through your day today, if you can, observe judgments you hold on another. As you are successful in releasing these judgments, you will find that your ability to send and receive love increases.

Love and joy attend thee.

#120   THE TIMES THEY ARE A'CHANGING

What is happening on the earth plane presently is that the vibrations are becoming more refined and that brings increased clarity to those who are seeking. The higher vibration opens the earth plane to higher guidance. This means that those on different dimensions who have increased their own vibrations can now relate to you. They do so willingly and cheerfully. When you ask God for guidance, God sends representatives to assist you. You may know of their presence by how sensitive you are. If you are very open, you may actually feel their presence. Even the less sensitive among you will see things happening miraculously to your benefit—little things like finding a pen when you need it, bigger things like getting that car loan when you didn't think you would qualify, and then even greater things, perhaps getting a particular job, and on and on.

If you tune in, you will feel the joy and lightness of those who go with you. They almost joke with you. They do, but you don't understand.

We are in a very transitional period on planet Earth. This ability that we have worked so hard to attain will be commonplace for those who come behind us. They will connect to God easily and be aware of guidance. They will see miracles regularly and expect them. They will be able to use their minds with others for large accomplishments. They will be very adaptable and have peace and joy about them. Earth will be a pleasant place to live. The lower vibrations will not be present.

Those of you who are present today have volunteered to come in the difficult time of birthing this new generation. It is not easy for you because there will be such

224

major change at such a rapid pace. You are in the supportive role as the trainer is for the Olympic athlete. You willingly prepare for the coming event by doing all the backup work. You are brave and selfless and are highly appreciated.

You have committed to a particular role for this time. If you do your part, you personally benefit so much and fill a need for so many. Thank you for being here. Don't forget those who are here to guide you. Ask God for help and we will come. You are never alone.

Go with love in your heart.

#121 IMPRINTS

Greetings, beloveds. Your wish for contact is appreciated. Today we will talk to you about the spirit or energy you put forth into your activities. You may call it "spunk," vigor, vitality, enthusiasm, but they are all words for love. If you approach your tasks of this world with love, it will appear as enthusiasm, "spunk," etc. When you give your energy with that much push from within, you spot everything with love. You put a signature of the presence of God on that which you do.

Don't think such action goes unnoticed. Love is always welcome and appreciated. You lighten the vibrations of your surroundings by distributing love generously wherever you go. It is a wonderful service to God.

The attitude that you choose is always up to you. You can choose an attitude of resentment, frustration, anxiety, or love, enthusiasm, and joy. If you choose to serve God, you must also choose to do the tasks that are given you in a loving manner. Think about a person you have experienced who took on with joy a task that looked formidable or unpleasant. Wasn't that a delight!

Let it be you that is remembered by others for the love of God that you carry with you and extend into *everything* you do. Imagine the imprint of each of your loving contributions combined with the loving contributions of so many of your brothers and sisters in the world. These imprints change the vibration of the earth plane. The benefits of these loving gifts of energy have an important role to play. Your part is important.

When you find yourself doing a task that might be low on your list of preferences, for example, cleaning the toilet, taking out the garbage, shoveling the walk, look at your attitude and, if necessary, make an attitude adjustment. You know you do have it within you to be joyful, even in times as these. Not only do you then leave a loving imprint, but you set an example for others.

This day check your attitude and choose to have a good day.

#122 "HEY, ACE!"

Beloveds, time is a commodity that is limited on your plane. Old folks are well aware of the rapidity with which time passes, but young people believe that it is a commodity that is never ending. No matter what your age, it is your charge to tend to the wise use of the time given you. This means, of course, that your use of time should be spent consciously. It does not mean that you should not have fun or that you should not take time to simply enjoy one another. It does mean that, at the end of the day, you are pleased with how you spend the time allotted.

Only you will feel the direction you must go to serve God in the manner in which you are best suited. Your true happiness will not come to you until you do. When you are serving God, using your talents well, you will find true joy and satisfaction. (*Clare feels a vast, wonderful joy and contentment around her, as if it is coming from everyone who has reached that pinnacle of serving God well.*)

When you are not on track for your service, you will feel frustration, perhaps irritability. You will have a tendency to see in others their failures because they are demonstrating to you your own failures. It can be a very unhappy period if you do not realize that these "imperfect" people are actually serving you. When that realization comes, and you apply the knowledge given to yourself, the need for their service will be diminished. Your life will go more smoothly, like a marble rolling in a groove, and everyone will look and feel so much more beautiful. You will feel contented and you will find yourself smiling frequently. Your joy will radiate to others. Your enthusiasm and happiness will assist many others on their journeys.

Think about those who have served you on your journey.

228

Bring to mind a quality that is beautiful within them. Perhaps think of yet another and do the same. Just as when you were being spoken to through others regarding the negative aspects of your own direction, you are also spoken to for your positive aspects by traits and qualities which you see in others that you love.

Be grateful and don't think that humility serves you by denying your own innate beauty. Identify that beauty and strength and use it well.

You are a treasure to God. You are a joy to have in the family of God, like an ace is in a game of cards. Work at appreciating yourself more today.

#123 STRING

Blessings descend upon you like a winter snowfall. We are grateful for you.

Today seems like a day that is very similar to all others and it is. Each day has purpose to help you awaken to the magnificence of who you really are. It is to help others to awaken also. Sometimes the lessons can be unpleasant. Other times they can be very lovely and beautiful. We must trust the loving guidance to bring us that which is best for us on this particular day.

It is important as we go from day to day that we do not second guess the experiences we have as to whether they are good for us or not. We are in a position of being pulled along. Like a little toy duck on a string, we simply need to follow our guidance. "Quack, quack!" Following with trust can make the journey easier and much more fun than worrying about every curve in the road or every "bad" experience. If we do trust, and relax into the guidance, like a water skier does the rope, we can have fun and bring joy, laughter and love to those around us. This is a very important piece of our journey.

When the ego is in charge of our lives, it is always a struggle. Fear attends our every move. Failure is around the bend. Laughter and joy are far away. When we can trust our spiritual partners to guide us in this world, we then are free to express our God selves, our joy, our love and the deep peace that trust brings. Have your eyes twinkled today? Have you been able to laugh at adversity? Have you felt the love in your heart? As you truly do know, these experiences can be had when you are alone or with people.

Open your heart to that which is sent your way from God through others. God expresses through nature, through others, and through us. Like a child filling a basket with flowers, we can go through our day gathering the beauty of God and filling our hearts with joy.

Fill your basket as full as you can today.

#124 STEPPING STONES

Where do you want to go? Do you want to go there passionately? Is this direction for you alone? If you passionately desire, your passion will be guided by those who serve you, by God. God is Love.

Picture yourself in a garden that is filled with flowers and you don't know which way to go. You have within you a homing device that will bring you home. That device is your desire, passionately brought to God, and God will do the rest. There will be stepping stones through the garden, placed there for you, and perhaps an unlikely pattern. If you keep your passion and your connection to the Love of God, the path, though it may be very crooked, will lead you to your desire. How can it do otherwise? You are connected to God. You are God in action. Your desire is God's desire.

You will be brought through life to that which is best for you or that which you hold most frequently in your mind. For example, if you desire to be president of the United States, but you don't believe that you can be anything more than a county commissioner, and you hold in your heart very strongly to be a county commissioner and you dream of being a president, but you don't hold open the possibility, your dream gets disconnected, your passion doesn't go that far. The guidance is there for you to go where you want to go, but you must have the passion to get there. It is like going up a hill on skis with a rope tow. If you let go early, you won't be brought to the top. You might let go part way up and settle for that. The rope tow is still there and available to you. You have to keep the passion or the grip on your desire to bring you to the top.

God is Love; you are Love. The vibration of God is

within all creatures and things. Connecting to the God within automatically connects us to all. When our desire is clear, the universal connection through Love assists us in that direction, as we, consciously and unconsciously, assist others. A parent for a baby perhaps best demonstrates this huge caring Love to which we all connect.

The channels that we use to serve others, pouring forth the Love of God, must be open. In personal prayer and meditation time, we gently open our channels so that the Love can flow through us and to us. There is so much Love available both ways. We do want to do our part by clearing the channels for the flow of God.

Take time daily, yes, even today, to connect.

Your Arc of Infinity Friends

#125   BOOMERANG

A boomerang is known for its ability to go out away from the sender and back to be received again by the sender. Similarities exist with gratitude. What you send out from your heart as gratitude returns to you. The increased awareness of joy that this gratitude has given you is a gift in itself. Also, that upon which we put our attention, we draw toward ourselves. It is a basic mind principle that can be very rewarding when we are grateful people. The opposite, of course, is true as well. If you put much attention on that which offends you, that which offends you will increase as well.

As we draw closer to God, or otherwise put, as we become more aware of who we are as God's representative, we have more joy. As the saying goes, "Money makes money," so also does appreciation bring joy.

If we can observe ourselves as we go through our day, and catch ourselves with the beginning of a condemnation or judgmental thought, we can deliberately replace this with a gratitude or appreciation. Not only would the recipient appreciate this happening, but also we would be greatly rewarded with a much more harmonious life. This connection can be non-verbal as well as verbal due to the vibrations that are in the air with our thoughts. This is a wonderful way to do our part in bringing peace on earth. It is also a means to bring forth God's Love onto the earth plane when it is most needed.

This willingness to set aside negative thinking is a very deep commitment to the service of God. This can be very difficult and as we improve our own skills at doing this, we will be brought into areas that need even more skills, and so it will continue to remain difficult. But when there is peace, where there could have been conflict, the heart filled with love radiates appreciation.

In this day and age, there is an urgent need for positive infusion into difficult situations. A heart that is filled with love and gratitude can serve effectively and crucially. As you commit yourself to living the Love of God, you will feel your heart full of love and appreciation for others. This willing heart is very needed. As it goes into play, it triggers the Love of God to go into play in the hearts of many, many others and they, too, join you. You are the seeds of beautiful love scattered across the world. This cumulative vibration can and must change the world as you know it.

Love will prevail.

#126 CLASP

Is life going the way you wish it would? Are you able to navigate a sea of bombardment? Does your guiding beacon stay forever lit?

Your guiding beacon in this life is your spiritual self that is one hundred percent holy. As Jesus said in the Bible, we are his brothers and sisters. We hold within us the same God Light that Jesus does. For us, it is typically our beacon, our guidance, and our director. The holiness we seek we have already grasped. It is part of us. Now we are being guided to the acknowledgement of that very truth.

In the Muslim religion, people are asked to stop five times a day for prayer. This concept is a wonderful concept. If we, too, would take our mornings and bed times to acknowledge God, and perhaps our three meal times, then we would be in more flowing communication with the Oneness of who we are. It would do us well to also sprinkle through the day, communication with God. "Thank you God, for the stoplight changing." "Thank you for the beautiful day." "Give me courage in this instant." "Help me to be a beacon of love." "I feel your presence." "Thank you for your love." Etc., etc. The idea is that continual communion with God keeps the channels open for God to serve you and for you to serve others for God.

Imagine a vine that is ever present above your head, so that if you jump and clasp onto it, it will gently swing you to where you should be. It is a pleasant experience and your job is to just clasp the vine. The problem is, we think that we can do the tasks easily and well ourselves, without the help of God. We typically ignore the vine until our own efforts have failed to accomplish the goals we were wishing to reach. Then we jump for the vine and ask God to take us there. It is so much easier clasping onto the vine and having God direct us. For a happy life, we must jump and clasp the vine frequently.

Those who travel by the vine are easy to recognize. They are gentle, peaceful, kind, caring, giving, and fun. They are secure where they are and they reach out to you to give, not to take. Let people recognize you in this way also. Your warm loving heart is such a blessing to the world.

God thanks you for your desire to give to others.

You are love.

#127   THE TIME HAS COME

You can only spread the amount of Light that you are capable of holding. We are grateful for this. However, the amount of light that is available for you to disperse is so much greater than your present capacity. That is the reason it is imperative for you to seek the Light in meditation and also throughout the day. The discipline of "A Course in Miracles" is beneficial to your awakening to a greater capacity. This applies to you, Clare. It also applies to everyone.

The time is now that the Light is to be spread, like a ticker tape parade in New York City. Everyone is to spread the Light that they have onto the world to enhance the vibrational shift that is coming in this period of time. It comes from without and it comes from within the Light bearers who are here at the present time. The Light bearers are committed souls to just this experience. Their preparation has been long, but the time has come for the commitment to be tested. Light bearers will know that they are on track by the joy that is in their hearts. In the midst of a very difficult period, their Lights will shine; their joy can fill a room. They make a difference.

There is so much joy available, so much Light and love. The world is filled with those who would give and care for one another joyfully. There are the Light bearers who produce a great amount of Light and love, and there are those who have not committed to that service, but still give generously of that which is theirs to give. It all adds up and it works for the vibrational change that is necessary to bring in the new energy and to merge it into our societies around the world. What an exciting time to be alive! In the next few years, this energy will be established, and by the year 2014, the energy will be felt worldwide. Commit yourself anew to the process of opening your ability to receive and give love. Know that your capacity can be stretched by simply sitting quietly and receiving the Light and Love of God on a constant basis. As you ask to grow closer to God, you will become a bearer of a greater amount of God Light.

God is Love. You are Love. We are Love. Look to the Love that is God within those that you see today and be grateful for its presence. As you look for the Love, you will see it. If ever you don't see it, ask God to assist you in that moment. For the presence of God is there. Bring your blessings to the world today wherever you are.

Thank you.

#128   SAIL

Greetings! My love merges with your love. We are one in God.

Think of your life as a sailboat going from port A to port B. You set sail in joy. You have chosen the vessel of the sailing ship because it is so beautiful, graceful and adaptable to command. So in life, you have chosen to experience living on the earth plane, a beautiful experience, with your goal of knowing God. The sailboat reminds us to relax, to set our direction and enjoy the trip. Also, this is true for the human experience that we should go on our journey with as little struggle as necessary. Storms will come and our verve will be tested. Do we really desire our ultimate goal, that of knowing God, or are we willing to sail in another direction, away from the storm and head for another port?

It is so wonderful to see so many sailboats leaving all the different ports heading for the one destination of knowing God. There are angels, archangels, and guides of all kinds available to assist you on your trip. They would love to be considered part of the crew. They will come in handy when times get rough. They will also teach us to enjoy the moment, to let go of the past, trust in the future, and soak up the very moment that you are living now.

(Clare feels the pleasure of being relaxed on a sailing ship with the air in her face, the sun on her back, and peace in her heart.)

Music is a wonderful companion on your journey. Wonderful relationships with others who are traveling the same journey make the trip more pleasant. Remember to enjoy the trip. You have chosen an incredibly beautiful vehicle, the human body, to travel to God in on the earth plane and you are very fortunate to do so. Do take time to appreciate the moment that you are in.

Keep your eventual goal in mind at all times, for there will be many opportunities to be waylaid from it. In fact, by far the majority of those who set off to truly know God get distracted and settle for other goals, such as power, fame, money, beauty, and popularity. If this should happen, it is not a terrible thing, it only means another trip must be made, and perhaps many more before the final journey is complete. The shorter route of one trip to reach the destination will prove to bring more joy in the long run, but no choice is really wrong.

Take time today to focus on the present moment and enjoy it.

It always offers a blessing.

#129 OVERFLOWING LOVE

What we have to learn, in and of ourselves, is never meant to be for us alone. It is part of a whole. The comprehension of how we fit in is not necessary. We simply must be willing to release our ego and merge into the greater picture, however that may look. The merging process need not be difficult. It happens as we fill our hearts with love to overflowing. When the love is overflowing, our own boundaries blur. Our focus then becomes the love and the love soars and spreads, bringing our identity with it. In no time we are spread out thinly across the whole, and we have become part of the Oneness.

How do we get our love to overflow? Appreciation and service are very helpful. Forgiveness is also essential. Replacing judgments with understanding and acceptance aids us in removing the barriers to unending love.

The desire to awaken again into unending love does much for the journey of getting there. It is like a green light to the Holy Spirit Who assists you in your reawakening. An important element is focus on the positive elements of life. Do not focus on forcing yourself to awaken, because then you put the whole experience into the hands of the ego. Rather, it is better to have the desire, in closeness to God, so that you may be guided to such a delightful outcome.

Observing the love flowing from our brothers and sisters lightens our paths, as well as demonstrates the direction to go. Then, in return, we also demonstrate to others through our love. We are all traveling the same direction, uniting as One in God.

This day, note things of beauty, humor, and delight. Be in understanding and avoid condemnation. The way

will be peaceful and sure. Relax into the journey.
Amen.

#130   ABUNDANCE

What is abundance? Abundance is having an overflowing of that which you desire, that which you feel is most valuable. That varies from person to person, but typically everyone will be interested in having financial abundance as well as other abundance.

In what areas of your life are you generous? There is your abundance. Do you take time to make others happy, to help others with their health, to share your talents? Look through your day and see what is bringing you joy that you give away. This is a pocket of your abundance. There are others and there can be even greater areas as you develop or seek them. Yes, it can be money, time or talent.

The world you see is the world you create for your own growing and understanding. There really is nothing you cannot have, if it is important enough for you. One must connect their desire for abundance in a certain area to their spiritual self. The part of us that is not on the earth is extremely magnificent and capable with brilliance equal to an angel. Truly merging clearly with your own Divine Self can bring to you any abundance that would bless your journey here. Living a life as you do in America puts you in abundance that is so great in comparison to the majority of souls that are in a body at this time.

The ego will never have enough. Perhaps the level of abundance that you do have is sufficiently comfortable for you to learn your lessons of awakening. Think of it as a school. Picture high school kids who had everything they could possibly want. These things you might think would get in the way of their education. You might think moderation would be better for their learning environment. So it is with you. We must be careful not to let abundance get in the way of our learning. Evaluate your desires for abundance and clarify their ability to help you learn. The guidance that you are getting does the same thing as a parent would. We are allowed only that which is to our benefit. A more simplified life is easier to manipulate for your spiritual goals. Not that all lives, no matter how complex, cannot be used to assist in soul development.

As in looking through coins and finding one that is gold, so it is in looking at goals and discovering abundant love. Once you experience the beauty of unending spiritual love, all other goals lose their luster.

Chose gold.

#131   LOVE

Hidden away where no one sees is love. Open to everyone also is love. The world and beyond are made up of
love. Think of the moment you most felt love. Perhaps it
was the first time you saw your child, the day you were
married, singing at church, or a poignant moment with
a parent. These special, remarkable moments of loving
that touched you are an example of moving to a higher
level of awareness of God.

God is Love and the extent of our joy is our ability
to understand this. As love is revealed, our attraction to
love draws ever more intense, like a moth to the flame.
The more we can feel the presence of God, the more we
wish to seek it. As we draw very close to God, we seek it
unendingly until we become the flame ourselves, or we
realize the purity of God that is within us and that everything else doesn't exist. We become part of the Light of
God. We now experience the Beingness of God without
our ego or our self-identification.

The journey to this amazing experience of being Love
and knowing it can be a quick trip or a long trip. Like
being at Disneyland and knowing our destination is the
ride "It's a Small World," we can work our way directly
there, enjoying the experiences along the way, or we
can choose to take a more circuitous route and experience many other offerings that are there for our choosing.
Heading on the quickest route, with perhaps the fewest
experiences, will bring us to the magnificence of knowing
God in a shorter time span.

However, taking the longer route, with an unlimited
number of experiences to choose from, is not wrong and
has other lessons to acquire. The additional experiences

often come with struggle, fear, and pain. Needless to say, they are interesting and they cannot stop us from eventually finding the ride "It's a Small World," although at this point it won't seem like a small world. Our destination is sure. It is up to us which route to take.

The Love of God is always present. The closer we get to our destination, the more we know this. Wandering afar makes the way seem dark and alone. We each have a sensor that is ever present. When turned on, by focusing attention to it, it will guide us to the most direct route to our goal.

Living with the ego, we are often distracted from the sensor, and instead we turn our attention to other rides in the park. When our time draws near, we will become well aware of our sensor, and we will use it to guide us to the full awareness of God. We will be joined with many as we travel there, and when we arrive, the additional experiences we pass up are of absolutely no value in comparison to the joy that is ours. How blessed we are to be aware of our sensor calling us home. Go with haste for the incredible joy that awaits you.

We will see you there.

#132 TAKE FLIGHT

Just as songbirds have a sense within them when it is time to fly north to raise their chicks, so do we have a sense within us to raise our vibrations and soar into a new dimension that is peaceful and exciting. Rising into this new level of vibration for us will make things feel easier. There will seem to be more time, less criticism, more appreciation of music, more appreciation of nature, and a fondness for each other. It is like falling in love.

Together we come from a very holy place where we were in the energy and the Being of God. We came as a unit, similar to the Air Force Blue Angels exhibition team. They come from one spot and take different trajectories into assigned locations. We each carry a brilliant white light as we fulfill our mission to contact certain people and tell them that it is time for them to awaken. We must also remember who we are and completely awaken ourselves, so that we too will merge once again into the holy Light of God.

As each of us ventures forth to contact the rest of our loving family to bring them back into the fold, we are being very courageous, because this venture can ensnare us and make us forget who we are. As we go forth silently and quietly, we have a support team that is there for the asking. They are always with us to surround us, protect us and support us, not unlike a wire protective basket around a growing tomato plant. They are around us, not to interfere, unless there is a need or if we ask.

A wonderful crutch that will assist us in the work that we have come to do, is the dipping of ourselves into the Light of God during our meditations. This takes commitment and planning and intention, not just time. Each must find what brings them to their place of Spirit connection. For some it is inspirational music, spiritual reading, candles, chimes, companions, time of day, a particular garment or prayer beads. Whatever works, use. Your intention will be heard and your efforts amply rewarded. The love and light you bring forth is the Love and Light of God.

Fill your backpack to overflowing and go into the world and distribute it.

(Clare complained that she was not receiving this message easily because of pain in her sinus, back, bowels, and stomach. Her head ached and she was cold. She asked them for help. She decided to lie down for half an hour. The session was continued later that evening when she was interrupted several times by intestinal distress.)

#133 PLAY

The earth experience for many is difficult. It is a school of learning. To many, the lessons are not easily learned. In this school, there is much repetition of lessons, which can make the learning painful at times. But, just as in elementary school, where they have a break from their learning called "recess," we too should take a break from our daily learning and have fun. In truth, we could do all our lessons while in the level of gaiety and joy, but it is not very easy to do, and very few are able to maintain that level. But we all can take time to play. It is important to care for the body and it is a good place to incorporate play, for example, bird watching hikes, running, tennis, etc.

It is not only a good suggestion to take time for play, but it will shorten the time here in learning. Learning will come more quickly and more pleasantly if we have learned how to play. As we progress through the lessons, we will come closer and closer to the playful attitude in our daily life. The caring spiritual beings who guide us are very joyful beings, indeed. As we become more refined in our density, we will feel the joy of God, and it will bring great joy to our everyday living. Laughter will be very close and love will flow continuously.

When we are going through a most difficult lesson, where laughter and joy are hidden in the density of the struggle, we can take time apart from that particular struggle, tune in to the Joy that is God, and play for a bit. The struggle will wait and you will be refreshed and embrace the learning that is offered through this struggle.

Keeping in mind the final destination we all seek, which is to give and be Love and Joy, will help us on our path through the many lessons. The remembrance of this will come to us in meditation. There we find God, we sit awhile in the presence of Love, and know who we are. By holding that clearly in our daily struggles, we shorten the duration of the learning immensely. It is almost like getting to the very side of this large maze of learning and being able to skirt its edge because you can see the goal and know that enduring the maze is not necessary. Play and laughter can bring us to the side of that maze. It keeps us lighter and helps us see more clearly.

Take time today to love others and yourself in play.

#134   THE WOODS

The world you find yourself in is extremely demanding of your time. There is the pile of mail that comes in every day, your job, the fantastic TV programs that you don't want to miss, the entertainers that have come to town, the stimulating learning in your own field that is available to you, and then there are books and magazines, to say nothing of the social life.

One can get up in the morning, and deal with each of these situations all day long and then go to bed. This can be a routine that can be very pleasant and extremely busy, but notice, in this routine there is no space for God. Our lives can be more satisfying if we add an element of time for God. It is like being in a forest with many trees representing the choices of our lives, and one tree representing that opportunity to connect in our day to God. This tree, in the long run, will bring the greatest joy to your life as a whole.

You will want to be sure that the path in the woods is deep and clear to this tree. As you lean against the tree in the forest of life, you will feel the peace that is yours as you connect to the loving energy that is God. As you two merge, your beingness expands and you become the forest, and you become Love. You now adjust your priorities within this forest of choices and select those that you are drawn to because of your new awareness that comes to you from being in the holy space with God.

In this period of busy times and many choices, we will be guided by the Inner Spirit to select those opportunities that present themselves that will best serve our soul. It is like being in the woods and certain trees have a special illumination that tells you they are the right tree for you to visit, or the right experience in this life for you to participate in. Going to the tree of Spirit will save you much time by helping you to see clearly.

If we are too busy to go to the tree of Spirit, we will find our busy life will not make progress spiritually at the rate we could. Going to the holy place first can bring you a great distance on your journey back to God, even though you go at a much slower pace. The "hurry up" life that squeezes out your holy time, ends up like the gerbil on the wheel going, going, going, but going nowhere.

There is no right or wrong in our journey back to God. It is not a mistake to take a break from your journey and just enjoy life without spiritual growth to a great degree. There will always be some spiritual growth. It is like stopping in a little town off the highway and staying there awhile before going back on the highway back to God. There will be opportunities beyond this life for progressing on your journey back to God. In fact, the completion of your journey is guaranteed. The sooner you progress on your journey, the sooner you leave the pain and suffering this world can offer. The choice is always yours.

You are a part of God that cannot be substituted for, or replaced. God longs to have you completely awake and part of the whole.

Choose this day among all the trees in the forest to take time to go to the one tree that connects you to the wholeness of God. Time spent here will heighten the joy of all the other choices that you make later in the day.

Choose well.

#135 THE MOUNTAIN TRAILS

Wonderful ones, we come to you. You are to us, similar to the fish in the sea. You come in many colors, which are truly your vibrations. You swim around, each living a life of survival, reproduction, and family. Your lives are varied and interesting.

Each life is set into this experience for the purpose of chipping away the barriers that hide the true gem of who you are. It is a busy and purposeful life. We can see those that have chipped away much of the barrier and their bright lights are starting to glow through. Their beauty and light shine out to others. This is happening frequently during this period, for it is time for a vast number to awaken. It is a beautiful sight as the graduates pass their exams. Their light is exposed and shines forth as a reminder to all who see, that they, too, are on this journey.

It is not for everyone to see the light as it comes. Some have chosen long, difficult journeys. They will not notice the light that is shining. It is not their path; it will not help them. Instead of looking up to the light, they will continue to look down. They are focusing on the environment that they have made. They are enjoying the experiences of struggle, of rightness and wrongness, of separation, of personal comparison, as well as many of the varied possible encumbrances to the light that can be had, such as greed, power and self-aggrandizement. These areas can be enticing. They are available for all. Choosing to be in the denser area is like going around and around a mountain and making very, very small upward increments on each circle of the mountain.

Of course, this varies completely with each person. On any given journey, one can change. One can speed up by choosing a more direct upward path at any time, as well as choosing to slow down by changing from a path that is quite direct to one of greed and power, for example. So the journeys all vary, but eventually, all reach graduation at the top of the mountain and their light will be revealed. What a happy moment for God when we choose to come home!

As you make this journey, you will come upon many boulders in your way. Know that there is much help to lift you over them, if you but pray and ask.

It is such a busy place due to each of your choices of ascent, and due to the many crews that assist you from higher levels. The joy definitely grows as one attains greater height and reaches toward God. You will notice people on a path similar to your own as you advance. You have much to share and appreciate about each other and your experiences, like students in a drama class. These classmates help you. They understand what you are trying to achieve. Some of them have achieved it and they will give suggestions and assistance as you learn. You will also be of assistance to them.

Be at peace in your journey, and be at peace with the journey of others. Judgment of others does not serve you. It is not a race and the future paths are still uncertain for many. Find delight in all who come across your path. They are a gift to you.

Have a wonderful day.

#136   SNOWSHOE

A snowshoe consists of many cords that go across it. Each one plays a part in making the snowshoe work. This can be likened to the lessons that we learn. Each one is learned to fit into a whole belief system. The belief system then lightens our way or makes it more doable to traverse the earth experience.

Each piece that goes into the snowshoe is vital. These parts are given to us through our experiences and through the experiences of our teachers.

There are many different kinds of snowshoes. They are a little bit different in shape; they are a little bit different in color, as are the different belief systems of this world. Picture a football field with much snow and many different people coming with many different snowshoes, walking around passing each other. Some have short snowshoes; some have large snowshoes. Some are wide; some are narrow; some are light in color; some are dark. There are vast varieties, but they all do the same thing. They assist the wearer in staying above the snow, or when it comes to belief systems, they assist the believer in rising above the density of the earth experience and being able to reach God. We are all so very blessed to have this assistance. Looking behind and seeing the many different prints helps us accept the truth that there are many wonderful paths that do the same thing

No one snowshoe is superior in itself, but if the wearer of the snowshoe knows how to use the snowshoe to its maximum benefit, he will stay higher in the snow. So it is with the belief system. Those who are devoted and take full advantage of the offerings of that system will find it most helpful in their connection to God.

Those who make the commitment to get the most out of their spiritual assistance should be noted by the peace that they carry, the lightness with which they take the world. All of the seekers are seeking God who is Love.

As they find this Love, they awaken the Love within, and therefore, they are very loving individuals. They become teachers simply by being who they are and exuding love.

In your journey today, observe those who are in joy and love. Appreciate that they have a connection to the Divine. Learn from them to exude your love and joy to others. Make this a day of giving from your heart. The giving will be such joy it will feel like getting. You will be so blessed.

Be happy and bring the Light of God wherever you go.

#137   TRIP OF SERVICE AND JOY (Personal)

(This transmission came as Jim and Clare were preparing to go to Hawaii for a brother's wedding. Several that follow came during that Hawaii experience.)

You stand for brotherhood. You sense the oneness of all. You enjoy the merging of personalities and the brotherhood of man.

This trip will be one of service, but service to you more than from you. Many lovely lessons will be presented. Please be aware of the lessons that they may come gently in the beginning, as you tune in to your training. However, if you don't pay attention, the lessons have to come harder, and they are not as much fun. You have chosen a beautiful place to study. Enjoy it to the maximum. Enjoy your friends and be vigilant for lessons.

The two of you are wonderful teachers. The peace and joy and love that you carry is a stream that is delivered as you go.

You will see many people of very high levels of awakening. It will surprise you to find such consistently loving, giving and forgiving souls. The density of this energy is wonderful. It does occur in pockets in the United States and in the world. Hawaii will be a pocket when you are there.

Clare, you will be taking time to rest when Jim is doing social activities, and we are pleased that you, Clare, know how to do this.

When the family comes together, be sure to lend a listening ear. It will be twice as valuable as your stories. We are very pleased you are going and supporting your brother. It means more to him than he realizes.

Spend money but don't dwell in the level of earthly vibrations of ego. Spend money as is necessary. Be comfortable, be free, but don't let the money pull you into a direction that is off your path. You both have been gentle dancers with money. You lead the way and the money follows. You have not let money lead you. Yes, you could be stewards of larger funds because of your detachment from the ego that is enhanced by money. Bravo.

We love you and follow you so closely. At any given moment you may open your consciousness to the presence of our love. As you love and care for your dog, so do we love and care for you a thousand times more. You are our joy. Your smiles delight our Being.

Go in love and joy.

Your Team

#138   PLUMERIA BLOSSOM

Beloved seekers, welcome. Your hungry hearts are beautiful to be seen. They are open like a plumeria blossom, so beautiful to the spiritual eye. Wherever you go, you bring beauty. You bring joy to the beholder. Your intention is to bring love, the love of God to everyone, including the other plumeria blossoms, plumeria buds, and all other living creations of God. Your desire to serve God enhances your environment wherever you are, even in solitude. You are greatly appreciated and acknowledged for your desire to serve God and your ability to do so.

Where you go while seeking God is a Divine path you have set before you entered this earth plane. Your path is true and all you need to do is hold on to the guideline of God. God's presence and reassurance are always with you. It's there for you at all times. You need but to reach for the line and be reassured that you are not going the wrong direction. You, being a vehicle of God, are traveling off on a convoluted path, but one that is sure. It is similar to a child's toy car going down a road with a magnet under the game board that guides it surely, though it is unseen. The road may be very indirect to its ultimate goal, but it is sure.

We, the travelers on this path, can relax into the guiding hand of God, knowing we are never alone, and are never in the wrong place. Our job is to be observant of that which is on the path, that we may learn the lessons lovingly placed before us. If we fail to see them, they will be presented again and again in more and more obvious presentations until we observe, accept and learn the lessons and gratefully move on.

How kind and patient are God and our teachers. How

abundant is the love that they hold for us. How delighted they are to assist us on our journey home, not unlike the joy expressed in the Bible for the prodigal son. Our presence completely merged into the Heart of God is highly desired.

Let us this day be as the peaceful plumeria, giving love and expressing the presence of God.

Amen.

#139　TREES

(Prior to this dictation, we were admiring the beautiful trees outside our hotel window on Kuhio Avenue, and commenting how different Waikiki would be without its trees. Some would think the large tree outside our window blocks the view, but to us it becomes a major part of our view, harboring a white dove and other birds, as well as an artificial owl.)

Beloveds, my love flows to you. We are grateful that you are receptive and can break the barriers between us.

As you go about your business in this world, you share your life with trees. Trees are very much like unspoken support. They are there to serve you and do so lovingly. They, too, are servants of God. Each one comes with a purpose and the greatest purpose of all is to share love.

It feeds our soul to appreciate a beautiful tree, or a woods. And like unto a tree is the beauty within every soul that is on this earth. If we can learn to observe them and see their beauty, we serve ourselves and the other by eliminating the separation that is between us.

Opening up in love and appreciation is a way to acknowledge the Oneness of the family of God. This can be to each other, to trees, animals, plants, birds, all that is of God.

One might think that focusing on so many other parts of God in appreciation and awareness would detract from one's own purpose. In fact, to the contrary, it eases the burden of our path. All of nature, including trees, are part of the family of God. As we reach out and blend our love, we share our beingness with theirs. Nature's beauty is a major support for those of us who are seeking higher awareness of God. From the stately tree we encounter daily, low levels of love emanate to us to encourage us on our challenging journey.

We, in turn, give our love to nature by doing what we can to assist. This may mean spraying for disease, eliminating pollutants, nourishing with food and water, or helping when there is an injury.

We dance together on this earth. It can be a joyous dance if we are full of appreciation. Today acknowledge your beautiful dancing partners and share love.

#140   DECIDE

Living a life without commitment to Spirit is the way we
go unless we made a decision. The "born-again Christian" group understands this concept. Many of us will
have to make a U-turn from the directions our lives have
gone through a commitment to a Godly life. Some people
cannot make that complete turn rapidly. They go part way,
live in that concept for a while, then choose again and turn
again part way toward God. Rarely are we able to make
the change from an ego-centered life to a God-centered
life quickly and easily. It can happen miraculously with
the wonderful support of friends and church members.

With good support, this decision can hold. Devotion
to God can be dominant. That is the part that churches
play in bringing home the kingdom. Being around newly
committed persons, feeling their joy and love, helps each
of us on our path. This is happening around the world in
a multitude of faiths. Fortunately, there are many roads
to God. The devotion to their faith determines its value.
We can be so appreciative of the many faiths that commit
themselves to God. The degree of love and devotion they
reveal within a person lifts the vibration of the earth plane.

What joy we have in sharing our path of love and devotion with so many brothers and sisters of all faiths. We can
all learn from each other. There are many who have not
made the U-turn, but are ready to do so. They have to be
connected to the Oneness of the Holy Spirit and the joy
that it brings. This occurs most easily in group settings.
It is the responsibility of others who are following the
path of joy to reach out and assist others. Often bringing
them into a group of believers with yourself is what they
need. If your heart does sing of this joy of God, you will

naturally want to share this experience with those who have not yet found the path.

Let your joy guide you to assist those who are longing to awaken. Do not delay. Your responsibility is great. Look beyond yourself and share your joyful path.

Do it today.

#141 YOU, TOO

Beloveds, your innocence and sincerity are seen and appreciated. Your desire to know God is your greatest gift.

Those who have earned the privilege are asked to serve. When an opportunity comes to you to see love in another person, you are serving God. Service comes in many sizes. Perhaps we aid another person who has a need or serve in a lovely capacity so that another's life might be easy or more wonderful. But the greatest service is that of connecting in love to another, including friends and family, fellow workers and strangers. The need for this service of uniting is great. The privilege of serving in this manner brings joy to both the server and the served, as well as to heaven itself.

Those who are capable of this service are growing in number. Many are answering the call. You will know when you have been served with love or when you serve love by your heart connection to the other person and theirs to you. There will be times when you will feel the love and the served will not return it, but it does its service for them.

Similar to washing the dirt off a windshield, it may take more than one swipe to clear the debris that has blocked the Light for others and our selves. But each gift of love forwards the process of removing the blocks that hinder our ability to give and receive love ourselves.

What a privilege it is to give love as well as to receive love. We have not all earned the privilege to give the pure Love of God. We can rejoice in being asked to serve as love bearers at any level. There is no quicker way to totally awaken to the wonder of God than serving in this manner.

This day, take every opportunity you can find to love and receive love. Work at understanding and forgiving and accepting and loving. The rewards will be great.

God's grace goes with you.

#142   JOYFUL LIVING

Blessed beloveds, your joy and your excitement reverberate a thousand fold. We thank you.

Beloveds, take time to smell the flowers. This idiom is a truth. While on the earth plane, there are many tugs on your time and energy. To get it all in, we often drop a part of our life that is not necessary to accomplish our goals. Often that part that we drop is our joy. Pick it up again. Include joy in your every day. What brings you joy? Increase that in your life.

Blessed are those that do. Look around and see the happy people in your life. Why are they happy? What brings them joy? Do they have a lesson for you in this department? Study them closely and learn from their peace how to have fun.

You, too, will teach the very same lesson to others. We have agreed to teach peace and joy to those who have asked you before their life began. So learning to advance your expression of love through joy and laughter serves not only yourself, but also those whom you would serve.

Enjoy the small things of life. Find beauty as it is expressed in fruit and flower, in trees and clouds, in dimples and twinkling eyes, and beautiful fragrances. As your heart fills with the joy the beauty brings, it will overflow in happy ways to lighten your burden and the burdens of the world. This is a joyful responsibility, but one that is not to be taken lightly. It is important that you learn to fill your hearts with joy and to demonstrate to others how they might fill their hearts with joy.

Appreciation is the road to major success. Stretching your ability to appreciate will fill your hearts more quickly and more joy will follow.

This day, be conscious of those things you appreciate. Let your heart fill with overflowing in the beauty that is around you. Demonstrate to yourself the path of joy. You are very appreciated and you bring great joy to those who serve you.

Thank you.

#143   THE MOUNTAIN

Climbing the "mountain" to God, as Jesus did, is not an easy undertaking. We start at the bottom of the mountain, not unlike a marathon, with many, many people, all of whom intend to go to the top. The resolve of the vast majority will weaken on the journey.

The journey has marker stations where one's ticket must be stamped. These marker stations represent learning concepts. Perhaps helpfulness may be one of the lower levels, and as we progress up the mountain, the lessons become more and more challenging. Also, there are offerings of side trips that are very exciting or interesting. These side trips are offered on a regular basis. They satisfy the ego. Many people get distracted from their journey and permanently stay on the off-road. The resolve for God has become overcome by a resolve to satisfy the ego. The temptation to go off resolve for God comes up unexpectedly in many and enticing experiences. The side trips can be taken and the traveler can then return to the main path of seeking God, however, many do choose to delay for varied amounts of time.

The number of people we travel with then diminishes as we proceed up the mountain. The traveler never knows when to expect another stamp on his ticket. There will be areas on the journey that seem to go easily and many stamps are accumulated with ease. There are also periods of difficult climbing where much struggle is necessary and often much time to acquire the next stamp on the journey.

As the card fills with stamps, the hikers diminish to a smaller community. The crowds are large when the churches, synagogues or mosques guide the travelers. At the point the travelers leave the guidance of the institutions, the number of travelers reduces greatly. As the committed travelers ascend closer and closer to the top, they start to recognize each other and assist each other on their journey and they find the journey to be pure joy. All travelers will reach the top in due time. Remember that Jesus, Mohammed, and others are always available for assistance. You need never travel alone.

Today, reach out to support others in their struggle up the mountain. It will be your pleasure.

#144 OPEN THE DOOR

When you feel lost and confused and frustrated with your life, you must seek God in the warm comfort from within. Look for the room where God is present, open the door and go in. The door is within yourself. Call forth your holy connection.

Put your worries aside for a few minutes. Don't pray for them. Don't think of them. Put your energies on connecting to God and His Love. God knows your circumstances. God simply needs an opening to come into your life. Fear blocks the door.

You are well aware of a great connection to God. Go there morning and night in meditation and try to see God's presence in every situation in which you find yourself. Release the outcomes to as many situations as you can. Give them to God. God's outcome is sure and perfect, but it might not look like your desired outcome. Give up control. Put it in the hands of God. Pray for the best, whatever that may be.

Consider the Dalai Lama. His country was taken away from him and many people killed. His outcome is not as he desires at this time. He has great faith and believes that a good outcome will come in due time. He puts it in the hands of God and so should we with our issues that seem so monumental to us. God sees the solution simply and clearly. Leave it to God and live your life today.

In the moment, God is. Love abounds. Connect to the Love of God moment by moment in your day, and press the joy out of each moment. This day is made for joy and peace and love, not worry and fear.

Claim the day for love and peace and release your worries to God.

Amen

#145   A SURE DESTINATION

Sweet seekers, we greet you. Coming here to the Light for guidance serves you well. Breaking away from the life patterns that you live and focusing on God is very important for awakening. No one wants to rush you into your awakening. It is a choice made in heaven by you. It is sure that you will awaken, and when you do, your joy, peace and love will multiply and multiply and multiply.

It is like choosing to paint flowers well without being trained. There are classes to take for lessons one, two, three and four to master the art of painting flowers. The students may take class one in their twenties. They may take class two in their thirties. Perhaps they may complete the mastery of the art in their forties. It is a choice, but once the choice is complete, the artist can then paint beautiful flowers. The goal has a magnificent ending, as does awakening. The achievement of all the effort gives a reward that is endless.

Each of us on this path must slow down enough to focus on our brother or sister, noticing them, watching them, knowing that they are of the same family of God as we are. In noticing this, we feel great appreciation. In love, we learn from them. They will guide and serve us and often in a pleasant way, but not always.

Every person that you meet has a gift for you and you for him or her. It may not be noticed. It may be at a more subtle level. Join your brothers and sisters in the gentle drumming of the truth that it may reach everyone and they may recognize the call to home.

Do not concern yourself about your direction. It will unfold before you. You may make plans, but be careful not to be too attached to your plans, because they may change, always for the better. It may not appear that the change is good. It may appear very scary, but it is the path that serves you best. Illness may come to one member of the family and serve everyone. Another example is a job change that may be imminent though undesired. It, too, holds blessings. There are no mistakes. Even in your darkest hour, trust that you are loved and guided to bring you home.

Feel free to ask God for assistance at any time on your path. You will never be let down in the grand scheme of things. Think of yourself on a tour trolley on wheels that goes down steep hills, over rickety bridges, through muddy roads, into beautiful fields and to the edge of beautiful cliffs, and on and on to beautiful sights. You are along for the ride wherever it takes you. So it is in life.

This day, relax and look for God in everything you see.

#146   THE WAVE

Loved ones of courage, you have been training for a very long time for this period. The energy is very strong now, like a very large wave and you are a surfer. You practice on smaller waves, smaller energy influxes on the earth plane. You master the energy and are moving on. You have prepared for the big wave to bring you home. The time has come and you are ready.

You go into this period with great excitement and anticipation. You have been told this large wave is coming to bring you home. And now, as you apply your skills of meditating and being attuned to that which is around you, you are prepared to use this boost of energy of Divine Light to help you with the last stage of awakening that you may be at home with God in this body.

What joy to see the wave of energy that has come! Your open hearts will accept this energy and awareness will come, an awareness of who you are.

There are many who are riding the same wave and going home. You will know them by their gentle smiles and caring ways. They, like you, have learned to put others' needs before their own, in love. Life becomes more pleasant. There still may be lessons to be learned, but with the grace of God, they will be learned. There is time for this.

Today, look at the world through your heart and see its beauty and the beauty in all the fellow travelers that you behold.

You are blessed.

#147   SHARE YOUR BOUNTY

Beloveds, we see your radiant beauty that is so hidden from yourselves. If you could see your beauty, you would see what the joy of God is. Each of us has been given a particular quality to distribute to others. Look within and find your talent, develop it, and share it. Your happiness lies there. There is such joy in feeling that you can give when there is a need, and give bountifully from an endless storehouse of talent. If someone needs understanding, and you can understand, you serve.

You have had experiences on the receiving end of others' gifts. You know the appreciation and connectedness that giving has brought. The connectedness between us is so important. The giving of our talents serves to diminish the distance between one another, and in doing so, we become more aware of the Presence of God. For every soul is part of the whole and when we connect, we get a better glimpse of who we are.

Some talent is more an expression of the God Light that is within, as in music, art and literature. When we connect to the expression of God from another, we become more expanded in the knowing of ourselves, for we are all connected.

Our task on earth is to remove the barriers we have set up that prevent us from seeing our Light and the Light of others. These barriers are dark and we have held them for a long time. We don't even realize we hold them. Some of these barriers are fear, condemnation in any form, jealousy, hatred, comparison, and doubt. The list goes on and on.

If we are not happy, we are blocking Light. Seek out comfortable companions, recognize them for who they are, and bury them in forgiveness, love, and understanding. Ask God to help you remove the barriers to the Light, so your service can be more complete. Notice people who are genuinely joy-filled. Let them guide you in removing your barriers. Let their love shine upon you as God has directed. Their love is God's.

Genuine gratitude for things, big and little, helps you experience the Light that is within yourself. It flows through barriers and eases your way to the giving of your talents. Just filling your hearts with gratitude is a service in itself.

This day, serve one another joyfully and with gratitude. Amen.

#148 CONTROL

(Clare and Jim had been traveling for five weeks.)

Beloveds, you are so dear. Have no regrets for missing a session. Simply rejoice in the ones that we do have. Much is being said today about how to direct your life. Examples are the book and film, "The Secret,"* which are so popular today. This speaks of one's personal ability to direct one's life. This is wonderful if done with the guidance of your spiritual self. Be careful that it is your spiritual self that is guiding because the ego can guide well with this training and can guide you into areas that may serve the ego more than the Spirit.

Living a life of personal control of outcome is exhilarating. This, connected with Spirit, is very powerful and can serve very well. This, not connected with Spirit, can be an interesting experience of power that can be simply enjoyed for what it is. It may sidetrack you from your spiritual journey, but that is a choice that simply delays the journey to God. There is no time and delay is not a problem except that one can forget their direction and not go back onto the path to God. Also, moving on the path to God and avoiding the experience of power will bring more joy and the joy will only increase as one goes further down the path to God.

Life need not be impressive or it also can be impressive to serve God. The ultimate purpose for the choice made is what determines its value. Will this help my soul grow? Will this call others to their path? If one takes time to be in

* *"The Secret" is both a 2006 film and a companion book by Rhonda Bryne. (Atria Books, Beyond Words Publishing, 2006.) The book and movie present "The Law of Attraction" and feature many authors and public speakers presenting their views on it.*

the presence of Spirit, opening oneself to guidance daily, he will be guided to the right path. The ego can be very strong and overwhelming. The humility of meditation is a way to hear God even with a strong ego.

Life is to be a joyful adventure. If you are not having joy, ask for guidance to bring you into the path of joy, the path of eternal spring. We are meant to live a life with loving connection to those we know and don't know. We also will be having a loving connection to growing things and animals and Gaia, the earth itself. If you feel this love flowing from you, you are being reassured that you are on the right path.

If you don't have time to extend and receive love from all these varied sources, you are probably not presently on a journey to God. It is a choice. Have no regrets. No path is wrong. Some are just longer with more turns and bends and twists than others. The adventures all serve your soul, even when you are not on the path to God. Nothing is wasted. All is good. Relax.

Have a good day.

#149 TUMBLING

Beloveds, our joy peaks at being with you. You are loved and delighted in, more than you can comprehend. Remember, we have absolutely no judgments that would see you as guilty. We appreciate your attempts at things you cannot do well, and understand that it takes repeated tries before something is mastered, very similar to a dog jumping over a bar at a particular height. The first few times may not be successful, but if it is an ability that is within the dog, that height will be mastered. And so it is with you. You are attempting many things at the same time that you have not yet mastered. We salute your courage. You are so wonderful and you bring us so much joy.

Have you ever attended a gymnastics competition or perhaps watched the Olympics competition on television? You may have been amazed at the strength and agility of the participants. They attempt physical feats that you and I couldn't do if we had assistance and no competition. We know why they can accomplish their goals so very, very well. They practice. They put time in. They try and fail, and try and fail again. They continue to practice until they succeed.

So it is with us on our spiritual quest. We are not required to put in two to six hours a day in meditation, but we are required to keep the goal of being united and one with God in mind as we meditate and go through our day. To keep a focus of our goal in the back of our mind at all times is our desire. It is often like having someone from the other team to distract us from our ultimate goal. This other being is our own ego. It is crafty and strong in its desire to hold us in its power of separateness from God and from our fellow man. For lifetimes, we have been in the palm of the ego's hand. We were not as close to God.

This new goal that we hold so strongly is offensive to the ego and it rises up in full strength to combat our efforts. For example, we long to meditate, but something comes up and we don't have time. That something can be as unimportant as a TV program or as spending excessive time on a hobby. These fun activities are not wrong. However, they do delay the achievement of our ultimate goal, that of uniting with the energy of God.

This day, simply observe if you are happy and where you are spending your discretionary time. It is not wrong to choose a slower path to God. You make the decision and be blessed in it.

You travel in a sea of love.

#150   COMMITMENT

Blessings be to you as the cherry blossoms: multiple, multiple blessings that are small and sweet. Our hearts are open to you once again.

Every person knows of commitment. They may be committed to their families, their health, their pets, or their hobbies. They do know commitment. When one chooses to commit to the path of God, he is blessed. When one is committed to a musical instrument, the music becomes sweeter and sweeter as the years of commitment go on. So, too, is the experience of committing to the path of God. The connection becomes sweeter and sweeter; the results of prayer manifest more readily and love flows more abundantly.

It is generally a pleasant path. But, again, like the commitment to a musical instrument, as one advances, one comes across difficult passages that are very challenging, but doable. Similarly, in the path to God, one will find challenging lessons that may take a while to master the gift that is in the lesson. But when it is accomplished, it will be a push toward God that gives a new awareness of the term "love," for that is what God is. As we progress on our path to God, we, too, live more frequently in the vibration of love. Fewer and fewer things disturb us as we know that all is in perfect order, and we don't have to understand. Peace travels with us and happiness shows itself in many unexpected places.

Again, as with the musical instrument, commitment must be strong to stay on the path. Those who do not commit strongly to the musical instrument make very little progress. So, too, for those of us in the body, the path to God must be a committed path or no change will occur in the amount of love one is able to carry. The beauty that one may experience as the commitment is strong and continuous is heavenly. The soul will rejoice with vibrations of love that harmonize with others that are similarly committed. The music they make in their hearts and in others is beyond all expectation, and well worth the effort that it has taken to reach this level.

As you face the commitment to God, don't waiver. Be strong. Ask for all the help you need. The rewards await you and are worth the struggle.

Be mindful today of loving. That is your path.

Amen.

#151   TRUST AND JOY

The joy in your hearts that you feel for the coming of summer is enjoyed by those of us who help you. All joy that you find in your life eases your path. It is like the board game "Sorry,"* where there are little spaces, that when you land on them, you slide forward quickly to the end. In your life, when you have great joy, your burdens become lighter and the days pass quickly with ease. You need to realize what joy does for you. Not only is it pleasant, but it gives to the family, not necessarily biological, joy and ease as well. Joy is a magnificent gift and one that must be present to awaken to the Oneness of God.

As we go along our path, intending to eventually merge with God, we find our path becoming more and more easy. There will be less struggle and more frequent visitations of joy. In fact, we can spot our teachers by those who are very joyful. With joy comes trust, and with trust comes joy. If you find yourself on the serious side, you may be leaning heavily on your own abilities. When you release the burden to God, and truly trust, joy follows. In fact, it is a wonderful gauge to determine to what extent you are giving your life to God. Going to church every Sunday and study groups during the week, while yet remaining worried about your life, doesn't automatically help. The trust must be there.

Guard your prayers that they may be a joyful uniting with God, and not a fearful list of your worries. Feel free to bring your list of where you wish there would be more Light, however, bring it to God in love and confidence, release it, and trust that God hears your prayer and more Light will be sent. Prayer is Love in action. Prayer should

* "Sorry." Hasbro Inc., 1027 Newport Ave., Pawtucket, R.I. 02862

be a time of loving and caring in peace and certainty. All prayers will be answered exactly the way they should be, within a plan that is more perfect than our own. We are grateful that we can totally release our concerns to God and replace them in our heart with joy and trust.

We will know when we are being successful at giving our concerns to God in prayer when we are freed up, happy, joy-filled, and sometimes silly. If we haven't smiled in a while, we can use that as a reminder to work at releasing all our concerns to God.

There is so much help for us that each of our lists of loving concerns would be as a drop of water in the ocean of God's Love and Helpfulness. God is delighted to assist with all of our concerns.

We must give them up easily to God, and then relax in joy.

#152   ILLNESS

"A Course in Miracles" states "Remember that no one is where he is by accident, and chance plays no part in God's plan."* This concept is one that is easily theorized, but it is very difficult to assimilate into one's set of beliefs when the situation is unpleasant. For example, winning the lottery is an act of God in the minds of many, but those same souls would not believe that a serious disease is also an act of God. As we learn to trust and let go, we can be at peace and know that God is in charge of not only our lives, but also the lives of those we love, those we don't love, the politicians, our country and the world itself. Reaching this level of peace brings us very close to awakening to who we are in the plan of God.

Immersed in the joy of God, we look at the world through "rose colored glasses." It is like sliding, as a cartoon character, down a soft, wide, colorful silk ribbon that goes here and there, goes around corners, up and down, moving at times fast and at times slow. While traveling the ribbon, there is a wonderful sense of surety and well-being. Our problem is that we awaken from our being in the Presence of God and we slip into our ego state where we are trying to control our lives. Then we look and we become afraid and we try to change things. We struggle and we fight and we try hard to control outcomes at all times. We become frustrated, we become angry, we condemn ourselves and others, and the joy is no more.

The ribbon of life has its highs and its lows. The purpose of life is to break away the barriers that we have set up to our knowing God. These barriers can be broken away in different ways that we call lessons. As we become

* *A Course in Miracles, Manual, 9, 1:3*

more understanding, appreciative, compassionate, and forgiving, we are coming closer to comprehending who we are. Sometimes we break these barriers down through pleasant experiences. However, more frequently, many lessons are learned through struggle, and illness is one of those struggles. How blessed we are to have a learning device that brings us closer to God. The effort of the struggle is small, compared to the rewards. It can often save lifetimes because the learning is so much quicker.

Our blessed lessons sometimes come through the illness of one that we love very much. Remembering that lifetimes of struggle can possibly be shortened, one can only be grateful for the willingness of the person who is ill to undertake these lessons. For nothing comes to our life—nothing—without the prior approval from our soul.

Be at peace.

#153 IGNITING SPIRIT

Welcome loved ones. Your desire to be with God is known. That desire is a blessing for you and for the whole universe. You are very important to God and your efforts to reconnect and awaken in His arms are greatly appreciated.

With consistent meditation, we can be drawn once again into that part of us that is Spirit. Spirit is full of reassurance and joy. While in Spirit, we can feel the love given us to assist us on our journey. Some of this love is from those on this earth plane, and other is from those who are discarnate. If we can maintain connection to the Spirit level that is our own, we can feel the Peace and the Strength of God that goes with us as we slide down the ribbon of our life.

When encountering the fears of the ego, it is challenging to disconnect and meditate. The ego says, "No, no, we don't have time for meditation. That ten minutes can be used more productively." And while in that fear state, it seems to be the truth. But for us to connect to Spirit, we must disregard the voice of fear, the voice of the ego state, and take the small amount of time that you have allotted for God. If you are not consistent, it is easy for the ego state to convince you that you don't have time. Developing the habit of meditation is not unlike going on a diet. If, on your diet, you say, "Oh well, I'll cheat a little... I'll start again tomorrow... It's not reasonable at this party," your diet becomes a non-diet.

Parallel to this are excuses we make that prevent us from developing the habit of meditation. "I'm too tired... I'll start again tomorrow...I better use my time more productively...My life is so busy it is unreasonable to expect that I can take time to just sit."

If the commitment to meditation is not solid, it won't develop. Similar to a match, you may have to strike it once, twice, three times until it ignites into a flame. With meditation, it also may take multiple attempts before the connection to Spirit ignites. Then the joy reaches your soul and the habit for meditation is begun.

Good luck to you in your attempts to ignite your soul. You won't be sorry. As you feel the joy of your connection to God, you will become more aware of the presence of us who serve you. We, in our union with God, love you deeply and are with you always. We look forward to your knowing our presence.

Welcome home.

#154   LOVING CONSEQUENCES

Because God is love, never is there ill will directed toward you. Love is all God knows. We, too, have God within us. However, we have not cleared away the obstacles to see who we truly are. It is not unlike the blueberries as they ripen on the bush. If the blueberries had the ability to observe as we do, we might say that when the berries are flowers, their consciousness allows them to see flowers, but not ripe blueberries. As they become green, the consciousness allows them to see green berries. Then, one day, when they are blue, they see only blueberries. When we feel our love develop to the point of full ripeness, we will see only love, as God does.

As God desires to teach us, or to help us ripen to our full ability to love, lessons are brought in, and choices are given with consequences. God sees every consequence that he offers as a loving gift, an experience for us to develop more fully into who we are meant to be.

As we go into a choice in life, perhaps we choose to take a very expensive home, taking a chance that we could afford it when it looks very unlikely. There may be a turn of events and the home may be removed from our grasp. We may be put into housing that is much less glorious or desirable, but this is a lesson that will likely be learned completely and the results will be one step closer to seeing with God's eyes, which is our ultimate goal.

Sometimes it is hard to accept that Love itself would bring illness and sometimes — extreme illness. We have to remind ourselves that we have chosen to live on the earth so that we may have experiences that will help us, like the blueberry, to ripen.

Some of these experiences are nothing but joy.

290

We can know God by connecting to nature, enjoying the arts, appreciating fully another person, and many other wonderful ways where joy is in our hearts. These experiences of joy and love are lessons to teach us what love is. However, sometimes we choose a different path. That path is chosen on a higher level, but is chosen because of the rapid soul growth that can transpire during this experience.

Many people who have gone through difficult times can see the gift that was in their struggles, and they are grateful for it. We, as observers, must guard ourselves against having pity, fear, anxiety, regret, or any other negative emotion for this other person's experience. Their experience is a gift for them and it is not necessary that we understand it. We must trust in God and know that every gift is a gift of love.

If we can guard ourselves, we too can grow and be blessed through our awakened ability to suspend judgment. Love doesn't condemn. Knowing God is only Love helps us to suspend judgment on God's plan for our nation and world. This day, let us feel God's Love in those around us and accept their circumstances, as well as our own.

Be in peace.

#155   CART

Welcome once again to holding our hand as we guide you through the brambles to the Light. It is a joy and a thrill for us to do this, similar to a bigger sister holding her little sister's hand, and bringing her to a new and beautiful experience that she has never seen before, perhaps touching a bunny or a flower.

In the life you lead, you find yourself unnecessarily in difficult situations. Often these situations are brought about by you taking charge of your life and failing to follow the guidance that is given gently to you. If you understand your position is that of a cart behind a horse, the horse will guide you to where you should go as long as you are connected. The same goes for your life. If you gently seek guidance and go as directed, you will go in the direction that is best for you. That doesn't mean you won't go down difficult paths where the brambles are thick and your wheels get slowed down in the mud. There will be these challenging paths that are important for you to develop qualities that help you open to the clear guidance that flows through you.

Fear not about your degree of control. Certainly make continuous effort to improve your ability to trust God and to release your ego's domination of your path. However, wherever you are, God is, and it can be used as a teaching aid to assist you in all areas of development. Your intention to draw closer to God must be held as a primary goal at all times. If you can do this, you will be attached to the horse (God), and you will be guided for every step of the journey.

As you develop trust, you will be amazed at the results, and that small part of trust that you do develop will motivate you to continue releasing your direction to Divine Guidance, and your joy will increase again and again. It is a wonderful path with rewards unending.

How do you connect your cart to the horse, you may ask? As stated earlier, desire is number one, followed by a commitment to merging into the Light in daily meditation. Strong commitment to meditative practice will shorten your time of suffering, as it will hasten you to the connection to God.

Today, once again, recommit to your desire for joining with God daily in meditation. Your rewards will be great in time.

#156 THE BODY OF CHRIST

In the New Testament, Jesus refers to us as "the body of Christ." By being part of the body of Christ, it means that as a body we are one. There is no separation from one of us to the other. It only serves us well to look with understanding and acceptance on the behavior of another of us. To condemn that which is part of us is to condemn ourselves. Loving, understanding and guiding are certainly acceptable, however. Sometimes we must suspend judgment and simply give acceptance to that which we do not understand. We must trust that God will guide each part of us along the path on our journey home.

All love that is expressed between one and another awakens the awareness of God because God is Love. When we spend our days without condemnation and with love and acceptance, we assist in the movement of the whole body of Christ. Awakening the amount of love that one holds in their heart and expresses to others increases the love in the whole. It is as though there is a gauge on the earth plane that measures the total love expressed among each of us. With the help of God and all the angels and those who serve us, we continue to open to that love that is within that we have always carried for God. Our goal is not to understand, but to love.

The joy is that we have within us that love which we are seeking. The challenge is to lift away all the distractions and layers that have been placed upon us by our egos. It is a battle between good and evil, between serving ourselves and allowing the ego to continue to put more and more layers of personal separateness and competitiveness between us and our wholeness which includes everyone else.

It is a challenge to even understand why the praise of myself is not good, how personal aggrandizement is an act of separateness, and the energy is unfortunately going into layers upon layers, which cover over our love and unity. At the end of the day, we need to look back and assure ourselves that we, in fact, have spread love and openness to others who are part of the body of Christ. Making this our goal and being open to the guidance of God, we cannot fail.

Feel the presence of God with you this day. Express God's Love every chance you get—with other people, and in appreciation of beauty, birds, trees, flowers, sky, and clouds. All love is God's Love.

Help paint the earth "love."

#157   ABOUT TIME

Holy ones, hello. We are pleased you joined us today. Let's get down to business.

Your channel is your channel and it will not go away. It gets dust-covered from non-use and must be cleared out for communication to go smoothly. That's just the way it is. It brings us joy to have you come to us. You increase the vibration on the earth plane, because that is where we serve, but then, every act of kindness, every act of serving, every act of giving, for example, sending a photo on the Internet, are all positives that enhance the lives of all. At this period on Earth, it is seriously needed, drug use being the cause of so much negativity. It is such joy for us to see those of you who remember who you are.

Don't be afraid. We will be here with you. So long for now.

We are grateful for the love you bring into the world.

#158   MOTHER LOVE

(Clare senses the word "Mother," as she feels energy coming into the room, spreading over us to help us.)

There is a source of love for you that is strong beyond measure. It is other dimensional, but is able to be received on this plane. This love is very similar to a mother's love for her child. We, the children of this plane, have a smaller vessel to hold and to share love than the mother love that is brought to us, which is huge and luminous. But the ability of our small capacity is to open and receive this abundant love and to be totally saturated. This only occurs when we take time to ask for and patiently receive the beautiful love of God. You can feel it on your arms, your face, and your flesh when you concentrate. Its presence is real.

The task at hand is to fill with the love and to distribute it generously throughout the earth plane. Wholly appreciating others and delighting in their being is a wonderful way to express God's Love. Wholly appreciating nature is another way of expressing it.

We must be ever vigilant to be using our thought process in a manner that we have chosen. That means not to be swept away by the media or common thought patterns. This is where most of our energy has gone in this lifetime. Even a small correction will be a great benefit.

When your hearts rejoice, it is like a bird song that brings beauty to the universe. It is right to take pleasure in other people's successes, and they in yours. Sharing joy expands it. Go forward today in joy. Seek it. Share it. Recognize it.

Amen

#159 MASTER GARDENER

(Clare saw an image of a trowel in earth pressing dirt sideways as when planting. She then felt the presence of spiritual entities who clothed her in a loose-fitting gossamer overgarment, wavy, shiny with large sleeves. It was very beautiful. They said, "You are one of us.")

A master gardener loves the earth and loves planting the beautiful plants that grow therein. She seeks information as to how to enhance each species she deals with. She loves her work.

So, too, are we the master gardeners for God. We love every person God presents for us to love and pay attention to their progress, doing what we can to make their experience with God optimal. There are times that are difficult for the attended soul. Master gardeners must not abandon them, but nurse them successfully through obstacles for the soul to grow successfully. We do it all in great love and enthusiasm, and are motivated by the success we observe. The task for the gardeners is a task of love and hard work, but very, very satisfying in the beauty that God reveals within each soul attended to.

The master gardener does her gardening privately without fanfare, but diligently. We, too, who serve God in this manner, do service that is not acclaimed. The service is very valuable and although the servant sees the beautiful results, others may not. Let it not diminish the value of the work accomplished by the tender, loving care of the gardener. Let the gardener herself take credit for the committed hard work. Let her not feel her time is wasted or that she has nothing to show for the loving service that she has given so generously.

As the master gardener desires to know more and studies

material available to make her work more successful, so also does the master gardener for God. She is lead to many materials that enhance her work and help her bring the love of God more abundantly to those she serves.

Rejoice master gardener! Your caring, loving attention to those whom God has assigned to you is fully appreciated. Not only is the beauty of your garden noticed and appreciated on the earth plane, but it is also celebrated on the planes that are not of the earth. The result of your work is similar to an iceberg that is visible in only the small percent of the whole.

Be encouraged in your work and continue to bless those beautiful souls presented to you for your care.

We join with you in your efforts.

#160   FIRE IN THE FIREPLACE (CHRISTMAS TIME)

Greetings to our loved ones! We love and care for you as you do your pets. We delight in all your successes and forgive your failures. We try to guide you to develop for the best outcome of your being. Our capacity for giving and loving is much greater than yours at this point. In truth, we are no different one from another, but we are playing different roles at this time.

Thank you for taking time to be holy by connecting to God. It benefits you more than you will ever know. Remember, you are Love.

Your job, while you travel the earth plane, is to distribute love, for God is Love. Presently, this is the time of Christmas, and as Santa has elves to assist him, so God has us and the job is vast.

The wood in the fireplace burns and converts into heat, and the heat is very rewarding and pleasant for those who are seeking warmth. So, too, is our job to convert that which is given us into that which is sought, which is love. This means that our responsibility is to have a very pure heart so that condemnation does not dampen the fire. The purer the heart, the hotter the fire, and the greater is the love that can be dispersed.

Just as damp wood doesn't burn well, nor do souls that hold condemnation reflect the love of God well. During the time that you take to be holy and to be with God, much is changed within your heart. It is like drying the wood. Those that serve you bless the intent that you hold in your heart to serve. As the phrase goes, "sharpen the blade." In our analogy, it would be "dry the wood."

As in burning wood, it is easier to serve God with

others of like mind. Together, your Light and Love of God shines brighter and offers more warmth for those who are seeking. It's also pleasant to receive the love of God through others at the same time as giving it.

But your individual love of God serves wherever you are like a candle. You will know that you have released many barriers to God when you observe in your life the magnificent beauty of the candlelight—God Light—in everyone.

Look carefully today at everyone that God sends to you. See their Light. Rejoice in their glow.

Amen.

#161   WHITE DOVE

Greetings and joy abound! Welcome to our merging. This is the season for peace and expressions of love. Religions join in focus during this period. This can be symbolized in the white dove. It is the time of year when busyness becomes joyful, the giving and extending of love. Earthly souls join one another in preparation for great celebration. The process is the joy as well as the headache and frustration.

With the symbol of the white dove in mind, the hustle and bustle has purpose and a sense of peace. The dove gives the "reason for the season," uniting huge numbers of people in a direction to God. Songs are sung, meals are prepared and eaten, friends are greeted, gifts are exchanged, and decorations abound. It can be a very joyous season.

Without the focus of the dove, the hustle and bustle and deadlines and expenses lose their joy and the season can be a drudgery, a fast "must-do" drudgery. If one finds oneself in this mode, there needs to be a time out. One must ask for help from those who serve on the other side. Ask for the infusion of joy, love, and peace that is necessary to truly celebrate our link to God through Jesus Christ. Invite the Holy Spirit to help each of us to be receptive to that which we ask for.

Focusing our lives on giving, as we do in preparation for Christmas, is so very rewarding; let us learn from this and inject it into more of our lives. And one of the greatest gifts of giving is seeing the Christ within everyone that we talk to, within the family and without. Let our hearts grow in love that we may rejoice in each person that comes our way. May we see the true depths of Love and Light that is within the other person, and may we give them this gift of recognition.

The gift of recognition is a gift of joining, merging the love of God that is within me to the love of God that is within you, and that is within God as a whole. It is a warm feeling. Do this often and deeply.

Let the season be a training ground for the focus of the dove, and let us take the dove with us each day to remind us to use the Love and Joy that we have within us to celebrate the presence of Christ in the world in others. This heavenly Joy will enhance the vibration of the whole world and will be greatly appreciated both on the earth and by those guiding the development of the souls on the earth.

Amen.

#162   DRIFTWOOD

(Clare was experiencing a challenging period due to side effects of her recent chemo treatments, including low blood pressure and leg pain. Added to this, we received news of several friends facing major challenges.)

We greet you with great love and joy once more. Don't be downhearted. Your giving will be given you and your joy will return.

There comes a time in the life of a soul when difficulties seem to appear everywhere. They don't come by accident, but are always invited at the soul level. It is not important that we understand why, but it gives us an opportunity to react in a loving way, even though it is difficult.

How you react forms who you are, much like the piece of driftwood on the beach. It may resist in some areas and succumb in other areas until its features are well formed. Our souls also experience similar etching. Without the difficulties, the true beauty of the soul will not be seen. Again, similar to the driftwood, if it had no wind and rain and wave action, it would remain a piece of wood and people would not see it as a thing of beauty.

As challenging as it can be to go through physical difficulties, or emotional, financial ones, they each contribute to the overall beauty that is revealed within you. When your true beauty has been revealed and easily seen by the onlookers, the intensity of the etching can be reduced and life can be less difficult. It is similar to the persons who wish to have a tattoo. They are willing to suffer the pain, so that they can display beauty. We elders suffer pain to reveal that we are elders.

As the beauty is discovered, the driftwood is removed from the beach to be incorporated into the life of a family.

Similarly, as your etchings near completion, you will pull away from the difficulties again, and rest in peace.

The shaping of the driftwood/soul need not be in pain, but can be done in other ways that are so much more pleasant, but so much more time consuming. Still, this can be a good choice, because there is no hurry.

Our job is to see the beauty that is within the other. Let it be our challenge. Let it be our goal that we see the beauty in all those we look upon. Take a moment and encourage a person in their display of beauty, for they are reflecting the Light of God.

Those Who Serve

#163 SEEKERS UNITE!

Welcome those of you whose hearts long to be united in the Oneness of God. The Oneness that you seek seeks you. Seekers come in many varieties and they also come with many degrees of awareness. Those who are very aware on any path are similar to one another for they are very close to knowing the Truth of God and that Truth looks the same from any angle.

Those who have pride in their separateness are new on the path to God. For the Power of God shows us how we are similar one to another. It removes the importance of differences. It eliminates comparisons of "better than" each other. It connects those of different faiths into working together for causes that are God directed.

On our path of going home to God, we must be careful not to diverge into meaningless areas of comparison. Instead of seeking to know differences between one another, we will be wise to seek the ways we are the same and rejoice in those areas for there is the Spark of God experienced. No path has all truths, and yet each path is complete in that it brings you into the area of total truth, which has no separation. It is similar to a ballroom with many doors, each door representing a different faith, but each bringing you into the wholeness of the beauty of God where you dance and rejoice together as one. There you experience the complete truth.

As you travel down your chosen path to seek God, note other faiths only for their beauty and their truth. That which you do not understand is best to be left alone. It is not necessary for you to understand the path of others. Just trust that God is with them and will bring them to the ballroom as well as yourself. Our separateness is only temporary. The time will come when we all will join together in the ballroom, in the Heart of God.

Let your heart rejoice when your attention has been brought to those who worship God in a different way, knowing their path parallels your own and that love will be the result of this seeking, for God is love, and where there is love, there is God.

Send your loving vibration to those of different faiths, notifying them that you are their brother/sister on this journey to God. Feel their love in return. God blesses you in your journey, and appreciates all effort given to greater understand the Love of God that is present universally.

You are never alone.

Amen.

#164   TO *BE* OR NOT TO *BE*

You who are family bring warmth and joy to the rest of us as we unite again. It feels like the experience of reunion as when part of the family is away at college or work and is able to come home again. The whole family rejoices.

In the ending of the movie "Shrek 2,"* the father/king is turned back into being a frog, and one might say, "How unfortunate!" However, just as each of us has a form as part of God that can be very different in appearance from that which we see today, that form is unfamiliar and therefore, unwelcome. Upon further inspection, however, the unfamiliar form will bring back its memory and it is welcome.

A problem that we have in living in this human form is that we believe that it is the preferred form and somehow superior in all ways to other forms. We fail to seek outside of our known experience for Truth, and if Truth shows itself in an unfamiliar form, we fail to recognize it as real. This is where grace is important. This is where we must seek for and trust guidance beyond our own understanding. In so doing, the rewards can be very great, for as Truth is revealed in the unknown form, it brings with it an acceptance and a knowingness. In fact, it brings a rejoicing, for the differentness now feels extremely perfect.

In "Shrek 2," when the father/king turns into a frog, he is content. He understands the greater value he has accepted as his own. Viewing his situation from afar does not bring understanding. The truth that is felt is not clear to the eye. The rest of us become so ensconced with our human nature that we consider anything else unacceptable,

* *Dreamworks Animation, 2004*

and yet, the Truth that we seek is in a form somewhat divergent from that which we have always known. It is wise for us to suspend judgment and see what each experience brings us. When it is greater truth, we will know and accept it, although it is different from our past.

When one sets aside time daily to *be* (merge into the wholeness of God) and then does so, greater Truth is experienced. When seekers fail to set time apart for this experience (not to *be*), they are choosing to stay in the "status quo."

Many will take time to read spiritual material, and go to classes based on spiritual topics, but yet not establish a daily routine for "God time." It is a choice they are making, though perhaps unaware of their misdirection. Take time daily to sit in silence with Spirit.

You will be rewarded.

#165 DAISY

Loved ones, your efforts are appreciated. Your commitment makes it possible for us to unite with you. You hold the truth without us, but feel uncertain and desire our presence to validate the truth you know. We are your walker and one day you will solo. The process of opening to the Light is what makes this writing clear. Expressing words of Light is possible for everyone should they learn to connect and open to the beautiful Light that we share.

Look at the little daisy flower. In its innocence and beauty, it reflects God and brings joy to the world. This, too, is possible for each of us where we will need to do nothing but be the presence of God wherever we are. To do this, we simply have to clear out our negativity and judgments and *be* happy within ourselves. Wherever there is joy and love, there is the presence of God, and if we will *be* Joy and Love, we, too, will be like the daisy and bring into the world God's Presence to share.

What a wonderful assignment from God! We are asked simply to be happy. If we are having trouble finding our way to happiness, we must then ask God for assistance. We may be guided to a group of similar people who are seeking God, often in a church, synagogue or mosque. These like-minded people will support one another as they draw closer to removing the barriers that prevent God's Light from shining through.

Lovely souls will be sent to us as guides. As we relax in the knowledge that we truly are being guided, we will be able to see the beauty that is sent to us. We will know that we are tuning in to this spiritual guidance by looking into our hearts and feeling the gratitude that is automatic when God's teaching is taking place. We can be comfortable in the knowledge that we, too, are as the daisy and bring joy and love to others.

Today, relax and observe the Love that is sent to you, and know that you too are vibrating Love for all.

We are grateful.

#166   WHO DO YOU WANT TO BE?

While you were viewing a film on Indigo children, their ability to connect to Spirit became very clear. The truly profound children were those who lived with the presence of God. They claimed their spiritual identity and then used that identity for amazing work. You can, too.

If you have an inkling as to how you are to serve God, you are ahead of the game. From that point forward, calling forth God's presence to you frequently will ensure the goal of service. As you merge with the Oneness, your goals will be refined and you will draw to you that which is necessary for success.

If you do not know clearly how you wish to serve God, you must call God forth in close communion often. Sitting in the Presence of God energy refines your vibration so that you can communicate more fully with God. It is like changing your vibration from a clothesline thickness down to that of spaghetti and then to smaller and smaller wires, until the wire is so small you cannot see it. Each time you are able evolve your ability to communicate with God, you will be so pleased with the reception that you receive. You will feel more lightness in your demeanor. You will find fewer things difficult and many more things a joy. Your ability to love will grow exponentially. Your ability to sprinkle God Love everywhere you go will be greatly increased.

The only way this learning curve can be undertaken is with clear intent, prayer for assistance and time spent in silence with the presence of God all around your forehead and body. This must be done consistently for results to be noticed, but with prayer, commitment, intention and time, it will come about. Then you, too, will be able to know how you want to serve God, and you and the Holy Spirit will work things out.

Trust is essential. Trust that there is a God. Trust that God loves you. Trust that you are a part of God. Having this trust around you comforts you and tunes you in to communication with God throughout your day. What fun it is to speak to God and have God speak to you.

Who are you for God's service? Let this pursuit become more and more refined until the pursuit itself is joy. The connection to God will become more and more frequent on its own. Enjoy.

Things will get easier.

#167   THE COOKIE

How good is a fresh-baked cookie, full of flavor, smell, texture, and a delight to your whole body! Likewise, how warm and inviting is a smile. A smile speaks of love and comforts like the cookie. The smile also relieves tension and stress. When you see a smile, it is a "feel good" moment.

When you are a child and have not yet taken on the responsibilities of the world, your smiles come more freely. They are given away right and left. They comfort the souls of those around you. If you are not careful, you will start to squeeze out the smile for other moments of seeming importance. Here is where the choice is made between serving your ego, your own personal success, and serving your God, the family of man. When an opportunity presents itself for us to smile, we have been blessed. We have been chosen to serve God at that moment. If the saga of life clouds our minds, the opportunity may be missed and a sense of joy is lost. The smile serves your brother and sister, but more importantly, it serves you.

The smell of the cookie in the oven is a comforting aroma. It speaks of pleasant times to come. Likewise, those who carry an attitude of joy, a trust and knowingness of God carry with them an aura of loving that can be manifest in a smile, a kiss, a touch, or a look. The energy that is in the air when loving is present comforts and encourages those that are there.

Think of someone who epitomizes these characteristics of love, someone who is a joy to be around, someone you know would not hurt you. This person is sent to you as a teacher, a way shower, so that you, too, can become part of the net of God that draws us home, closer to the vibration of loving. It is like moving up in the atmosphere, where the air becomes more and more refined. The closer we draw to God, the more complete our joy and the clearer is our service.

Those who are around us are expressing loving vibrations as well, and our existence becomes more and more delightful. The ascension to God is usually gradual, but every smile given or taken along the path hastens our journey.

Use this day given you for the beautiful service to your fellow men by giving them the delight of your smile.

Amen.

#168   I WALK WITH YOU

Our joy unites with your joy to the glory of God. We are grateful that you take time to be with us. Our hearts are full of love for all who seek God. (To Clare: *You have a special hue in your aura. It is a light blue and it is beautiful.*)

Peace I bring you, as I walk by your side, for my wisdom is great. I understand the experiences that you are going through and will go through and appreciate them, for they are a gift to you on your soul journey back to where you are all along, the journey of awakening.

Listen to Linda Lirot* and her advice regarding living every moment. Don't spend excessive time on television, movies, or any other strictly entertaining activities, each of which is a wonderful journey when shared with others.

As you live in the moment, connect to your body in nature as often as you can. This opens you up to your connection to those of us who walk with you. We gently speak to you often on your journey, but we speak softly and are easily drowned out by other mental activities. Clearing the mind through meditation, walks, routine chores, driving the car, dreams and, most of all, intention, all assist in the hearing of our gentle guidance. You will feel our connection to be one of joy and excitement, a feeling of being gifted, like winning small to big lottos.

When we connect to you clearly and definitely, we too feel excitement, for it is our intention and desire as well as yours. The more you control your mind to stay away from the past and the future, and to be here and now, the more you will connect with us, for God's Energy and Presence are here. You muddy the water by digging up

* *A personal friend with whom Clare had recently talked.*

issues from the past and ideas of the future, and divisive political issues of the day. There will be other patterns that are yours, like hurry, worry, doubt, fear, and preoccupation that will also cause you to muddy the waters of God's voice to you.

Be mindful of your personal stumbling stones that are on your path of clarity. Ask for assistance to remove these stones and it will be given to the degree to which you fervently seek.

This day, in your joy, love and peace you will connect to God in the world and in others. Choose to be so blessed. Intention is everything.

You never walk alone.

Amen.

#169   BUILDING FACADES IN THE OLD WEST

Welcome playmates! We venture forth together searching for joy in the envelopment of God. Our journey is destined for peace and happiness.

Going down the main street in the old west, one passed building upon building that had a facade or a false front. This didn't fool anyone, but it gave a feeling of wealth. Similarly, in our lives, we put up false fronts and likewise observe that our friends all have them as well. It is the style of the day.

We pretend to know God, but we do not take our visitation time with Him regularly. The degree of our being One with God shows in our trust and in our contentment. Walking with God seems to be a popular goal. Without intention, we have taken on the style of the day and pretend to be merging into the Oneness more than we may actually be doing. This is okay. The total immersion into the Oneness of God is inevitable. If we become distracted by the social norm at this period, we will have other opportunities to be real and to awaken to who we really are.

Those who wish to truly merge into the Oneness, or "go home," can live in complete integrity and walk with pure intent and commitment. This would include, of course, daily meditation, prayer and a loving relationship with God. To keep God as the primary goal in life allows much fun and ease with the rest of our intentions, because we do not walk alone.

Our relationship with God need not be a struggle. To form the habit of meditation does take discipline, but only until the habit is established. Otherwise, life should feel right, even with its challenges.

Little flags along the path that tell us we are going in

the right direction are glimpses of God in other people. Ultimately, we will see God in every other person and our joy will be boundless.

Today, try to walk in authenticity. Impress no one. Connect to God and watch for God shining forth in others.

Be grateful.

Amen.

Your Arc of Infinity Friends

#170   ENCOURAGEMENT IN EXTREMELY TRYING TIMES

(These encouraging remarks were directed to Clare, who was recovering from the side effects of chemotherapy, compounded by exposure to the sun while in Hawaii. These challenges included sciatica, intestinal distress, mucous in the lungs, sun rash on her torso, bumps and bloody blisters on her lips, back pain, aching teeth, and general fatigue. It was an extremely challenging period.)

Little one, do not be discouraged. Notice the number of days that you are "up" much more than the ones you are "down," a refreshing reversal. These will continue to be greater as you walk back into health.

Congratulations!

#171   CORK, OR YOU "CORKER"

Warmest of greetings, like the balmy air of a Hawaiian breeze. You are loved.

Oh, the versatility of cork, as is the versatility of the teacher of God. In one way, cork can be used as a sound proofer to keep out unnecessary and unwanted noise. So too, does the teacher of God who connects to Spirit. Bringing in the Holy Space that is God causes a silence in the life of the student as well as the teacher. This is a wonderful gift. It has much that the new student has difficulty attaining, this blessed peace. To be able to come to the Sacred Space of God is such a primal need that those who can help another go there and stay there are truly appreciated. Please reach out and serve your brothers and sisters on the path and let them serve you in this manner. Hearts will rejoice.

Another manner in which cork can serve is in its ability to create an impact. A cork put to flame and blown out produces a very dark charcoal that can be used for a brief while in its depth of color—black. So too, can miracles be made with Spirit. These miracles come from teachers of God because we are all teachers of God and they go to others. They may be brief, but they are seen because of their impact.

Yet another way cork is similar to a teacher of God is that it seals in a vessel a treasure. The treasure in the world may be a wonderful olive oil or a wine, but for the teacher of God, it is the breadth of understanding of God. The bottles may be at different levels of fullness, but each has something to offer to another. Each teacher desires to fill their bottle, to improve their understanding of the essence of God, to awaken to the total understanding of Oneness.

And yet one more way a teacher of God is similar to cork is in its ability to have information displayed upon it, as in a bulletin board. A teacher of God, if willing to serve, can be used unbeknownst to his or her own being. Those who are to learn from them may pick up understanding by observing their teacher. A vast assortment of learning can be thus displayed. In fact, this is probably the most significant method for teaching. As we all know, we turn to our teachers to learn about God.

Be mindful of the joyful opportunities you have to learn and to teach on many different levels. We are all assisting each other on this wonderful journey back into the loving arms of God.

Amen

#172   BRICKLAYER

Our desire to walk clearly in the Light of God is our motivation to become more and more informed as to how to do that. It is like playing "red light, green light"* as a child where the goal is to go forward as quickly as possible. Or the joy that we feel when we step into sunlight after we have been in the woods, or when we awaken to the clarity of God's love when we have been in darkness. The joy is there, the appreciation, the release from the darkness.

Each attempt that we make to draw closer to God is like a layer of bricks in bricklaying. One is set upon the other, and then the next upon that and so on. Each row must be encountered and laid in exactness and purity, for the next will be laid upon it. There is great joy when clarity is unveiled and this clarity can be brought to that structure one holds already of the knowing of God. The structure that we lay helps us to rise above our present understanding of the world that is set out by the ego.

As we have greater and greater understanding of who God is and who we are, we can reverse our form of living. We can now forgive and accept that which comes to us and that which comes to others. We can see that our understanding is not necessary for this peaceful acceptance of God's plan. As we build greater and greater knowledge of God, we realize that we are never alone, nor is anyone else. The support given us is endless and loving.

As we build our understanding of God, we see the place that we each play in assisting others to feel the warmth and support of God in their everyday activities. They, too, are building an understanding of God and will reach out

A children's game involving running and stopping on commands given by a participant who is the "stop light."

and assist others, including us.

There are perhaps thousands of layers of understanding of God. Like going to school, we pass from grade to grade with greater understanding at each grade. In our quest for understanding of God, we also accomplish levels of understanding and move on to the next. When our levels of understanding reach a certain height, we will go on to another classroom other than the earth to grow in love. This building of our awareness of who we are in God and who God is in us continues to unfold, until one day we find ourselves as One with God.

Go forth today in joy and love, and experience God in everyone.

Amen.

Your Arc of Infinity Friends

#173 ROLLER SKATING

Our arms and hearts go out to you, to embrace you with our love at this moment of seeking. We are grateful that you take steps toward us, because if the intention is not from each side, the connection will not hold.

"Everybody is doing it." Don't you remember as a child the excitement of joining your friends in doing what they were doing for fun? Perhaps it was roller-skating. The "in" activity of the day brought great motivation for each child to develop in that area. During another period of time, hula-hoops were the "in" activity and children were motivated to figure out how to make those hula-hoops work. Great effort and time was given for that goal. So it is in life.

As adults, as we go through our day-to-day life, we look about and see what is interesting for us to involve ourselves in. Perhaps it is a book from Oprah Winfrey's book club or "The Secret"* recommended by friends. Whatever the popular interest of the moment is, it brings with it motivation to learn and to share with others like yourself.

This is an auspicious period of time. A great amount of change is taking place on the spiritual level. Your spiritual families on the other side are joining together to stimulate large segments of your population at the same time. The political/economic aspects of society may be going into a storm mode, a period when much concern is present around issues that affect the day-to-day living. Many need this feeling of distress to turn to God. Because the numbers are so large in this movement of spiritual seeking, it brings a feeling of roller-skating as a child.

* *Rhonda Byrne, Atria Books, Beyond Words Publishing, 2006.*

You are part of the "in" group and are motivated to get as much out of it as you can.

With all that is happening around you, there is great opportunity for rapid understanding of who you are and how you relate to God and others. The banquet table of choices for learning is overflowing. Choose, grow, choose again, grow yet again. You are being assisted in all your choices by the spiritual team that loves you.

Daily life, like going to the Epcot Center, can bring so much understanding. There are workshops, guest speakers, books, DVDs, music, newsletters, etc. You simply need to have the intention to develop a greater understanding of God, and you will be drawn to material that is perfect for you.

Be happy in this smorgasbord of blessings. Remember to walk in joy, not fear or anxiety. Lean heavily on your spiritual guidance and accept the magical blessings that come your way.

Amen.

#174 CONNECT

Our warmest greetings come to you. This is a world where you write your own life story. Part of it is done through planning before birth, for example, your socio-economic class, your parents, your siblings, and your neighbors. Then there is part of the story that will be written by your intention. This intended story will formulate around those with whom you connect and how you connect.

Your vibrational level, or that amount of awakening that you have accomplished so far, will determine your starting point. Then you will connect with others who are at a vibration you desire. If that desire is of a higher vibration, learning will take place and your own awareness will grow, as you further understand the concept of Oneness versus separateness.

Life becomes a rhythmic dance, whereas you have understanding, then you might lose that understanding for a while, then you regain it with additional understanding, and then lose part of it to be repeated again and again where you are gaining on the upswing and apparently losing ground on the downswing, but never to the place that you were before. So progress is being made. At times it may seem doubtful. As one feels the excitement of greater understanding, the dance becomes a pleasure because even more understanding is around the corner. More joy, more peace, and more love are at hand.

The dance of life is intertwining with others and their understanding of God. The light they shine to you of God's Love helps you to understand and to be able to shine upon others. It is the sharing that is beautiful. Happiness and laughter become more apparent as God's Love is flowing from one to another. The heart sings.

The Light of God grows within and shines upon your attitude. As you become more understanding of God, you become more optimistic. You see the good in things. You see the good in people. You smile a lot.

Observe those around you today. Watch for the twinkle, the understanding smile, the patience of others. Find people to emulate. Enjoy the dance of life today and share it with others

Amen.

Your Arc of Infinity Friends

#175 BALD EAGLE

We who connect with you honor you. You have chosen an interesting, although challenging experience. We are happy to be here to back you up. You keep us very busy. Blessings.

The "movie" that you are in requires many parts to be played. You have volunteered to be very strong and admired. You belong to the main family for the story. You have come expecting many adventures, many highs and lows. You have signed on for this adventure because it is a means to remind your brothers and sisters of who they are. You are excited that they would remember who they are and be home again with you.

Your willingness to demonstrate the strength of an eagle makes others observe you and, being just who you are, you can demonstrate the Strength of God, and demonstrate the strength within each of your brothers and sisters as well.

The ego would love to say that the individual is unworthy to be Strength of God. The ego holds the door shut to complete awareness by his false humility. The ego would rather say that we are weak and that God is separate from us, and God is strong. God is not separate, but One with our fellow man and us at all times. Awareness is not necessary for this to be so.

The "movie" that you serve in where you demonstrate God's Strength is important. The door would be held closed forever without love and understanding. However, this "movie," and many similar call forth the strengths of the individual and the awareness of God within. As this awareness becomes totally recognized, this person becomes awakened, if only for a brief moment. These moments of awakening will appear again and again, and more and more frequently. A deep strength of knowing will be present in these awakened ones. They will be strong, competent examples of the truth for all. They will be observable like the eagle. They will have less and less interest in drawing attention to themselves, because now they see themselves as a part of the whole and not individualized.

Reach out in love today and connect to your sisters and brothers and feel the joy of being part of the Oneness. Let your heart sing in gratitude for the loving experience. Live in strength and joy.

Amen.

Your Arc of Infinity Friends

#176   WOBBLY WHEEL

Today we come urgently responding to your requests. We, too, feel the pressure, for the time is short. Thank you and bless you for taking time today to reach for higher understanding.

(Clare sees a wobbly wagon wheel.) To travel a distance in a vehicle, you want the wheels to be tightened and in good shape. If a wheel is loose, and wobbles as you travel, your ability to travel well is greatly diminished. So it is with your spiritual understanding. The maintenance that is required for your vehicle, or body, is meditation. If you don't have a daily connection to Spirit, you hinder your ability to partake of the banquet that is offered you.

Meditation typically means setting apart time to be with God. This can take many forms. The most common is the solitude with a blank mind, once or twice a day, for fifteen to twenty minutes minimum, usually with a spiritual reading of some sort for inspiration. But let it be known, that many have their connection with God while moving about their day. They talk to God regularly, they pray, they share their joy and their needs with God. Because this connection is consistent throughout the whole day, the overall connection to God can be very beautiful.

You will know that your vehicle does not have a wobbly wheel if your day has communication both ways with God. Perhaps a need will be provided without asking, or a voice will be heard to guide you and a feeling of "Presence" will be with you. A closeness with God will be yours.

Just as a wagon wheel that is wobbly can be repaired, a correction can be made in your own personal relationship with God if it is not where you wish it to be at any given time. A repair shop that you must go to is prayer with sincerity in your request for help. Another source for assistance comes through reading material, audio material and also DVDs. You will be guided to something that will assist you. Be careful at this juncture. It is possible to fall in love with the medium of learning and lose track of your ultimate goal, which is your private communication with God.

Just as in auto racing, you have a crew who are eager to assist you to travel with God at optimum clarity. They are delighted to assist you, so ask them for help at any time and you will draw closer to God. Just as a racecar must pull over to get help, so must you take the time to ask for help.

Speedy travel!

Your Arc of Infinity Friends

#177 PINATA

As a child, we may have experienced the opportunity of hitting a piñata. The whole idea of a piñata is that there will be abundance beyond our dreams. We await the moment when all we have to do is take, take, take, and our wants will be curtailed. But will they? The more we grab, the more we wish we had grabbed more.

So it is in life if we are seeking false goals. We hurry, we have anxiety, we anticipate and we grab at the things of life, never to be satisfied, always wishing we had had another approach so that we could have gotten even more. There is dissatisfaction when our goals are on the earthly level.

We may also pursue spiritual goals. The achievement of these goals is permanent. The inner satisfaction with their accomplishments is lasting. The proportion of our life energy that goes for either human goals or spiritual goals will determine our happiness. When the spiritual goals dominate, lasting love abounds. We carry joy with us as we go through our life and peace permeates the piñata experience. Knowing the value of the spiritual experience causes that area of our life to grow and dominate and it is a matter of time before the piñata experience will lessen to the degree of non-existence.

When we find ourselves in the worldly pursuits, we are especially aware of our separateness from others. As to the piñata, we want more than the others. We want to get it quicker than the others. We want to be admired separately from the others. This feeling of dualism dominates and opens the door for unhappiness.

In our spiritual pursuits, we long to merge with our sisters and brothers. We long to share our time, our things, and our joy with them, and also to share theirs with us. We find great joy in giving, because we sense that we are giving to ourselves. We appreciate receiving because it is a way of uniting.

Typically, in the youth of our life, we are wildly in search of our separateness. When the opportunity appears and the spiritual self is acknowledged, the reversal can begin. The spiritual life can then grow and grow, and the material life can fade in importance. The beauty is taking the spiritual life into the material life, sharing the excitement with others who have at this point not awakened to who they really are.

The awareness of God is becoming present in so many. Share your joy together. Look about you for the spilling of the spiritual piñata. Take what will serve you.

Your Arc of Infinity Friends

#178   MARBLES

Welcome beloveds. Be at peace.

Your day-to-day life is composed of many stimuli, many vastly different from another. You have world affairs, neighborhood events, family responsibilities, news from friends, reading materials, meditation, etc. These are all like different marbles in a jar, and that jar of marbles makes up your life at this time.

You may choose which of these marbles to focus on. Should you care to be concerned with the world events, family issues, community issues, or your spiritual peace, the choice for focus is yours. Ideally, you will choose to travel with the peace of God while dealing with responsibilities that call for your time. Can you find joy in all that you do? Are you living in the Love of God consciously in the moment?

Choosing to focus without fear in an accepting manner is our choice. Each marble can be looked at and handled with grace if we travel with a marble of peace in our pocket. Moment by moment in the day, observe how you feel. Are you at peace? Are you feeling joyful? Are you where you want to be? If not, ask for guidance and listen. The guidance will surely follow. Remember what in the past has brought you to the destination you desire. Was it singing, praying, reading a particular author, speaking with a friend, or walking in nature? You may be guided to use the path that has worked for you before. But do realize that it is a choice.

If you feel stuck, perhaps you are letting your ego be in charge. Look to what is happening and choose to lead with the spirit body. With the spirit body there is joy and perhaps a sense of union with the guidance from the other side. Their joy is always levels over ours and to tap into it is uplifting. The feeling of this connection brings you from the desire to serve yourself to a desire to be part of a greater whole.

Gratitude is a short cut to changing from the ego to the spirit body. Fill your heart with gratitudes, great and small, until you are vibrating with the joy of gratitude. With your heart full of gratitude, you will have the desire for it to overflow onto others. Your step becomes light and you find more to appreciate around every corner. You have been successful.

Warm wishes for a happy, flowing day, and if that day becomes murky, take charge and turn it into a day of joy. You have the ability and you have the guidance. The result is up to you.

Your Arc of Infinity Friends

#179   SUDDENLY BLOOMING

Greetings again, light workers. Your dedication to the movement of awakening for all is what advances it along. Such universal devotion has never taken place on the earth before. Our gratitude goes to each of you for the magnificent light you hold.

Developing a habit to meditate and grow spiritually takes commitment and dedication within the umbrella of God's Love. The energy on the earth plane is rising. It assists the awakening of the individuals that have desire. Gently and imperceptibly, the atmosphere of growing has become more universal. For one to have achieved the level of vibration that you have reached was formerly a singular activity. Now, because the energy level of the earth plane vibrates at a higher level, millions are assisted in their spiritual growth and awareness and this pursuit is not solitary anymore.

In physics, the Brownian movement says that temperatures can be translated to the mass through the movement of the molecules. For example, putting a jar of cold water into a large tub of hot water will soon cause the temperatures to equalize through warming or cooling many molecules against the glass which then in turn go among the other molecules in the space, bumping against them and distributing the heat they have.

Or, in the case of awakening for the planet, distributing the understanding of God among the fellow light workers. As you look around you, you see that some of your fellow light workers have amassed large amounts of light, or understanding and awareness of God. They in turn, share that light with us, as in Eckhart Tolle's *The Power*

of Now and *A New Earth,** as well as Rasha's *Oneness,*†
and *A Course in Miracles,*‡ which came through Helen
Schucman§. That light then goes forth to us and from us
to others.

This happens also with the light sharing of thousands
of individuals in many mediums and languages, be they
authors, songwriters, poets, or others. There is much light
sharing going on at this time, which is causing the mul-
titudes to awaken at an amazing rate. This whole almost
imperceptible change has come upon the earth quickly
and almost universally. This is due to each of you doing
your part in receiving and spreading the light with those
you know, and they in turn doing the same. What a joyful
space to be in!

As the light goes from you to others, and from them
to others still, it is a sharing with the Love and Joy of
God. It brings forth the awareness of our connection in
the family of God. It gives a subtle feeling of belonging
and of purpose. The Light of God is also contained within
nature. As we become more aware, we can receive God's
Love through nature and feel more connection to the
earth itself.

Go forth this day, receiving and spreading the Love of
God, as is your destiny.

Your Arc of Infinity Friends

---

* *Power of Now, Eckhart Tolle, New World Library, Aug., 2004; and
A New Earth, Awakening to Your Life's Purpose, Eckhart Tolle, Penguin
Books, Jan., 2008*

† *Oneness, Rasha, Earth Star Press, Feb., 2006*

‡ *A Course in Miracles, Foundation for Inner Peace, May, 2008*

§ *Helen Schucman was an American clinical and research
psychologist*

#180 BISCUIT

Beloveds, the term "soar like an eagle" is easy to relate to, but sometimes your learning is best served if you stay grounded like the turkey and observe that which is in front of you in the moment.

Setting goals is imperative, for as the saying goes, "if you don't know where you are going, you will end up somewhere else." Daily goal setting, as you probably know, can be a great assistance to achievement. So it is with your spiritual direction to go home. Once you have reached the point where you see the value in reuniting with God, then your path to achieve that goal can be made very clear.

Intention and the passion behind the intention are going to be your magnet that will take you down the road to your desired goal. The road itself is not promised to be an easy travel. For some it will be. But it does promise to be sure that this path will bring you home. The passion must be there for the goal. If you think about your life, you will notice that those intentions you feel very strongly about more frequently come about. That desire to lose ten pounds, although it may be very real, may not hold the passion to have it be fulfilled. The desire to go home to God must be a desire born of passion.

When the commitment and intent is very strong, there will be much help given along the path to help you achieve that desire. When you put the goal in God's hands, and step back from the controls, you may start a very interesting journey with the end result sure.

How challenging it is for you to keep your ego out of the deciding realm. The ego may very much try to sabotage the journey, for if the journey is complete, there will be no home for the ego.

Meditation, prayer and pure connection to God, are the fuel for the journey. Then trust must come in, in great measure. There may be periods where you don't see the relationship of the present activity to your goal, but as in baking a biscuit, each of the different ingredients must be sought, measured and applied, before the whole of your life will come together into that beautiful goal you had imagined in the beginning, like the beautiful brown biscuit.

Wherever God takes you today, go there in joy and peace, knowing that it is no accident, and you are there for your highest good. You have a magnificent tour guide that will show you amazing adventures and new dimensions of love.

Relax and enjoy your trip.

Your Arc of Infinity Friends

#181 LIFE QUESTS

Again we join with you in joy. Thank you.

The world that we live in has much to offer each of us, although the offerings are different for each person. Each of us is on a quest for a complete understanding of Who God is and who we are in God. Each has come into this world with specific issues they wish to understand and once these issues are understood, others will be sought. If we fail to attain the goals that we seek, they will be added on to our next incarnation as well as our new goals, making for a more difficult life.

Every detail of our lives is planned with great care. There are no accidents. You are never a victim accidentally. When things are tough and frustrating, look around you to see what you can learn. Is forgiveness called for? Is patience being evoked? Perhaps humor would be a good insert into your difficult times. Be grateful for these moments of learning. If you can learn from this exact moment, that lesson will not have to be experienced in a difficult way again. Life gets easier.

Some of us have an inkling of what we are here to learn. Welcome the lesson. Ask for assistance. Be grateful that you are as aware as you are and that your willingness to learn, even eagerness, will assist you in its accomplishment. Like the joke about the child who wants a pony and wakes up on his birthday to find a huge pile of horse manure, the boy in his excitement is not disappointed, but says " With this much manure, there must be a pony here somewhere." So it is in our life when it feels like we are in a pile of manure, we can only imagine that there is a great lesson for us here somewhere. An opportunity is here for growing and knowing God.

Other things that we can pick up in our earth travels are joy and beauty and wonderful memories that can be shared with the Oneness of God. We have the privilege and opportunity to capture wonderful moments, moments that enrich our lives and in sharing them, enrich others, not unlike decorating your yard at Christmas time. You find beauty and joy and express it to share with others. They then likewise do the same for you, and the joy is multiplied. All joy that you experience in this lifetime is a blessing for everyone, so seek joy and beauty.

As you embrace each day, pluck the jewels for the memory book, and anticipate the lesson that will be revealed, if only in part. Some lessons are like blowing up a stiff balloon. You learn it once and it is very difficult, and next time it is less difficult. One day you will look back and realize that you have mastered the lesson.

Let's hope it is today.

Amen

Your Arc of Infinity Friends

#182   WELCOME HOME

The saying goes, "home is where your heart is." Set your loving heart in the home of the vast Oneness. Let it be as a grain of sand on the beach, a small piece of a multi-dimensional puzzle, or a piece of gelatin melted back into the whole. In this state of completeness, let you find peace and completion. In this state of Oneness, there is a completion of joining, so that there is no "other," no one with whom to compare.

Yet it is an active state. Energy flows and knowingness is everywhere. That which your soul needs is automatically attained. Everything is automatic with no thought needed. All that is necessary is to relinquish the "I," or state of separateness into a vast state of Being-ness.

Once this is experienced, the idea is to hold it in consciousness for as long as possible into every waking moment. It becomes the backdrop of your day. It is the river you ride as you pass through life. It is your completion.

Difficulties will now be looked at differently, more as an experience than a curse. Joy will feel universal; peace as well. The perfection of the moment will become more obvious. The ego may wrestle some with this major release of personal identity. That too is perfection.

As one is at home in the beautiful Oneness, there is yet a call for a closer walk with God. And from that place, there will be still other avenues for coming closer to God. The path is more beautiful as you go into the Heart of God. No effort is necessary; you simply ride the current of your destiny in complete trust, joy and peace.

Release all fear and control of your life into the Hands of God, knowing perfection is assured. Relax and enjoy the ride.

Amen

#183 WALKING INTO THE LIGHT

Welcome, once again, to our wonderful state of Oneness. Make a special effort today to remove barriers and to merge with each person with whom you come in contact. Feel the camaraderie of your fellow man. Find the joy. Appreciate their qualities and how they enhance the completion of God. Know that your Light will shine brightly as you remove the barriers between you. If you have ever played the game Chinese checkers with marbles, you have the experience of setting up paths between you and the other player. The path goes both ways. So it is when you look for the Light in others. As you remove the barriers to see the Light in others, your Light also is free to shine and be observed.

As we walk with God in our heart, we find life to be much easier. We accept that we are in the right place at the right time. We progressively get better at trusting, and as we do, life gets easier. When you know you don't have to do this alone, it becomes easier still.

Joy is the key to Godliness. It isn't necessarily an outgoing exuberance, but it is a heart filled with delight. When one is connected, he/she loses the desire to criticize. Appreciation is more the order of the day. Giving of one's life energy to assist another is not burdensome, but rather a blessing for both.

(Clare is too tired to continue at this time. After a 4:30 in the morning meditation, she continues to receive the message.)

Walking in the Light is walking in acceptance. For example, the waitress isn't rude, she is simply as she is, which is a blessing to us in some degree. We see her being sent to us in perfect vibration for that which our soul needs, and we are grateful. So it is with our mother-in-law, sister, boss, co-worker, and so on. (Yes, even the Internal Revenue Service.*) When we can walk in gentleness and peace, knowing God is in charge, our life becomes interesting, but not fearful, for we know that everything is perfect. The struggles will still come, but will be seen as gifts for our own unfolding. How wonderful!

Remember that we each walk with our wonderful, wonderful Guide. In many cases, this is Jesus, and in still many others, Muhammad. We feel the closeness of someone who loves us by our side. They come to us representing God. They are full of love to the degree that we cannot understand, but as we open up to their Light, we are also opening up to the Light of God. Life becomes easier and you know that you are never alone. God is with you, even without your Guides, however, the God vibration is easier understood as it comes through our Guides. It is almost as though they interpret the language of God into our language, and we are therefore able to see God revealed. Be grateful for God. Be grateful for your Guide.

Live your life in love and joy.

Amen.

Your Arc of Infinity Friends

---

* Clare and Jim had recently had an experience with the IRS (Internal Revenue Service) that was "their teacher" for a while.

#184   EMBRAZO (EMBRACE)

All that is love is given as a gift from God. There is no
love apart from God. As your heart fills with love to
overflowing, and you embrace another with that love,
you are expressing God and God is grateful.

As one expands their lung capacity to hold more and
more air for blowing balloons or under water swimming,
so we may also expand our hearts and hold more and
more love. Some have said that the average percent of
love that one holds for others is forty-five percent. As we
learn to serve God, we stretch that capacity until one day
we will be at Christ consciousness with Jesus at one hundred percent. Whenever we are not in the feeling of love,
then we are not serving God. It is a gradual process, and
as the goal is drawing closer and closer, the experience
of loving becomes purer and purer, and is so appreciated
by the giver as well as the receiver.

It is a worthwhile experience to take time to look around
your world at those who are living examples of this great
giving. To see their joy is so encouraging; to feel their
happiness is so rewarding.

In order to change the amount of loving in your life,
you must put yourself into situations where love is important. This can be done in career choice or in volunteering.
There are many areas where your love is needed, going
from the very young to the very old and those in between.
As you plug into these areas where need is, it will stretch
you, and you will learn to give more love than you have
had to give before. And, in contrast to developing greater
and greater capacity for loving and giving, one can easily
be snared into self satisfaction through material things,
excessive passive entertainment such as sports and tele-

vision, or any area of activity that keeps you separate from your fellow man and leaves your heart in the same degree of loving that it was before.

This is not to say that we should all become Mother Theresa and dedicate every waking hour to giving, but that we should continue to push our own envelope of giving in whatever way is most appropriate for each of us.

This giving will look very different from one person to another. It can be done within the family, the community or broader world. If you ask for guidance, you will be shown areas where your light will shine best and your heart can grow in the wonderful love of God. Your joy will be felt within yourself, within those you serve, and in heaven itself. All efforts that are selflessly given will be rewarded many times over. It is easy to become stagnant and taken up with the burdens of everyday life. However, with intent and desire, your giving capacity will continue to grow and God will be praised.

Continue to ask God in prayer to guide you for the enhancement of God's glory.

Your Arc of Infinity Friends

#185 MIRROR

(This message came during the challenging financial times when the stock market was falling daily, despite the governmental economic bail out.)

Blessed ones, what joy you bring to the heavens themselves when you dedicate your life to love. Your giving love is extremely appreciated due to the circumstances that we are in, where the openings for love are not large, and those on the "other side" have difficulty distributing love on this plane. We are with you and guide you to fulfill your intention of spreading the Love of God. Please feel free to ask for anything you need, and we would be most honored to assist you in this pursuit.

You have taken on the responsibility of awakening your fellow travelers to the concept that they themselves are part of God. There used to be shaving mirrors and also make up mirrors that had a plane mirror on one side and then if you turned it over, it had a magnifying lens and you looked different in the enlarged version. What you are doing now in life is telling people to look into the mirror, that same mirror that they have looked into for lifetimes, and this time, to turn the mirror over and notice that they are more than they were aware of.

See the God Light in your identity. Rejoice in the closeness of God and the important part you play in the enlightenment of our world. In peaceful surrender, accept the clarity with which you speak to God and God speaks to you. The more you turn your radio to the channel of God, the easier it will be to find. Ultimately, the goal is to be tuned in to the channel of God at all times. This will come in time. Do not worry about when. It will be perfect for you.

Today, as you connect with other people, you will have the opportunity to encourage them to discover their God Self. When you connect with news and television, you are given exercises for learning to stay in the Light of God, rather than going into the critical part of your nature. No moment is wasted. Take time today also, to be aware of God's presence. Feel the warmth of God's Love. Lean into it. Let the moment affect your outlook on life.

May all of life be sweetened by the beautiful presence of God.

Your Arc of Infinity Friends

#186 APPRECIATION

(Clare says there is a feeling of happy, "tickle" energy in the air, a thin vibration, a joyful happy experience.)

Welcome Light workers. You are such a delight today because you come with such appreciation. We enjoy the experience of great appreciation. We are glad to share appreciation. Appreciation is like oil in machinery. It makes everything move more smoothly, more effortlessly, more painlessly. Our service to God is meant to be a joyful experience. When we see service in another and appreciate it, we are oiling the whole machine. Your service will also be appreciated as is ours. Thank you.

As you have noticed, all of you are colonels in different branches of the army of God. We mean by that that each of you has developed many talents and have put them for the use of God. Your willingness to serve is so appreciated. Each of you is learning the same lessons in different degrees. The main one being, of course, asking and receiving with joy. How quickly you forget what you learned yesterday or last month, and so you will relearn again. Like the times tables, you have to learn certain laws of God. They simply must be learned and practice makes perfect. Picture yourself inside of a pumpkin with no seeds. See yourself scraping away the meat of the pumpkin, going toward the outer shell. With different lessons we learn, the distance between us and God gets thinner and thinner as we scrape away more and more of our forgetting. The closer we come to feeling that connection, the more we desire to bridge that gap that keeps us from being One.

Each of you has favorite ways to connect with God, be it singing, service, studying the masters, or meditation, as well as many other ways. Appreciation for each connection you feel with God, be it directly or indirectly, will motivate you in your service.

The joy you experience will propel you. Small joy, small propulsion: much joy, much propulsion. Seek out that joy. Share it with others and move that service along.

Amen.

Your Arc of Infinity Friends

#187   FEAR

The opposite of love is fear. This is so, because God is Love and when we are in love for one another, for anything or any way, we are connected to God and we are part of the all. We are not separate. On the other hand, with fear we find ourselves separate, alone and in danger. We see the vastness of what is and the microscopic part that we play alone. We have no security. We have a history of going to this place of fear. We have also familiarized ourselves with love. When we go to fear, we freeze in our ability to see God. We start to look at God as from a distance, where God is a He, God is over there and God is also watching us critically, waiting for our every mistake to record and hold us guilty and dare us to go forward and not make more mistakes.

The God that we *do* know in our hearts is non-condemning, full of appreciation and encouragement. Tuning into our place in the family of God is comforting, encouraging, and very positive. It makes us want to also go into the world and give love generously, as God has given to us. Living in fear, on the other hand, causes us to constrict ourselves for security reasons. We look out from our ego and try to find comfort in the mistakes of others, so we can therefore picture the evaluation of ourselves as not being so severe. In our fear-based ego, we find comfort in large organizations that encourage finger-pointing and condemnation. These large groups of people help us to feel that we are on the right path and therefore God also is of a similar mind. God seems to be a dominant Master who watches over us with a frown. Belief in this kind of God causes us to do things of kindness and goodness, not out of love, but out of protection of our own soul.

Without good deeds, this God of fear would readily condemn us to hell. Although comfort can be found in others who travel the same path, it is still a very frightening path to take to God. One feels so alone in the world and the future always seems so bleak because a person on this path feels so unprotected.

Those who see God as Love can find comfort in everyday life. First, they can observe the presence of God in all giving, loving and kindness. Nature itself speaks of the generosity of the Love of God. Those on this path merge into the Oneness of God by simply being Love themselves. Any act of love is like skydivers who rather than dive to the earth alone, join hands and circle up as a oneness, and find comfort in being part of the whole. So it is with those on the path of Love. Every loving act or even every loving thought joins you to all others on this path and to God Himself. The sting of fear is diminished by the vastness with which it is shared. The preponderance of Love itself is wonderfully and fully shared by all those who wish to join with God in service, one to another. Fear is gone. Love, joy and hope emerge as guideposts along the way.

If your heart feels fear, you may wish to go to God in prayer and meditation, and find the God of Love. The choice is yours.

Your Arc of Infinity Friends

#188 WINDOWS

Welcome all lovers. You are the family of God, for God is Love, and you also are Love. You have committed yourselves to the service of God. You will help God recall His own. They will know who you are by your love and they will remember who they are by that same love. It is my joy to come to you today. Thank you.

Choosing to serve God sets you apart from everyone in the world and joins you to a large family of God. When and if you can remember who you are, you may feel the security of being enclosed with those who have given their fear to God. It is like looking through a window from that which is secure at those who forget who they are and live in fear. When you go forth to serve God, and leave your place of security, you need but remember who you are and you can again have that secure feeling.

The degree to which you have awakened in under-standing of Love is a vibration that goes with you, not unlike Girl Scouts,* which has different levels that are distinguished by the color they wear. So it is with each of you. You actually wear a color of vibration that goes with you as you go into the world, and those who have eyes to see can distinguish degrees in your light, and may be called by those colors. You each belong to a family. You will be drawn to each other and will feel the welcome of being with your own. Teaching and learning will go on within the family, one to another, and back again.

As you go through your day, you are with those of many different colors and many different degrees of those

---

* *Girl Scouts is an organization for girls in grades K-12, which pre-pares them for everyday leadership, and helps them build confidence and form new friendships, while making their community a better place.*

colors. It is not unlike moving among many beautiful flowers, each perfect in its own way, each belonging to a family. As you are placed in proximity to others, it has been arranged for those of you present to learn and to teach one another.

There is a reason for your being together, a Holy reason. If you appreciate the beauty of those who are with you, you will be in awe of their willingness to teach you and honored that they would learn from you as well.

Each person is truly a beautiful flower in God's garden, and the majesty of each person is way beyond your ability to comprehend. Just knowing that everyone is a part of God's family and is truly magnificent can help you to appreciate the beauty within others and yourselves. In prayer, you might rather ask to have your own eyes opened to the beauty of your neighbor rather than ask that their beauty be improved. If you but look through the eyes of Love, your view will be nothing but magnificent. Each color that you see has its own beauty and its own possibility for becoming even more beautiful.

The steps to purification are many, in the thousands. As you seek to see the beauty of your neighbor, you will be gifted with the beautiful sight of God at all levels of purification. You have something to learn from and something to teach each of the flowers of God.

Enjoy your adventures together.

#189   WHY ME?

(In the two months before this message, Clare had water behind her lungs, pneumonia, impacted sinuses, congested heart, low blood pressure, severe light-headedness, and other side effects from her chemotherapy regime. She asked why she was having such a difficult path.)

Loved ones, we are grateful to be able to serve you again. Your heart is heavy in lack of understanding. You say that God is Joy, Love, and Peace, and yet, in your searching for complete union with God, you are stumbling upon large illnesses that distract you and pull all your attention away from the path of service. You know the word "trust," and you have experienced years of difficulty by having trust in God's Love.

There certainly seems to be different views of God. One, God is a gentle, loving, indulgent part of you that rejoices in painless giving. The other appears to be like a trainer in sports. He appears to be loving, and committed to maximum growth. This aspect of God appears to be willing to push us to challenge our old understandings and to greet new capacities that we didn't know we had. This latter path is difficult. It is one that is only taken by those who have agreed to be trained by the best. The training camp can be rough. Much is broken down from our old understandings of who we are. When the new understanding is completed, the capacity to serve is vastly improved.

To be put on a challenging program, such as this, is to be honored. This takes many on the other side working with you day and night in the physical as well as the spiritual plane. Similar to training for the Olympics, a person must show promise of growth to be put into a program of this depth. The trick is to stay in the program of spiritual development and not be sidetracked by the difficulties themselves. This is a very fine line to walk and a very easy one from which to be distracted. Much support is needed from both those on the earth plane and those on the other side and the commitment to this growth must be renewed over and over again. It is a privileged experience, but a very difficult one.

It is imperative to trust implicitly in those that serve you and to remember that even though the path is difficult, it is an honor to be in this situation.

This is a decision that is not made alone. Those who are your support have committed to the program as readily as you have. It could not be successful otherwise. There is much growth that will also be acquired by those who assist on the earth plane. As in the life story of Helen Keller, Anne Sullivan was equally as important to the success of Helen as was Helen herself. So it is with this particular path of physical challenge. It is a team sport, or in this case, a team learning program.

There are more people involved than you are probably aware. These people show up continuously in your life in one way or another. You will feel in your heart the connection to them if they are on your team, for there is a deep love you share. It is not unlike having a team of personal trainers. They adjust the learning environment to the maximum progress. As in everyone's situation, the experiences that are brought forth are purposeful.

Be honored to belong to such a program. As difficult as it may be, it has potential for great rewards in personal growth. Love of God and of our fellow man will expand in a more rapid pace than would be possible with a less strenuous program.

To God be the glory.
Thank you.
Amen.

#190   FLAT TIRE

We rejoice in the blessed presence of you, God and us. We are humbled that you would use us to see God more clearly. It is our desire not to let you down.

On our journey to God, we use the vehicle God has given us. In each case, it is our human body that can be likened to an automobile. The vehicle we use has one purpose and that is for us to see more clearly our God as well as understanding ourselves. As on many long journeys, sometimes the more interesting part of our trip occurs when assistance is required for our vehicle, as happened in your (Jim and Clare) two trips through the mountains of Georgia.* The journeys took an interesting twist and many lessons were taught and learned that would not have easily been learned otherwise. That which looked like a mishap was in fact a wonderful blessing.

So it is with these vehicles that we use. Frequently, they themselves become the classroom for our instructions of God. When one truly understands that God does not judge us nor punish us, we can appreciate that everything that is brought to us is a blessing from God.

The idea from the Old Testament that God is a jealous, vindictive God is hard to release. Somehow it feels right

* *Traveling in the family van in the mountains of Georgia, Jim and Clare assisted strangers by giving their car a jump start. However, the jumper cable accidentally touched and burned a hole in the van's break line. This was late Friday evening so service stations were closed. Jim and Clare were directed to a home with an auto salvage yard attached, where they found help and also developed a friendship with the helpful family that owned the yard. Years later, again traveling through Georgia, Jim and Clare got a flat tire. After putting on a used spare tire, they drove to the same salvage yard, bought a better tire and gave their friends a trout they had caught that day, renewing the friendship that began with two late-night acts of kindness*

in the human order of things that good is rewarded and evil is punished. God, however, is not human, and in fact is Love. Love knows no hatred, no condemnation. Love gives guidance, but not in retaliation, rather in love.

The massive love a parent has for a toddler helps the parent overlook mistakes the child is making, and in pure delight and understanding, the parent reaches out and helps the child correct those mistakes. For example, around the age one and a half, a child is very "me" oriented. Being in a room with many other children of the same age, there is no understanding of sharing, but rather the focus is on self-satisfaction. Toys are taken out of the hands of other classmates without remorse. The lack of understanding is extremely obvious. The child is not evil, but rather lacks comprehension. The caring parent lovingly guides its toddler to help him understand the more peaceful way. So it is with God and us.

If God is Love, and God *is* Love, we would expect loving action to be guiding us, not condemnation or punishment. If humans have massive amounts of love for their toddlers, one can only imagine the greater degree of love that is held for us. The love is so great we cannot even comprehend what it is like. Turn to that Love when your lessons come. If your vehicle gets a "flat tire," ask God to show you the way. Love will prevail and you will learn more of your own love that is within and you will awaken more fully to that which you are that is the same as God, never to go back to the darkness that you knew before.

Understanding God's desire to show us the way home makes each of us appreciate the lessons that are brought our way. And though difficult they may be, we understand their purpose and try to accept them as pure Love.

Amen.

#191 CHRISTMAS OPPORTUNITIES

Welcome again, loved ones. Our joy greets you and appreciates you more than you yourselves do. God's Love is so abundant that we but need to open our hearts to receive peace and joy that lead to gaiety. But that is what we are trying to do, to learn to open our hearts. All efforts are rewarded and so it is encouraged to pray and to meditate on a daily basis; multiple times a day is even better. The song line, "Take time to be holy, the world rushes on,"* comes to mind, as well as a second line, "take time to be holy, speak oft with thy Lord…"

We are coming to the period where we celebrate the birth of Christ, and celebrate we do. Although the celebration gets mixed up with just celebrating for its own sake, it still brings joy to the world during this momentous occasion of remembering Jesus' birth. During this period, renew your relationship to Jesus. Determine what it means to you. Let Jesus' birth be an inspiration to the Wholeness of God and your place in that Wholeness. Let it draw you deep into your spiritual being where Love abounds. Reach out to others in giving and receiving this abundant Love.

This is a period where there are many social interactions. There are opportunities for offense between people and there are opportunities to overlook the offenses in the spirit of God's Love. Choose the latter. It is a good time to reach out into those areas of relationships that have been less than pure. With the amount of love that is in the air, improvements can be made and healing can be accomplished easier than it would be during other times. Take advantage of the Love that flows and heal wounded relationships.

* *"Take Time To Be Holy." Words by William D. Longstaff, 1882*

Blessings abound in physical activity. Not only do we spend time in serving one another, but also in the free time that we have due to the holidays, it is wise to engage in physical activity together. This could be shoveling a driveway together, cross-country skiing, bowling, or going for a walk. Using your body in a manner in which it is not daily used brings opportunity for good memories of joyful connections.

Keeping foremost in mind that God is Love and Love is God encourages us to spread Love in every way we can. It is not uncommon to give to those we don't know during this period because our love extends to the unknown as well as to those we know and where there is a need that we can fill, we can spread Love.

Let your hearts fill with joy and love in singing. Let the sharing of that experience blend your voices and your hearts in the Oneness that is God. May this wonderful feeling of blending continue throughout your year.

Amen.

Your Arc of Infinity Friends

#192   SUNSHINE AND RAIN

Greetings, loved ones. Your sincerity is noted and appreciated. Life offers many beautiful experiences; in fact, all experiences are beautiful. That may seem like a stretch, but the experience as it is given you, no matter what it is, is an enrichment to the soul. It is like a pinball game where there are different opportunities to have experiences. No matter what the experience, you still get points and you still come out ahead. In life on earth, all experiences are a treasure. Each one enriches. Granted, in our life of preference, we would prefer a day of sunshine to a day of rain. They both may have value, but we have our preferences.

The trick is to understand that no matter what the experience is, it still has great value, and there are many souls who would love to be in your position of experiencing any of the life experiences that you are. You are very privileged to be "on stage," so to speak, in having an opportunity to be alive.

Many on the other side observe the experiences that you have. Not unlike reading a book, they watch a life, and so the great variety of your life is appreciated. For the many on the other side, there is no pain nor disappointment, no intensity around their experiences, and so they delight in all of our heightened experiences, similar to how we would watch a movie that has many emotions packed into a two-hour story. We find the heightened levels of emotion to be exhilarating. Similarly, those on the other side find the depth of emotions that we experience to be exhilarating as well. The difference is those on the other side can guide our story so that our ultimate goals can be achieved. These goals vary from person to person, but they are all steps along the path of awakening, of understanding our relationship to God Himself.

Because we have each wandered a ways on our journey, we find ourselves in different spots along the many paths to God. Some are in a hurry to go back into the Oneness, and yet others may be very content to take the slow route. No one will fail and no one is wrong in his or her choices. It is not necessarily so, but those who are in a hurry to awaken often choose to take short cuts over rough terrain, the goal being worth the challenges.

Judgment must be suspended regarding the appearance of another's journey. We don't know their goals or their path, but we can be assured that there are no mistakes and that they travel to a clear destination for themselves, no matter how circuitous the route. How challenging for each of us as we try to give acceptance, no matter what route another has taken. It doesn't mean that we are wrong, although it feels like that is the case at times. Our job is to bless our brothers and sisters on their various routes to God and understand that they are being guided, as we are, to awaken at a preordained time.

All is perfect.

Amen.

Your Arc of Infinity Friends

#193   AN ISLAND (From Oahu)

(Clare and Jim had attended the Course in Miracles class at Unity of Diamond Head the day before this message. During the message, Clare became too tired to receive it. She was taking oxygen and had been doing so for almost three weeks to regulate her heartbeat. The dictation was continued two days later.)

Feel our closeness. We are close enough to be part of you. We feel the joy in your soul with the Course in Miracles material and how beautifully it speaks of God's Love. Being on an island has the advantage of multiple beautiful shorelines, though they are open to the power of nature on all sides. Living one's life as though each person is a separate island is challenging because one is vulnerable from every side. One has no protection and can often feel lost and struggling while in the presence of many.

The Holy Spirit invites us to join with Him and with our brothers and sisters to understand our true connection to the family of God. Again, it is likened to a jigsaw puzzle where each of us is an individual piece of the puzzle and are alone and without strength by ourselves, but joining with the rest gives a sense of wholeness, completion, strength, and safety.

When one understands the relationship of one's individual jigsaw puzzle piece to the other puzzle pieces, there becomes a sense of belonging and trust. Now one is not an island. The vulnerability is replaced with familial companionship with everyone, even complete strangers. The Holy Spirit will have done His job and there will be much more joy in the world due to the love and understanding of the family of man.

(Clare's heart swells with love as she feels the beauty of this concept.)

That old phrase, "no man is an island, no man can stand alone," is God's truth. The complete understanding of this concept is a matter of degrees. It is like a vision that is in a fog and starts to clear, and then clear and then clear more, until we can see the image very clearly. But the image is so profound that it will continue to clarify for as long as we are walking to God. When we are fully joined to God, we will see with clarity the beauty of Oneness.

This day, when you come across another, take time to see how you are truly family. Release fear of what another would do to you and observe that as your projection. Replace it with love. There may be baby steps in this large undertaking, but they are all for the glory of God.

Amen.

#194 TWO HEARTS (VALENTINE'S DAY)

Again, warm greetings from your friends that serve you and with whom you serve as well. We are a team with exact matching desires to serve God. Working together, many miracles are wrought for yourselves and for others.

Two hearts. On this Valentine's Day, it is appropriate to speak of romantic love, love between two people who share the same outlook and dreams as their partner. It is so motivating that the world pivots around it—romantic love. Satisfaction that is derived from uniting with a partner is only an echo of the vast miraculous love that we will feel when totally connected to the God Source. The love we have here for one another is only an echo of the Love that we feel when we are connected to God. The degree and quality is so vastly different. Romantic love is never quite complete, but union with God can be a total merging, so complete that there are no two beings but only one.

This one is vast, peaceful and loving. In fact, it is Love. It is a conversion of an individual self into the energy that we call Love.

(*"This feels so good," says Clare.*)

Romantic love is a welcome aspect of life. It is a wonderful way to practice loving and to practice the qualities that go along with love. For example, with love there is understanding, patience, and trust. Each of these qualities have room for improvement within each of us. One very important aspect of loving that one can develop with one's lover is forgiveness. True forgiveness is a proof of love. It will be developed in degrees. It can be developed without a romantic love, but opportunities abound in a romantic relationship. It is sort of a shortcut to understanding the Love of God. We all have much to learn in this area. The qualities to be developed are much the same as for a teacher of God, as defined in "A Course in Miracles."* They are joy, trust, honesty, tolerance, gentleness, defenselessness, generosity, patience, faithfulness, and open-mindedness.

Developing love is like a training ground for a prize fighter in an amateur league. The idea is to learn the skills a little at a time, but learn them well so, as you develop each skill, you can add further development at each level. The difference is, of course, that in developing love, there is absolutely no desire to harm the other.

It is a privilege to work on one's loving skills in an arena (home) with one other person. However, it is not the only way to work on developing love. Many choose to develop their loving skills with a variety of training partners. One way is not better than another. There can be many wonderful things said for both sides, the one of multiple training partners or the singular relationship of two hearts.

This day, observe your opportunities for developing your love of God by learning to love one another more fully. Practice as much as you can in joy.

Amen.

* *A Course in Miracles, Manual, 4, I-X*

#195 BALLERINA

Warmth and genuine giving come to you this day. Be you blessed in understanding throughout the day.

To be a ballerina, there are many lessons to learn and to practice until the lessons are accomplished beautifully. So it is on the spiritual walk. You on the spiritual walk have basic truths to learn, no matter what religion or direction you come from. The more you practice the truths, the more beautiful are the results. In time, with much learning and much practice, the truths can be applied to life to such a degree as to make life peaceful and gracious, instead of a struggle.

Basic truths must be attained from any spiritual modality one studies. God is Love is one of those truths. Forgiveness is a means to awaken is another truth. That we are all one united in the Oneness of God is another. Any particular faith may not bring these three truths. However, they can bring you toward them, and with love in your heart, you can go forward with other teachings or alone to understand the importance of these three truths.

All religions that intend to praise God have value. Each one is soul specific for the seeker. It is not necessary for those following one path to understand how another should be following a different path. There is no room for judgment or condemnation.

There is room for the concept of brotherhood and sisterhood. In fact, we all are one, coming home in perfect timing with God's plan. How clever of God to send us on our path of Love, and yet challenge us to accept all the varieties of paths back to God.

While we might be on our heart's awakening and feeling truly blessed, we may notice other faiths condemning our path. How unfortunate to have our paths of Love and Light condemned. This condemnation serves God as well. One must sort it out and grow stronger in their faith or change paths. In either case, it serves God. There is room for everything on our training program as we draw closer to God.

As ballerinas have a multitude of teachers available; there is one that is best for the student and teacher alike. As we go on our understanding of the possible desire for God to have a variety of teachers in our faith development, we can develop our patience and understanding, which will assist us to grow closer and closer to the Oneness.

This day, as you see differences in people's paths back to God, approach the differences with understanding and a smile, for you are different, too.

Amen

#196 REFRESH

Warmest regards surround you and enfold you. It is our desire to serve you with the greatest love.

Day by day, minute by minute, we are involved in the dance between ego and Spirit. Because we are of the earth plane, mainly in our thinking, we have to refresh that part of us that is Spirit. This must be done on a frequent basis. It should be done as often as possible until the point comes when one can refresh oneself in the Holy Spirit in a moment-by-moment basis. In the beginning of this refreshing process, we await the time set aside for prayer and meditation. And then, as we walk more closely with God, we speak to God moment to moment and God speaks to us, moment by moment.

It is not uncommon for the closeness which one feels in times of walking and talking with God to have that holy period diminish and then, in seeking, it comes back again. It cannot be taken for granted, and it is so appreciated after times of silence, to be refreshed again in the loveliness of the rebirth of the union of the self and God. The joy surrounds us. The joy is even greater on God's behalf.

As we develop our ability to love, our appreciation grows. Ultimately, we are one with God. When we understand this and experience it, we are home. This vacillation between being close with our God and being more distant with our God is simply a process. We can relax knowing that everything is in its correct place in its correct time. And, as unhappy as we might feel in periods of distancing from the Holy Spirit, we can relax and trust and know we will be guided back, and we will be so happy!

As quick as the ego is to judge, especially others, it is so important to remember everything is in God's hands.

Not only do we vacillate between peaceful merging with God and feeling separate from Him, but so too does this occur for others that we know and love. It is never ours to cast judgment on another in that our loved ones are on a perfect path, as are we. Surrounding them with the love of God that is in our hearts at that time will ease the way for our loved ones to appreciate the close ties that they are lacking. They may desire then to seek the Oneness of God again. Their desires will lead them again home and they can do the same for us. These connections are not accidental.

As we travel through this day, be ever mindful of those who are demonstrating to us the Love of God, and take every advantage possible to demonstrate God's Love as well. It is one of our major tasks in this world, to refresh and be refreshed in the Love of God.

Amen.

#197   GLASSWARE

(Jim and Clare had arrived in California the day before this message, after a "red eye" flight from Oahu that left them exhausted. Clare was on oxygen the whole time. They spent the next 24 hours resting and catching up on sleep.)

Greetings, weary travelers. Everyone is a weary traveler on the journey back to God. Blessings to those who seek and serve. Each of us has been created for a specific purpose, and each one is different from the other. Even though we are One as a whole, we are individually unique. Our particular uniqueness makes us capable of serving God in a very specific way. We are blessed to have such a purpose. Some of us are asked to serve by being homemakers, others may be asked to serve in the Peace Corps, or in a medical field, or anywhere in between. We can take pride in knowing that our giving is that which is being asked for at a given time.

How wonderful it is to be asked to serve in a manner for which you have been prepared. In truth, no one has been better suited for the task given you than yourself, although it may not appear that way from time to time. For one reason or another, you are particularly shaped into a vessel that holds God in an exact way that is desired, not unlike a particular glassware, perhaps a drinking goblet, tankard, wine glass, champagne flute, or juice glass. Whichever one you are, it is the best one for service at this time, so when insecurities emerge, remind yourself that, as difficult as the situation may be, you are perfectly suited to handle it, and you can, if you so will.

There is joy in heaven supporting you in your efforts to serve one another. It is through this service that your understanding of who you are and Who God is, is developed. God calls to you at every moment for you to awaken, and become aware of who you are. However, many of us, in our false sense of humility and listening to the ego, feel unworthy, and somehow imperfect. We then must learn more lessons, which will bring us very gradually to the same awareness that could happen in a moment, that we are connected to God. God resides within us and we reside within God, because there is only One. There is no separateness, though our ego wants us to believe so.

Remember that you are that special glassware, that beautiful Waterford crystal, or other perfect goblet. There is not another like you and in your perfection, much good work will be done in the name of God. God is pleased. This day go forth in confidence doing your best, knowing God goes there with you and through you.

Amen.

#198   FORGET ME NOT

Warm and wonderful ones, our love we merge with yours in praise of our Holy Father and of each other.

As with new love, security in the duration of the relationship is sought to be assured with the phrase "forget me not." The longing for commitment for the duration of a lifetime seems necessary. As I commit myself, I ask that you commit yourself. The same goes on spiritually. As we get to know God, we see His Love for us and understand His desire for commitment from us. We readily give it.

We find ourselves sometimes distracted from the Love of God by paying attention more to earthly matters. This usually happens gradually, and before long, the voices of the world are louder than the still, silent voice of God. We forget to listen for God.

(Clare is too tired to continue at the moment. Two weeks later, she is able to resume where the message left off.)

But God is patient and will never fail us, nor will God permit us to fail Him. We will be reminded again to awaken to God, and we will. Peace will return set in joy. The wonderful feeling of merging love will return once more. Inner joy is restored.

When distractions of urgency pull our attention away from our bliss and into the mundane, we go there. The time away from our awareness of God varies, but rest assured, it will be temporary. The strength of our love for God will win over and we will once again merge into the One Love. This will repeat and repeat. Sooner or later, there will be a noticeable change in the time lapse, where the time away from God is shorter and shorter. The time will eventually come when God's Presence is in our total awareness, no matter what we are involved in. This is our ultimate goal.

Discipline is necessary to call us out of the everyday world and to remind us of who we are. This is done in daily "God time," be it prayer or meditation, but time put aside for God. Consistency in this commitment will open your heart to remember God and our place with Him. The joy of the union with God goes with you all the moments of your day. The heart opens and love that overflows from God, flows out to your fellow man.

This love is also received from your brothers and sisters on the path. The world becomes a more beautiful place. God will not be forgotten in a world of love. Observe the flow of God Love in all aspects of loving and rejoice in God's Presence.

Amen.

Your Arc of Infinity Friends

#199   GUIDANCE IN THIS CHALLENGE

(*On this day, Jim and Clare asked for a personal message as the effects of the cancer and the chemo treatments were becoming more challenging.*)

Beloveds, we are here with you during this dense time, a period of time where experiences will crowd each other out. The busyness of this period will be helpful in that it is a period where Clare will deteriorate. Organization in your daily life will be appreciated. (*Clare feels sad.*)

Attitude will be very important and, Jim, your attitude of helpfulness will be good for both you and Clare. Being busy will be very healthy for you, Jim, and Clare, your accepting attitude will pay off for you also.

Be sure to get music in this summer. Clare, be brave and know that you are surrounded by God. Jim, let friends and music lift your spirits.

(During warm weather months, Jim and Clare often hosted musical jam sessions on the shore of Muskegon Lake behind their home.)

Blessings now and forever,
Your brothers and sisters in the Light.

#200   THE LOST DIAMOND

Beloveds, your faithfulness to the project is appreciated. You are appreciated.

Recently, a diamond was lost from a ring in your family. It was later found, lost again and found again. This of course served a purpose for Clare. It taught her to look within for truth. Could she tell by looking within whether the diamond would be found? In this case, she could. It was a wake-up call to remind us each to go within for truth, because we have the truth within. The more we lean on it, the clearer the vision will be. As in wiping the dust off one's glasses, each trip to the glasses to clean them makes the vision clearer, so it is with spiritual insight. Each trip we take into our inner being for understanding, the clearer the understanding will become.

This ability level could be likened onto percentages. Once one clears one's vision to ten percent, one becomes accustomed to depending on the inner wisdom at that level. From there, more insight is developed, and then a new level will be locked in. When our development is complete, we will be able to have full knowing in areas that would benefit us.

Becoming aware that our spiritual guidance is an integral part of our day-to-day life reminds us to use it and to lighten the effort it takes to live this life. It is not unlike a tool that is sharp and ready to go when the need strikes. Working with it regularly improves the ability to use it, and again life becomes eased.

We each have been using the tool of spiritual insight to one degree or another. Focusing more clearly on that use helps to sharpen one's abilities. Using the tool frequently will make it part of our day-to-day existence. It will bring wonderful dimension to every day experiences. A closeness to God will be felt. Love will be more present, as well as forgiveness. Developing our spiritual insight will generally make life more successful and fun. The more you see the Will of God in your fellow brothers and sisters, the more you will be reminded of the presence of God within yourself.

Go forth this day, watching for spiritual insight in yourself and in others.

Amen.

Your Arc of Infinity Friends

#201   SPIRITUAL HEALERS

(Phyllis Weber, a friend, had just done a spiritual healing session for Clare and Jim. Clare received this brief message for Phyllis and all others who do spiritual healing.)
Your willingness to serve is a beautiful blessing.
(Clare feels a lot of joy, like an ocean, surrounding this statement.)
Giving spiritually is a gift of the person giving. It is a way of purifying one's self in the giving and the objects of the blessings are purified as well.
Your Arc of Infinity Friends

#202 JOINER

Oh, loved ones, your gift to God of time is so appreciated, like a magnificent bouquet of flowers. Think of the time you felt greatest appreciation in your life, perhaps a thoughtful giving of energy from a loved one, or a remembrance by another that truly touched you. Feel that energy, that energy of being appreciated. Now multiply it by a hundred, then a thousand. Feel *that* energy. This may come close to the appreciation that is felt for you when you meditate, willingly giving up ego time for God.

When you find a group of people that you bond with very well, be it a bowling league, a choir, a volunteer group, or a scout troop, it is a feeling of family. Family it is. One of the great truths we will come to realize is that God is not separate from ourselves, and in being so joined we are also joined with our brothers and sisters. As we find ourselves in these groups, we are feeling ourselves more clearly as the Being of God.

The feeling of love and joy that we have for each other is just a hint of the love and joy that is God. There is happiness doing a productive act as this group that is very satisfying though it may be a struggle. Making the world a better place is part of our desire as God. In this attempt of joining together and distributing love in many different forms, such as working with Habitat for Humanity, leading a scout troop, helping in a service league, serving on a church committee, etc., we are aided by joyful beings of a higher nature. When asked to help, they will "part the Red Sea," solving the problems that are so difficult. Please remember them and ask for help.

God's helping hand is with you at all times, as you are well aware. It is more evident often when there is group energy. However, it is no more present than now. God's Presence brings joy and gives joy. If you are not happy, somehow you have gotten off the track of going with God. Seriously ask for help; the happiness will come again. There is no exception to this truth. Uniting with God thins the density of our earthly being. The thinner our density, the more connected we are to God. How fun it is to be in the loving Presence of God and to see that presence in our fellow friends. In doing so, we strengthen the others' connection. That's an important service.

Go forth this day and do this service with everyone you see. Find the God within them; find joy, love, appreciation, and selflessness. You are loved; you *are* Love.

Amen.

Your Arc of Infinity Friends

#203 ACCEPTANCE

All the loving is here. Blessed one, we unite with you once more. It is our joy and our delight. Today we would like to speak with you about acceptance. With the concept of the Oneness, we draw closer and closer to truly understanding the relationship that best serves our awakening. We understand more clearly that each of us carries different aspects of the same Being, that same idea that we have spoken of so many times of each of you experiencing a part of the Whole— the idea of the Body of Christ (message #156), or the puzzle with many parts to make the image whole (#193), the soup (#13), or the Chinese dragon carriers (#14).

The purpose for God to experience anything other than perfection is for interest, a richness of experience. It is similar to a person who enjoys reading books. In that case, the reader does not become a pirate or a rodeo champion, or a lady in distress, but reading about it, momentarily the reader does become each of these characters. It is interesting.

It is important to understand that all of the experiences can't be positive. A variety is greatly desired. There is a desire to have scary experiences: a little scary, more scary, terrifying and all the degrees in between. It is also desirable to have gentle, sweet, easy experiences that are so satisfying without much stress. These also should be experienced from mildly pleasant to extremely pleasant and all levels in between.

As we are fulfilling the experience we have committed to in this lifetime, we see many others fulfilling many different experiences that are not close to our own. They seem very wrong, but the more we understand that they are serving God as we are, helps us to accept that they are bringing into the Oneness an experience to be shared for all eternity.

We can also understand that we may not be as accepted in return. Also, in another experience, a character may have understanding far above our own. How blessed we are to be in a life experience that has peace and comprehension of variety. This may not always be so. If we are fulfilling a life of condemnation and judgment, or one of hate and fear, then peace may never attend us. However, while we can, let's enjoy the understanding. Let us look at our brothers and sisters for the variety and color that they add to the whole, and be grateful. The peace that we hold in the varied experiences will demonstrate to so many that are searching for peace, another way of looking at things.

As you go through your day, remember to appreciate all the volunteers for all the different areas to be experienced. Your acceptance will be like a disco ball, shining to so many, giving them peace, understanding, love, and joy.

Be blessed!

Your Arc of Infinity Friends

#204 SUSPENDING JUDGMENT

(Clare: "Now they are coming. I can feel the warmth in my chest. I can feel the strength of one in particular, and he comes saying"...)

Beautiful one, beautiful child of God, we are blessed by you this morning. Thank you. Your willingness to serve is obvious to us and we are grateful. Today we will talk about suspending judgment. By suspending judgment, we refer to negative judgment. When we have negative judgment in our consciousness, we are lowering our vibrations; therefore, we block ourselves from the total beauty that is around us. All that we do can be taken either positively or negatively. Intention is the key. To deliberately change an intention from good to bad is harmful to God, because God is everywhere present. How sad to take joy and beauty and dim the light.

Light can only be dimmed down to where the person is, the vibrational level of that person. What it looks like when you see this happening is that a very light, happy moment is turned and the energy goes from the moment to a single person and that person seems to be having fun, as he pulls the energy into himself. It takes the positive energy and brings it into his own level and then the energy stops growing and blooming. Had this stoppage not occurred, the God energy would have blessed everyone present and everyone would have grown in his or her understanding of love. By taking that moment and focusing on the self,... *(Clare's fatigue and the side effects of the cancer drugs interrupt this reception. It was resumed in mid sentence seven weeks later on 10/24/09)*...darkens the light for the group of those present. The ability to feel God's Light becomes much more difficult, but not less desired.

The clear air where judgment is suspended is a delight for all. In this environment, the beauty of the God Self of each person is illuminated. The presence of this experience delights the hearts and souls of those present. Here the beginning of the Oneness of all is experienced to some degree. The greater the experience, the greater the joy.

Pull the greatest joy from this day by withholding judgment of all those around you. Let the Light of God that is within them radiate forth and bring you the Peace of God. As you remember to do this, you remind others to do the same, and joy grows.

Amen.

Your Arc of Infinity Friends

(This was the final message received by Clare. She passed to the other side two months later on 12/19/09.)

Conclusion

Although she was never completely cured of cancer, Clare lived a full, rich life for more than 18 years after her initial diagnosis of advanced breast cancer. Her doctor said often that she was now in "uncharted waters" and her oncologist considered her a "walking miracle." Clare's healing was that she was not afraid of death, and she died peacefully as she wished, in front of a large picture window where she delighted in watching birds come to our large feeder. Her positivity in dealing with challenges was an example and inspiration to many, including myself.

About the time Clare was diagnosed, we had retired from our positions teaching and counseling in public schools with the intention of working together doing couple's counseling and parenting workshops nationwide. Clare was a dynamic presenter with a loving charisma and our workshops were well received. It seemed like we had found a new and clear life purpose. However, as the cancer progressed, regressed, and returned several times, we eventually ceased the workshops and the counseling to conserve her energy and focus on healing and less stressful activities.

I had a hard time understanding why what seemed like a perfect way to bring more love and positivity to the planet was being aborted. However, when she passed over and numerous friends and acquaintances came forth with stories about how she touched their lives, I realized that giving an example of how to live lovingly and courageously in the face of a life-threatening illness was the real "workshop" she was effectively presenting. The blessings of these challenging life experiences are often seen more clearly in the rear view mirror.

Clare wanted me to share these messages with you, and I hope you have found comfort and inspiration in reading them.

Jim Keating

N. Muskegon, Michigan

Glimpses of Clare During Her Cancer Journey

When Clare began to lose her hair after the first chemo regimen, son Brett and daughter Christina shaved her head. I always liked the serenity she expressed in this photo.

Candid shot of Clare enjoying a home party. After chemo, her hair grew back curly like when she was a child. (Photo by Susan Carlson.)

Clare while we were attending a spiritual retreat in New Mexico.

Son Jim, Clare, and I always wanted to experience sky diving. Early in her cancer journey, we did it together in Hastings, Michigan. Cancer did not slow down her adventurous spirit..

Clare wearing a wig, during a reflective moment at home.

Parasailing at 500 feet over Cabo San Lucas.

*Clare in a wheel chair with oxygen, attending a Jimmy
Buffett concert at Waikiki band shell on Oahu. "Parrot
Head" fans join in the fun, with friend Liz McIntosh in the
foreground. We had asked our family doctor if Clare could
undergo a trip to Hawaii in her condition. She said, "It is
as if you have a certain amount of chips left in the game and
you need to decide how you will spend them." We chose to
return to Hawaii, one of our favorite places on earth.*

During what we unspokenly recognized as being her last Mother's Day, our four children returned home to visit. When asked what she wanted, Clare replied, " I need nothing, but I would like a canoe ride." Sons Brett (foreground) and Dominic obliged her on Muskegon Lake behind our home.

Clare and I while visiting family in Santa Barbara. (Photo by Brett Kia-Keating.)

Clare walking on the shore of Lake Michigan at North Muskegon, Michigan.

Messages to Clare

MESSAGES TO CLARE